Mastering Windows PowerShell Scripting

Second Edition

One-stop guide to automating administrative tasks

Chris Dent
Brenton J.W. Blawat

BIRMINGHAM - MUMBAI

Mastering Windows PowerShell Scripting

Second Edition

First published: April 2015

Second edition: October 2017

Production reference: 1251017

Published by Packt Publishing Ltd.
Livery Place
35 Livery Street
Birmingham
B3 2PB, UK.
ISBN 978-1-78712-630-5

www.packtpub.com

Credits

Authors
Chris Dent
Brenton J.W. Blawat

Reviewer
Paul Broadwith

Acquisition Editor
Meeta Rajani

Content Development Editor
Mamata Walkar

Technical Editor
Varsha Shivhare

Copy Editors
Safis Editing
Ulka Manjrekar

Project Coordinator
Kinjal Bari

Proofreader
Safis Editing

Indexer
Tejal Daruwale Soni

Graphics
Kirk D'penha

Production Coordinator
Nilesh Mohite

About the Authors

Chris Dent is a professional PowerShell developer based in and around London with over 8 years experience in that language alone. He is also proficient in C#, VBScript, Perl, and Python, but PowerShell is his favorite by a wide margin. He is also the author of dnshell.

He describes himself as being a toolset or module developer (he rarely writes scripts in the one-off sense); he has a deep interest in formalized development approaches, continuous integration, secure coding practices, and creating supportable automation frameworks within organizations.

Brenton J.W. Blawat is an entrepreneur, strategic technical advisor, author, and enterprise architect, who has a passion for the procurement of technology in profit-based organizations. He is business-centric and technology-minded. Brenton has many years of experience in bridging the gap between technical staff and decision-makers in several organizations. He takes pride in his ability to effectively communicate with a diverse audience and provide strategic direction for large and small organizations alike.

In 2013, Brenton authored his first book, *PowerShell 3.0 WMI Starter*, Packt Publishing. In March 2015, he authored his second book, *Mastering Windows PowerShell Scripting*, with Packt Publishing.

Brenton currently works at CDW as an Enterprise Architect in strategic solutions and services. CDW is a leading multibrand technology solutions provider in the fields of business, government, education, and healthcare. A Fortune 500 company, it was founded in 1984 and employs approximately 7,200 coworkers. In 2016, the company generated net sales of more than $13.0 billion.

His current specialization sits on top of 15 years of experience spread across (predominantly Microsoft) systems, (Juniper and Cisco) networking, and security.

About the Reviewer

Paul Broadwith is a senior technology professional freelancing in Scotland. He has over 25 years of experience in diverse sectors, from manufacturing and financial services to the public sector and managed IT services.

With particular expertise in Microsoft and Linux technologies, he has interest in PowerShell on both platforms. An advocate of a common-sense approach to coding, best practice, and code reusability, he enjoys practicing what he preaches in his code and mentoring new professionals.

www.PacktPub.com

For support files and downloads related to your book, please visit www.PacktPub.com.

Did you know that Packt offers eBook versions of every book published, with PDF and ePub files available? You can upgrade to the eBook version at www.PacktPub.com and as a print book customer, you are entitled to a discount on the eBook copy. Get in touch with us at service packtpub.com for more details.

At www.PacktPub.com, you can also read a collection of free technical articles, sign up for a range of free newsletters and receive exclusive discounts and offers on Packt books and eBooks.

https://www.packtpub.com/mapt

Get the most in-demand software skills with Mapt. Mapt gives you full access to all Packt books and video courses, as well as industry-leading tools to help you plan your personal development and advance your career.

Why subscribe?

- Fully searchable across every book published by Packt
- Copy and paste, print, and bookmark content
- On demand and accessible via a web browser

Customer Feedback

Thanks for purchasing this Packt book. At Packt, quality is at the heart of our editorial process. To help us improve, please leave us an honest review on this book's Amazon page at `https://www.amazon.com/dp/1787126307`.

If you'd like to join our team of regular reviewers, you can email us at `customerreviews@packtpub.com`. We award our regular reviewers with free eBooks and videos in exchange for their valuable feedback. Help us be relentless in improving our products!

Table of Contents

Preface

PowerShell scripts offer a handy way to automate various chores. Working with these scripts effectively can be a difficult task. This comprehensive guide starts from scratch and covers advanced-level topics, along with tips to make you a PowerShell scripting expert.

What this book covers

`Chapter 1`, *Introduction to PowerShell*, introduces PowerShell and why it is applicable to the IT community. This chapter discusses the types of Microsoft systems that leverage PowerShell and why it's important to learn this scripting language.

`Chapter 2`, *Working with PowerShell*, talks about finding and using commands and parameters.

`Chapter 3`, *Modules and Snap-Ins*, shows how to use PowerShell modules and snap-ins.

`Chapter 4`, *Working with Objects in PowerShell*, shows how to work with objects in PowerShell.

`Chapter 5`, *Operators*, shows how to use operators to test and manipulate data.

`Chapter 6`, *Variables, Arrays, and Hashtables*, explains the different mechanisms within PowerShell that are able to store data. These include variables, hashes, and arrays.

`Chapter 7`, *Branching and Looping*, shows how to explore conditional statements and how to implement loops in PowerShell.

`Chapter 8`, *Working with .NET*, shows how to work with existing classes from the .NET framework in PowerShell.

`Chapter 9`, *Data Parsing and Manipulation*, explains different methods to manipulate simple types in PowerShell.

`Chapter 10`, *Regular Expressions*, shows the usage of regular expressions in PowerShell scripts. This will provide the user with the ability to provide quick data comparisons.

`Chapter 11`, *Files, Folders and the Registry*, explores different methods to interact with common items on the file system and registry.

`Chapter 12`, *Windows Management Instrumentation*, explores PowerShell's ability to interact with WMI. This includes methods by which users can manipulate the WMI to obtain information pertaining to an operating system.

`Chapter 13`, *HTML, XML, and JSON*, explores the XML structure and how PowerShell can interact with XML files. This chapter will also explore how to use XML files as answer files for PowerShell scripts.

`Chapter 14`, *Working with REST and SOAP*, shows how to use REST or SOAP interfaces.

`Chapter 15`, *Remoting and Remote Management*, explores the use of Windows remoting and remote sessions to execute against remote systems.

`Chapter 16`, *Testing*, shows how to use PSScriptAnalyzer and Pester to improve the quality of your code.

`Chapter 17`, *Error Handling*, shows how to leverage PowerShell's error handling to work with errors.

What you need for this book

For this book, you will need Windows 7 or 10 and PowerShell 5.0 or 5.1. Nothing else is mandatory or used.

Who this book is for

If you are a system administrator who wants to become an expert in controlling and automating your Windows environment, then this book is for you. It is also for those new to the PowerShell language.

Conventions

In this book, you will find a number of text styles that distinguish between different kinds of information. Here are some examples of these styles and an explanation of their meaning.

Code words in text, database table names, folder names, filenames, file extensions, pathnames, dummy URLs, user input, and Twitter handles are shown as follows: "Use `Get-ChildItem` to list all of the environment variables:"

A block of code is set as follows:

```
function Get-IPConfig {
[System.Net.NetworkInformation.NetworkInterface]::GetAllNetworkInterfaces()
| ForEach-Object {
        $ipProperties = $_.GetIPProperties()
        $addresses = $ipProperties.UnicastAddresses |
            Where-Object {
                $_.Address.AddressFamily -eq 'InterNetwork'
            } | ForEach-Object {
                "$($_.Address) $($_.IPv4Mask)"
            }

        $gateway = $ipProperties.GatewayAddresses.Address |
            Where-Object {
                $_.AddressFamily -eq 'InterNetwork' -and
                $_ -ne '0.0.0.0'
            }

        [PSCustomObject]@{
            Name       = $_.Name
            Id         = $_.Id
            Addresses = $addresses
            Gateway    = $gateway
        }
    } | Where-Object { $_.Addresses }
}
Get-IPConfig
```

Any command-line input or output is written as follows:

```
PS> Update-Help -Module DnsClient -Verbose
VERBOSE: Help was not updated for the module DnsClient, because the Update-
Help command was run on this computer within the last 24 hours.
```

New terms and **important words** are shown in bold. Words that you see on the screen, for example, in menus or dialog boxes, appear in the text like this: "Press the **Initialize git repository** button, as shown in the following screenshot:"

Warnings or important notes appear in a box like this.

Tips and tricks appear like this.

Reader feedback

Feedback from our readers is always welcome. Let us know what you think about this book-what you liked or disliked. Reader feedback is important for us as it helps us develop titles that you will really get the most out of. To send us general feedback, simply email `feedback@packtpub.com`, and mention the book's title in the subject of your message. If there is a topic that you have expertise in and you are interested in either writing or contributing to a book, see our author guide at `www.packtpub.com/authors`.

Customer support

Now that you are the proud owner of a Packt book, we have a number of things to help you to get the most from your purchase.

Downloading the color images of this book

We also provide you with a PDF file that has color images of the screenshots/diagrams used in this book. The color images will help you better understand the changes in the output. You can download this file from `https://www.packtpub.com/sites/default/files/downloads/MasteringWindowsPowerShellScriptingSecondEdition_ColorImages.pdf`.

Errata

Although we have taken every care to ensure the accuracy of our content, mistakes do happen. If you find a mistake in one of our books-maybe a mistake in the text or the code-we would be grateful if you could report this to us. By doing so, you can save other readers from frustration and help us improve subsequent versions of this book. If you find any errata, please report them by visiting `http://www.packtpub.com/submit-errata`, selecting your book, clicking on the **Errata Submission Form** link, and entering the details of your errata. Once your errata are verified, your submission will be accepted and the errata will be uploaded to our website or added to any list of existing errata under the **Errata** section of that title.

To view the previously submitted errata, go to `https://www.packtpub.com/books/content/support` and enter the name of the book in the search field. The required information will appear under the **Errata** section.

Piracy

Piracy of copyrighted material on the internet is an ongoing problem across all media. At Packt, we take the protection of our copyright and licenses very seriously. If you come across any illegal copies of our works in any form on the internet, please provide us with the location address or website name immediately so that we can pursue a remedy.

Please contact us at `copyright@packtpub.com` with a link to the suspected pirated material.

We appreciate your help in protecting our authors and our ability to bring you valuable content.

Questions

If you have a problem with any aspect of this book, you can contact us at `questions@packtpub.com`, and we will do our best to address the problem.

1
Introduction to PowerShell

I write this as PowerShell approaches its 10th birthday since its release. PowerShell has come a long way since that time.

For me, PowerShell has gone from being a speculative replacement for a mixture of VBScript, C#, and Perl to a complex language with a great community.

This book is split into a number of sections. Much of the book is intended to act as a reference. We will cover the following topics in this book:

- Exploring PowerShell fundamentals
- Working with data
- Automating with PowerShell
- Extending PowerShell

In the first section of this book, while exploring the PowerShell fundamentals, we will look at the use of language and cover as many building blocks as possible.

In this chapter, we will briefly look at a number of short, diverse topics:

- What is PowerShell?
- Quick reference
- PowerShell editors
- PowerShell on Linux

What is PowerShell?

PowerShell is a mixture of a command line, a functional programming language, and an object-oriented programming language. PowerShell is based on Microsoft .NET, which gives it a level of open flexibility that was not available in Microsoft's scripting languages (such as VBScript or batch) before this.

PowerShell is an explorer's scripting language. With built-in help, command discovery, and with access to much of the .NET Framework, it is possible to dig down through the layers.

This book is based on PowerShell 5.1; some of the features discussed in the book may not be available in the earlier versions of PowerShell.

Quick reference

There is a wide variety of quick references available for PowerShell. This particular reference is intended to kick-start the book, as a lot of this is either not explicitly explained or used often before in a more detailed explanation.

Comments

Refer to the following table:

Line comment	#	# This is a line comment
Block comment	<# #>	<# This is a block or multi-line comment #>

Special characters

Refer to the following table:

Statement separator	;	Get-Command Get-Process; Get-Command Get-Help
Call operator	&	& 'Get-Process' # Invoke the string as a command & { Get-Process -Id $PID } # Invoke the script block
Dot-source operator	.	. C:\script.ps1 # Execute the script in the current scope (instead of its own scope)

Tick in PowerShell

PowerShell uses a tick as a multipurpose `escaped` character.

A tick may be used as a line continuation character. Consider the following example:

```
'one' -replace 'o', 't' `
      -replace 'n', 'w' `
      -replace 'e', 'o'
```

When using a tick to split a long statement across several lines, the tick must be the last character (it cannot be followed by a space or any other character).

A tick is used to construct several characters that can be used in strings:

Description	String	ASCII character code
Null	`` `0 ``	0
Bell sound	`` `a ``	7
Backspace	`` `b ``	8
New page form feed	`` `f ``	12
Line feed	`` `n ``	10
Carriage return	`` `r ``	13
Horizontal tab	`` `t ``	9
Vertical tab	`` `v ``	11

The `tab` character, for example, may be included in a string:

```
PS> Write-Host "First`tSecond"
First Second
```

Alternatively, the bell sound may be played in the PowerShell console (but not ISE):

```
Write-Host "`a"
```

Common operators

Refer to the following table:

Equal to	`-eq`	`1 -eq 1      # Returns $true` `1 -eq 2      # Returns $false`
Not equal to	`-ne`	`1 -ne 2      # Returns $true` `1 -ne 1      # Returns $false`

And	`-and`	`$true -and $true     # Returns $true`
		`$true -and $false     # Returns $false`
		`$false -and $false     # Returns $false`

Or	`-or`	`$true -or $true     # Returns $true`
		`$true -or $false    # Returns $true`
		`$false -or $false   # Returns $false`

Addition and concatenation	`+`	`1 + 1              # Equals 2` `"one" + "one"     # Equals oneone`
Subexpression operator	`$( )`	`"Culture is $($host.CurrentCulture)"` `"Culture is $(Get-Culture)"`

Dropping unwanted output

Refer to the following table:

Assign to `null`	`$null = Expression`	`$null = Get-Command`
Cast to `void`	`[Void](Expression)`	`[Void](Get-Command)`
Pipe to `Out-Null`	`Expression | Out-Null`	`Get-Command | Out-Null`
Redirect to `null`	`Expression > $null`	`Get-Command > $null`

Creating arrays and hashtables

Refer to the following table:

Using the array operator	`@()`	`$array = @()     # Empty array` `$array = @(1, 2, 3, 4)`

Implicit array	`Value1,`
	`Value2,`
	`Value3`
		`$array = 1, 2, 3, 4`
		`$array = "one", "two", "three",`
		`"four"`

Using the `hashtable` operator	`@{}`	`$hashtable = @{}    # Empty hashtable`
		`$hashtable = @{Key1 = “Value1”}`
		`$hashtable = @{Key1 = “Value1”; Key2 = “Value2”}`

Strings

Refer to the following table:

Expanding string	“ “	`“Value”` `$greeting = “Hello”; “$greeting World”   # Expands variable`

Expanding here-string	`@”`
	`“@`
		`$one = ‘One’`
		`@”`
		`Must be opened on its own line.`
		`This string will expand variables like $var.`
		`Can contain other quotes like “ and ‘.`
		`Must be closed on its own line with no preceding white space.`
		`“@`

Non-expanding string	‘ ‘	`‘Value’` `‘$greeting World’    # Does not expand variable`

Non-expanding here-string	`@’`
	`‘@`
		`@’`
		`Must be opened on its own line.`
		`This string will not expand variables like $var.`
		`Can contain other quotes like “ and ‘.`
		`Must be closed on its own line with no preceding white space.`
		`‘@`

Quotes in strings	“ \`” “ “ ““““ “ ‘ \`’ ‘ ‘ “ ‘	`“Double-quotes may be escaped with tick like` `` `”.”`` `“Or double-quotes may be escaped with another quote ““““.”` `` ‘Single-quotes may be escaped with tick like `’.’ `` `‘Or single-quotes may be escaped with another quote like “.’`

Common reserved variables

Refer to the following table:

Errors	`$Error`	`$Error[0]     # The last error`

Formats the enumeration limit. Dictates the number of elements displayed for objects with properties based on arrays.
The default is `4`.
	`$FormatEnumerationLimit`	`$object = [PSCustomObject]@{`
		`Array = @(1, 2, 3, 4, 5)`
		`}`
		`$object     # Shows 1, 2, 3, and 4`
		`$formatenumerationlimit = 1`
		`$object     # Shows 1`

Holds data of the current PowerShell host.	`$Host`	`$host` `$host.UI.RawUI.WindowTitle`
The matches found when using the `-match` operator.	`$Matches`	`'text' -match '.*'` `$matches`

The output field separator.
The default is a single space.
Dictates how arrays are joined when included in an expandable string.
	`$OFS`	`$arr = 1, 2, 3, 4`
		`"Joined based on OFS: $arr"`
		`$ofs = ', '`
		`"Joined based on OFS: $arr"`

Current PowerShell process ID.	`$PID`	`Get-Process -Id $PID`

Holds the path to each of the `profile` files.	`$PROFILE`	`$profile.AllUsersAllHosts`
		`$profile.AllUsersCurrentHost`
		`$profile.CurrentUserAllHosts`
		`$profile.CurrentUserCurrentHost`

PowerShell version information.	`$PSVersionTable`	`$PSVersionTable.PSVersion`

Present working directory.	`$PWD`	**`$PWD.Path`**

Quick commands and hot keys

Refer to the following table:

`ise` `ise <file>`	Opens PowerShell ISE. **Opens a file with ISE if a filename is given.**
`code` `code <file or folder>`	If Visual Studio Code is installed (and in `%PATH%`). Opens the VS Code. Opens a file or folder with the VS Code.
`Get-History` `history`	Shows command history for the current session.
`<Text><Tab>`	Autocompletes in context. `Tab` can be used to complete command names, parameter names, and some parameter values.
`#<Text><Tab>`	Autocompletes against history (beginning of the line). Typing `#get-` and repeatedly pressing *Tab* will cycle through all commands containing `Get-` from your history.
`ii`	`ii` is an alias for the `invoke-item`. Opens the current directory in Explorer.
`start iexplore`	`start` is an alias for the start-process. Opens Internet Explorer.
`start <name> -verb runas`	Runs a process as administrator.

PowerShell editors

While it is possible to write for PowerShell using the Notepad application alone, it is rarely desirable. Using an editor designed to work with PowerShell can save a lot of time.

Specialized PowerShell editors, at a minimum, offer automatic completion (IntelliSense) that reduces the amount of cross-referencing required while writing code. Finding a comfortable editor early is a good way to ease into PowerShell: memorizing commands and parameters is not necessary.

Two editors are discussed, as follows:

- PowerShell ISE
- Visual Studio Code

PowerShell ISE

PowerShell **Integrated Scripting Environment** (**ISE**) was introduced with PowerShell 2 in October 2009 and has been updated with every subsequent release.

ISE has an immediate advantage over other editors. It is installed along with PowerShell itself and is likely to be available in some form wherever PowerShell is. ISE consists of a text editor pane and a script pane, as shown in the following screenshot:

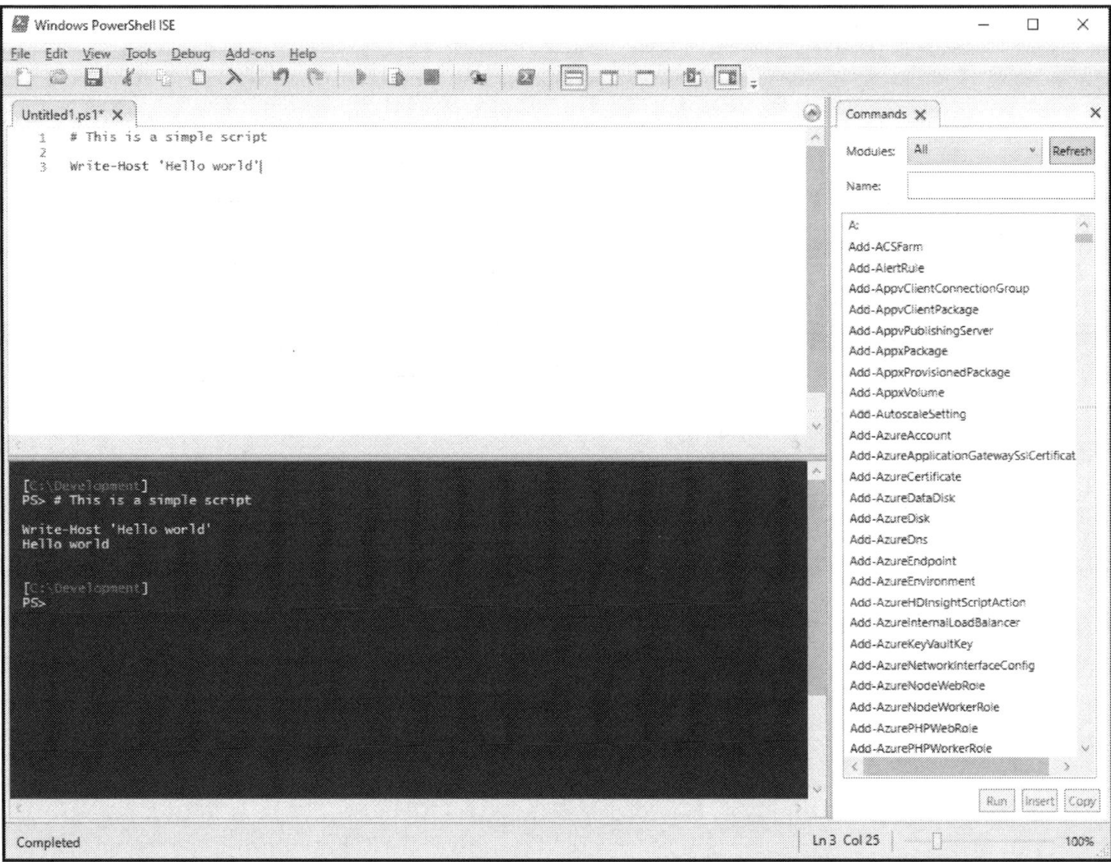

Features

ISE is a rich editing environment that includes IntelliSense, built-in help, syntax checking, debugging, and so on.

Additional features are available for ISE from the following add-on tools website:

`http://social.technet.microsoft.com/wiki/contents/articles/2969.windows-powershell-ise-add-on-tools.aspx`

If you are developing code for use on production systems, I strongly recommend adding PS Script Analyzer. PS Script Analyzer will highlight areas of your code that do not conform to its rule set; for example, using an alias instead of a command name would be highlighted.

Community and commercial add-ons can greatly extend the functionality of ISE to simplify day-to-day use.

Installing ISE Preview

In PowerShell 5, the distribution model for ISE is in the process of changing. Until version 5, ISE was released as a part of the **Windows Management Framework** (**WMF**). New features were introduced with each version of WMF, but the time between the versions was long.

ISE Preview may be installed from the PowerShell gallery using the following command:

```
Install-Module -Name PowerShellISE-Preview
```

Once installed, the `update-module` command may be used to bring ISE up to par with the published version.

ISE Preview can coexist with the version of ISE installed by the WMF package.

Starting ISE

ISE may be started from the start menu; however, running the `powershell_ise` command (from the **Run** dialog, **cmd**, or the search box) is sufficient. In PowerShell, the simpler `ise` command is aliased to `powershell_ise.exe`.

If the preview version from the PowerShell gallery is being used, the following command will start that version of ISE:

```
Start-ISEPreview
```

This first preview version differs a little from the version of ISE shipping with WMF 5. If the distribution model is successful, the PowerShell team hopes to release a new version of ISE every month, with each release fixing bugs and/or adding new features.

Visual Studio Code

Visual Studio Code is a free open source editor published by Microsoft. VS Code may be downloaded from `http://code.visualstudio.com`.

VS Code is a good choice of editor when working with multiple languages or when specifically looking for an editor that supports Git in a simple manner.

Features

VS Code does not come with the native PowerShell support. It must be added. Once VS Code is installed, open it, and select the **EXTENSIONS** button on the left-hand side.

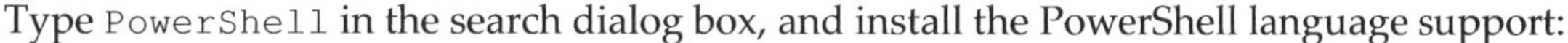

Type `PowerShell` in the search dialog box, and install the PowerShell language support:

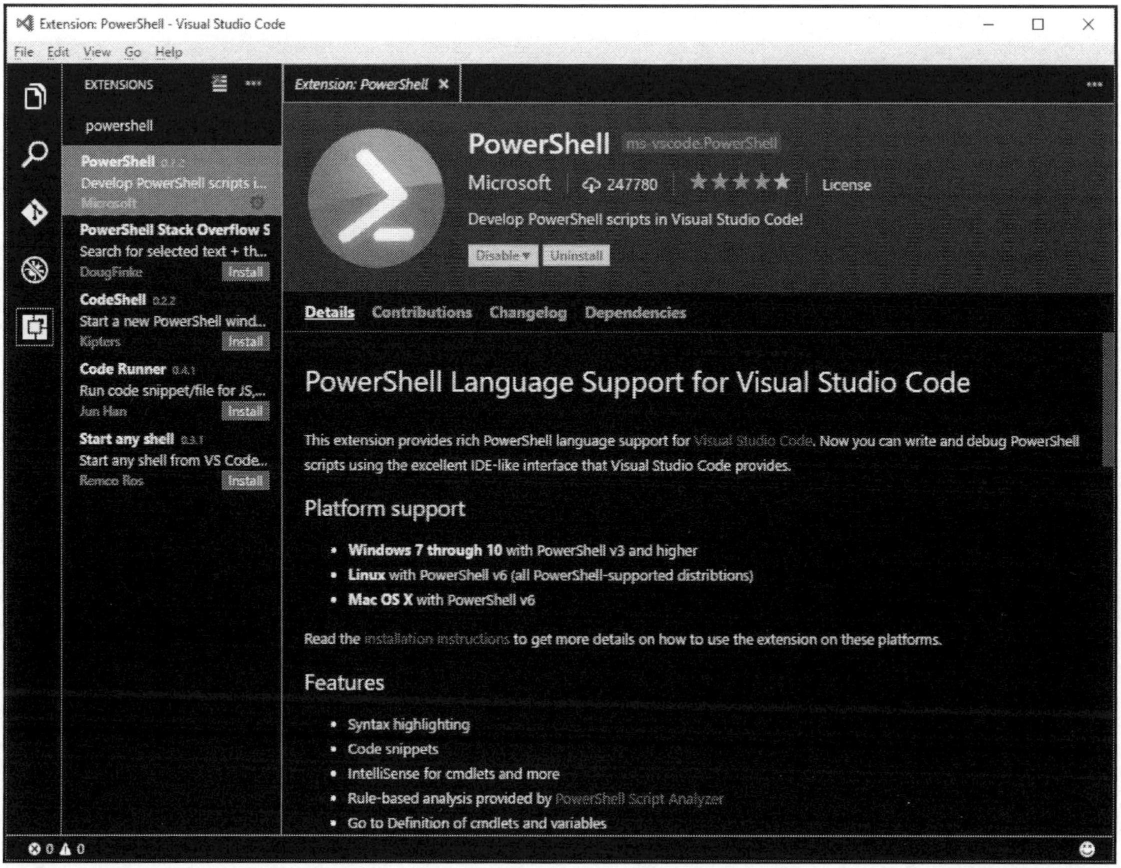

After installation, the extension provides **Syntax highlighting**, testing using **PowerShell Script Analyzer**, debugging, and so on.

Console

Unlike ISE, the console (or terminal, as it is named) in VS Code must be configured. By default, the terminal in code uses `cmd.exe`.

The following process is used to make the terminal use PowerShell:

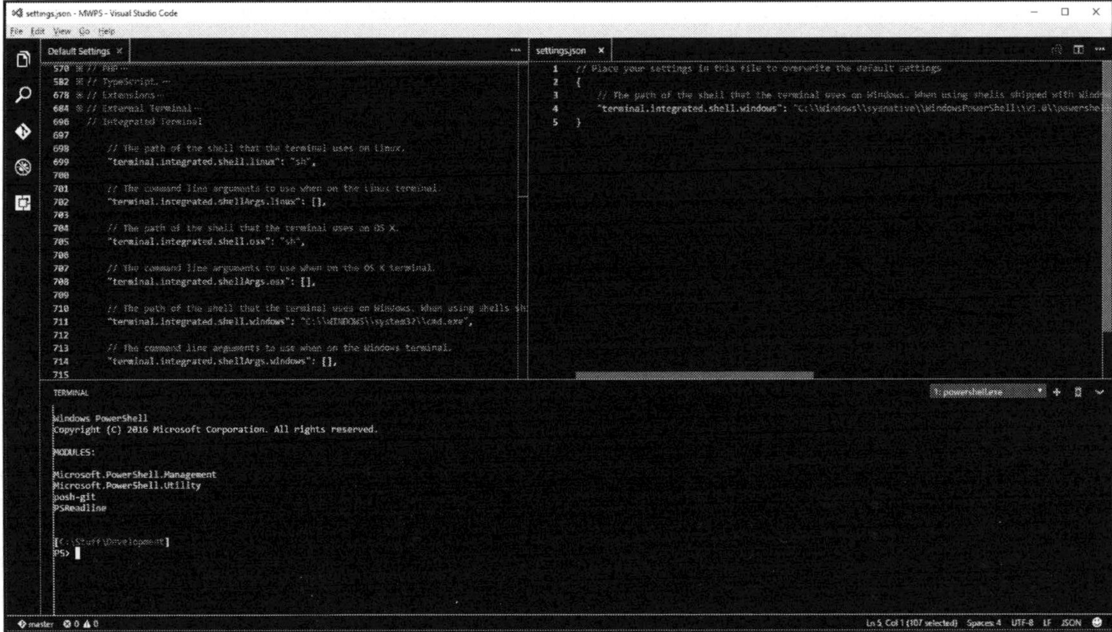

1. Open **User Settings** from **File and Preferences**. The same may be achieved by pressing *F1* and typing `user settings` followed by return.
2. This opens two windows: a `Default Settings` file on the left and a `settings.json` on the right. The file on the right holds user-specific configuration that overrides or adds to the default.
3. Expand the `Integrated Terminal` section in `Default Settings` (by clicking on the **o9** symbol) to show the default values.
4. On the right-hand side, enter the following between the curly braces:

```
"terminal.integrated.shell.windows":
"C:\\Windows\\sysnative\\WindowsPowerShell\\v1.0\\powershell.exe"
```

5. Save the changes, then press *Ctrl* + *Shift* + *'* (apostrophe) to open a new PowerShell terminal. *Ctrl* + *'* (apostrophe) toggles the visibility of the terminal window.

This is not ISE
In PowerShell ISE, *F5* + *F8* may be used to execute a script. This is not the case in VS Code. A selection may be executed by pressing *F1* and typing `run selected` to filter options to `Terminal: Run Selected Text in Active Terminal`.

Version control (Git)

Visual Studio Code comes with integrated support for Git version control. Git is a distributed version control system; each developer has a copy of the same repository.

Setting up a repository is simple, as follows:

1. Open a folder that contains a project. Then, select the **Git** button (or press *Ctrl* + *Shift* + *G*).
2. Click on **Initialize git repository** button as shown in the following screenshot:

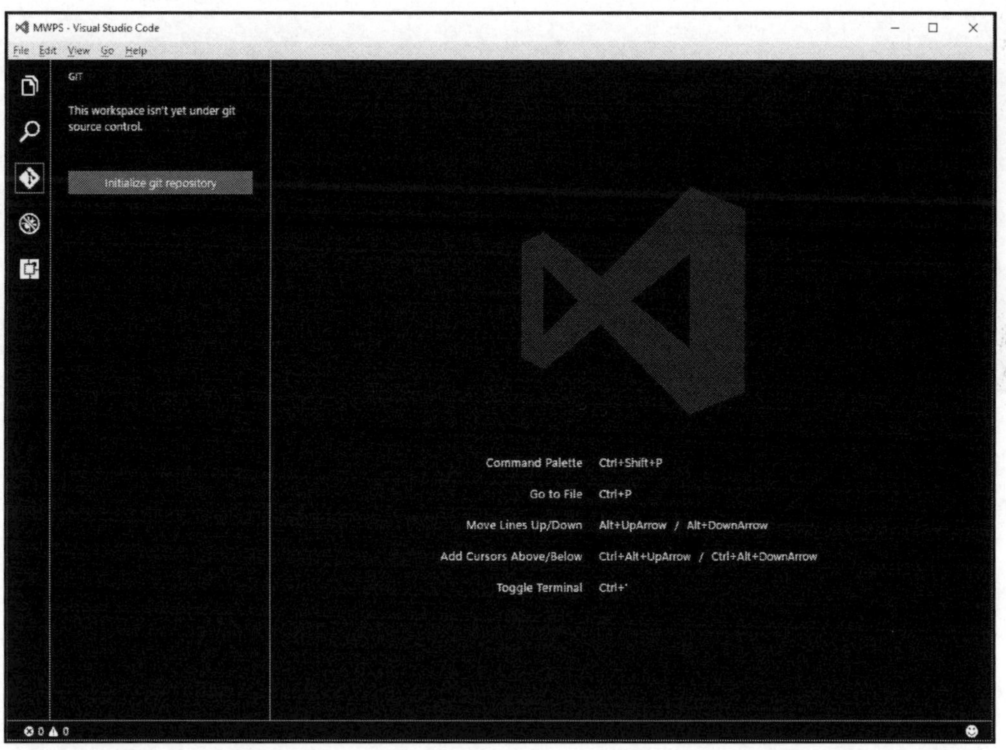

3. Once you have done this, files may be added to version control when committing (applying a change).

Subsequent changes to files may be inspected before committing again:

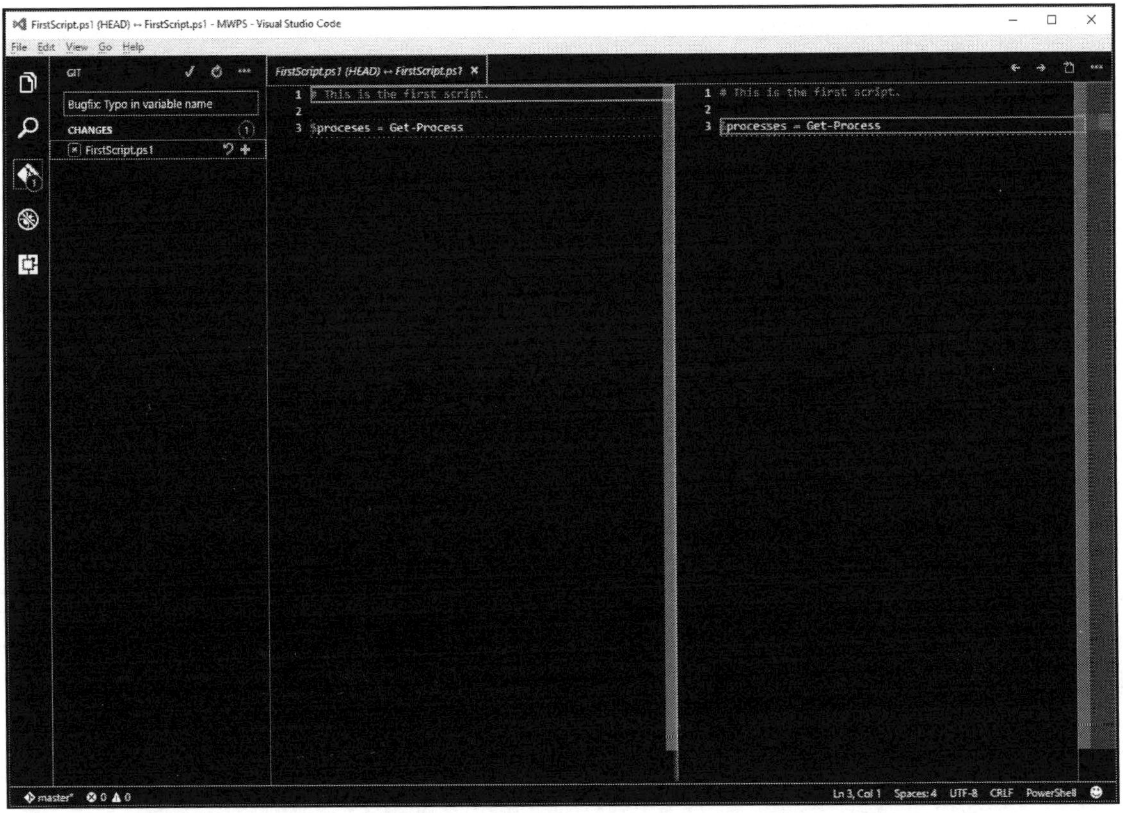

PowerShell on Linux

PowerShell for Linux is, at least at the time of writing, in alpha. The current release is still worth installing even if only to see what having a unified shell may look like.

What about Cygwin?
PowerShell is not the first to give a hint of a single shell across different operating systems. However, until PowerShell matured, it was a serious challenge to manage Windows and Microsoft-based systems from the command line alone.

Some familiarity with Linux is assumed during this process.

Installing PowerShell

This installation is based on PowerShell 6, alpha 12 as the latest at the time of writing. The package can be downloaded from GitHub with `yum`, which will also install the dependencies (`https://github.com/PowerShell/PowerShell/releases/latest`):

1. The following command will install PowerShell and any dependencies (`libicu`, `libunwind`, and `uuid`):

   ```
   sudo yum install
   https://github.com/PowerShell/PowerShell/releases/download/v6.0
   .0-alpha.12/powershell-6.0.0_alpha.12-1.el7.centos.x86_64.rpm
   ```

   alpha 12 is the latest release but it may not be when you read this.

2. PowerShell can be immediately started by running the following command:

   ```
   powershell
   ```

3. Create a few files in the `home` directory as a test:

   ```
   Set-Location ~
   1..10 | ForEach-Object { New-Item $_ -ItemType File }
   ```

4. The previous command creates `10` empty files named `1` to `10` (with no file extension). Ensure that the new files are now visible using `Get-ChildItem`:

   ```
   Get-ChildItem
   ```

ls versus Get-ChildItem:
On Windows, `ls` (list) in PowerShell is an alias for `Get-ChildItem`. On Linux, `ls` is the original command. See `Get-Alias -Definition Get-ChildItem` to view what still is.

Where are the PowerShell files?

Several of the following used paths are specific to the installed release (in this case, alpha 12).

As with PowerShell on Windows, the `PSHOME` variable shows where PowerShell itself has been installed:

```
PS> $PSHOME
/opt/microsoft/powershell/6.0.0-alpha.12
```

The paths for module installation may be viewed using the environment variables:

```
PS> $env:PSMODULEPATH -split ':'
/home/psuser/.local/share/powershell/Modules
/usr/local/share/powershell/Modules
/opt/microsoft/powershell/6.0.0-alpha.12/Modules
```

Case sensitivity
Linux has a much higher regard for case than Windows. Environment variables, file paths, executables, and so on, are case sensitive. The previously used variable name must be written in uppercase.
Use `Get-ChildItem` to list all of the environment variables using the following command:
`Get-ChildItem env:`

Changing the shell

Once installed, PowerShell is visible in the list of available shells:

```
chsh -l
```

Set PowerShell as the default `shell` for the current user:

```
chsh
New shell [/bin/bash]: /usr/bin/powershell
```

Profiles

The current user profile on Linux resides under the home directory:

```
~/.config/powershell
```

Two profiles can be created: `CurrentUserCurrentHost` (`Microsoft.PowerShell_profile.ps1`) and `Current User` (`profile.ps1`). Inspecting the automatic variable, `$PROFILE` shows the first of these:

1. The directory will need to be created prior to use; the following command creates it:

```
New-Item ~/.config/powershell -ItemType Directory
```

2. Create a simple profile file by sending a string to a file:

```
'Write-Host "Welcome to PowerShell" -ForegroundColor Green' |
    Out-File .config/powershell/profile.ps1
```

3. The `AllUser` profile may be created under PowerShell's installation directory, in this case, alpha 12, as this is the version I have installed:

```
/opt/microsoft/powershell/6.0.0-alpha.12
```

4. Writing to this area of the filesystem requires the `root` privileges:

```
sudo vi /opt/microsoft/powershell/6.0.0-alpha.12/profile.ps1
```

5. Inside `vi`, press `i` to enter insert mode and then type the following:

```
Write-Host 'This is the system profile' -ForegroundColor Yellow
```

6. Once completed, press *Esc*, then type `:wq` to save and quit `vi`.
7. As with PowerShell on Windows, this will be executed before a user-level `profile` that shows the following in the console when the shell is started:

```
This is the system profile
Welcome to PowerShell
```

Multiplatform scripting

PowerShell on Linux (and macOS) has a long way to go to reach maturity. Our experience writing for these systems has to make a similar journey.

One of the most important facets is that Linux and macOS run PowerShell Core. It lacks some features we may have become used to when writing for Windows.

Line endings

Windows editors, including ISE, tend to use a carriage return followed by linefeed (`\r\n` or `` `r`n ``) at the end of each line. Linux editors use linefeed only (`\n` or `` `n ``).

Line endings are less important if the only thing reading the file is PowerShell (on any platform). However, if a script is set to executable on Linux, a sha-bang must be included and the line-ending character used must be linefeed only.

For example, a created as follows named `test.ps1` must use `\n` to end lines:

```
#!/usr/bin/env powershell
Get-Process
```

The first line is the sha-bang and lets Linux know which parser to use when executing the shell script.

Once created, `chmod` may be used to make the script executable outside of PowerShell:

```
chmod +x test.ps1
```

After being made executable, the script may be executed from `bash` with the full path or a relative path:

```
./test.ps1
```

Editor defaults
PowerShell ISE uses carriage return followed by line feed (`\r\n`). This behavior is by design and cannot be changed.
Visual Studio Code uses `\r\n` for line endings by default. This may be changed in **User Settings** by adding the following command:
`"files.eol": "\n"`

File encoding

Windows editors, including ISE, tend to save files using what is commonly known as ANSI encoding; this is more correctly known as Windows-1252.

As Windows-1252 is a Microsoft native format, it may be more appropriate to save files in a universally accepted format such as UTF8.

Editor defaults
PowerShell ISE defaults to saving files in UTF8 with a **Byte Order Mark (BOM)**.
Visual Studio Code saves files using UTF8 (without a BOM) by default. The setting may be changed in **User Settings** by adding `"files.encoding": "utf8bom"`.

Path separator

Testing shows that PowerShell on Linux is forgiving about path separators; that is, Microsoft Windows uses the backslash (\), where Linux uses a forward slash (/).

If anything outside of PowerShell (including native commands) is to be used, a correct separator should be chosen.

The **`Join-Path`** command will merge path elements using the correct separator for each platform. Manual path construction (based on merging strings) should be avoided.

Example

The following function uses the `System.Net.NetworkInformation` namespace to discover IPv4 address information. This allows us to return the same thing whether it is run on Windows or Linux.

If it were Windows only, we might have used WMI or the `Get-NetIPConfiguration` command. Creating something to work on both operating systems is more challenging:

```
function Get-IPConfig {
[System.Net.NetworkInformation.NetworkInterface]::GetAllNetworkInterfaces()
| ForEach-Object {
        $ipProperties = $_.GetIPProperties()
        $addresses = $ipProperties.UnicastAddresses |
            Where-Object {
                $_.Address.AddressFamily -eq 'InterNetwork'
            } | ForEach-Object {
                "$($_.Address) $($_.IPv4Mask)"
            }

        $gateway = $ipProperties.GatewayAddresses.Address |
            Where-Object {
                $_.AddressFamily -eq 'InterNetwork' -and
                $_ -ne '0.0.0.0'
            }
```

```
            [PSCustomObject]@{
                Name       = $_.Name
                Id         = $_.Id
                Addresses = $addresses
                Gateway    = $gateway
            }
        } | Where-Object { $_.Addresses }
}
Get-IPConfig
```

Summary

This chapter featured a brief introduction to PowerShell itself and provided a quick reference for some of the syntax and features.

A reasonable PowerShell editor is a great tool to have for any scripting language. A number of excellent options are available for beginners and veterans alike.

Recently, PowerShell has moved onto GitHub as an open source project. At the same time, versions of PowerShell for Linux and macOS have been developed. Installation of PowerShell on CentOS was briefly demonstrated.

In `Chapter 2`, *Working with PowerShell,* we will look at the help system and how to discover commands.

2
Working with PowerShell

A grasp of a few basics about PowerShell will go a long way. These basics will always be useful no matter how long you work with the language.

In this chapter, we will cover the following topics:

- Getting help
- Command naming
- Command discovery
- Parameters and parameter sets
- Providers

Getting help

Gaining confidence using the built-in help system is an important part of working with PowerShell. In PowerShell, help is extensive; authors can easily write their own help content when working with scripts and script modules.

A number of commands are available to interact with the help system, as follows:

- `Get-Help`
- `Save-Help`
- `Update-Help`

Before exploring these commands, the concept of updatable help should be discussed.

Updatable help

Updatable help was introduced with PowerShell 3. It gives authors the option to store the most recent versions of their help documentation outside of PowerShell on web servers.

Which modules support updatable help?
A list of modules that support updatable help may be viewed by running the following command:
`Get-Module -ListAvailable | Where-Object HelpInfoURI -like *`

Help for the core components of PowerShell is no longer a part of the Windows Management Framework package and must be downloaded before it can be viewed. The first time `Get-Help` is run, you will be prompted to update help.

If the previous prompt is accepted, PowerShell will attempt to download content for any module that supports updatable help.

Computers with no internet access or computers behind a restrictive proxy server may not be able to download the help content. If PowerShell is unable to download help, it can only show a small amount of discoverable information about a command; for example, without downloading help, the content for the `Out-Null` command is minimal, as shown in the following code:

```
PS C:\windows\system32> Get-Help Out-Null

NAME
    Out-Null
SYNTAX
    Out-Null [-InputObject <psobject>] [<CommonParameters>]

ALIASES
    None

REMARKS
    Get-Help cannot find the Help files for this cmdlet on this computer.
    It is displaying only partial help.
        -- To download and install Help files for the module that
           includes this cmdlet, use Update-Help.
        -- To view the Help topic for this cmdlet online, type:
           "Get-Help Out-Null -Online" or go to
           http://go.microsoft.com/fwlink/?LinkID=113366.
```

`Updatable` helps as a help file that may be viewed using the following command:

```
Get-Help about_Updatable_Help
```

The Get-Help command

Without any arguments or parameters, `Get-Help` will show introductory help about the help system. This content is taken from the default `help` file (`Get-Help default`); a snippet of this is as follows:

```
PS> Get-Help

TOPIC
    Windows PowerShell Help System

SHORT DESCRIPTION
    Displays help about Windows PowerShell cmdlets and concepts.

LONG DESCRIPTION
    Windows PowerShell Help describes Windows PowerShell cmdlets,
```

The help content can be long:
The help content, in most cases, will not fit on a single screen. The `help` command differs from `Get-Help` in that it pauses (waiting for a key to be pressed) after each page. Let's look at an example:
`help default`

The previous command is equivalent to running `Get-Help` and piping it into the `more` command:

```
Get-Help default | more
```

Alternatively, `Get-Help` can be asked to show a window:

```
Get-Help default -ShowWindow
```

The available help content may be listed using either of the following two commands:

```
Get-Help *
Get-Help -Category All
```

Help for a command may be viewed as follows:

```
Get-Help <CommandName>
```

Let's look at an example:

```
Get-Help Get-Variable
```

The help content is broken down into a number of visible sections: name, synopsis, syntax, description, related links, and remarks. Syntax is covered in the following section in more detail as it is the most complex.

Syntax

The syntax section lists each of the possible combinations of parameters a command will accept; each of these is known as a parameter set.

A command that has more than one parameter set is displayed as follows:

```
SYNTAX
    Get-Process [[-Name] <String[]>] [-ComputerName <String[]>]
    [-FileVersionInfo] [-Module] [<CommonParameters>]

    Get-Process [-ComputerName [<String[]>]] [-FileVersionInfo]
    [-Module] -InputObject <Process[]> [<CommonParameters>]
```

The syntax elements written in square brackets are optional; for example, syntax help for `Get-Process` shows that all of its parameters are optional, as shown in the following code:

```
SYNTAX
    Get-Process [[-Name] <String[]>] [-ComputerName <String[]>] [-
FileVersionInfo] [-Module] [<CommonParameters>]
```

`Get-Process` may be run without any parameters at all, or it may be run with a value only and no parameter name, or it may include the parameter name as well as the value. Each of the following examples is a valid use of `Get-Process`:

```
Get-Process
Get-Process powershell
Get-Process -Name powershell
```

Later in this chapter, we will take a more detailed look at the different parameters and how they might be used.

Examples

The examples section of help is often invaluable. In some cases, a command is sufficiently complex to require a detailed example to accompany parameter descriptions; in others, the command is simple, and a good example may serve in lieu of reading further the help documentation.

Examples for a command may be requested using `Get-Help`, as shown in the following example:

```
Get-Help Get-Help -Examples
```

It is common for a command to list several examples of its use, especially if the command has more than one parameter set.

Parameter

Help for specific parameters may be requested as follows:

```
Get-Help Get-Command -Parameter <ParameterName>
```

This option allows quick retrieval of specific help for a single parameter; for example, help for the `Path` parameter of the `Import-Csv` command may be quickly viewed:

```
PS> Get-Help Import-Csv -Parameter Path

-Path [<String[]>]
    Specifies the path to the CSV file to import. You can also pipe
    a path to Import-Csv.
    Required? false
    Position? 1
    Default value None
    Accept pipeline input? true (ByValue)
    Accept wildcard characters? false
```

Detailed and Full switches

The `Detailed` switch parameter asks `Get-Help` to return most help content. This adds information about each parameter and the set of examples to name, synopsis, syntax, and description. Related links are excluded when using this parameter.

The `Detailed` parameter is used as shown in the following example:

```
Get-Help Get-Process -Detailed
```

Using a `Full` switch adds more technical details (compared to using the `Detailed` parameter). Inputs, outputs, notes, and related links are added to those seen using `Detailed`. For example, the sections detailing input and output types from `Get-Process` may be extracted from the full help document:

```
PS> Get-Help Get-Process -Full
...
INPUTS
    System.Diagnostics.Process
        You can pipe a process object to Get-Process.
OUTPUTS
    System.Diagnostics.Process, System.Diagnotics.FileVersionInfo,
System.Diagnostics.ProcessModule
        By default, Get-Process returns a System.Diagnostics.Process
        object. If you use the FileVersionInfo parameter, it returns a
        System.Diagnotics.FileVersionInfo object. If you use the Module
        parameter (without the FileVersionInfo parameter), it returns a
```

Save-Help

The `Save-Help` command can be used with modules that support updatable help. It saves help content for modules to a folder; for example, the help content for the `DnsClient` module can be saved to `C:\PSHelp` (the directory must already exist):

```
Save-Help -DestinationPath C:\PSHelp -Module DnsClient
```

Alternatively, the help content for all modules may be saved, as follows:

```
Save-Help -DestinationPath C:\PSHelp
```

The process creates an XML formatted `HelpInfo` file that holds the source of the help content and a CAB (cabinet) file named after the module and culture.

Opening the CAB file shows that it contains a number of XML formatted help files, as shown in the following screenshot:

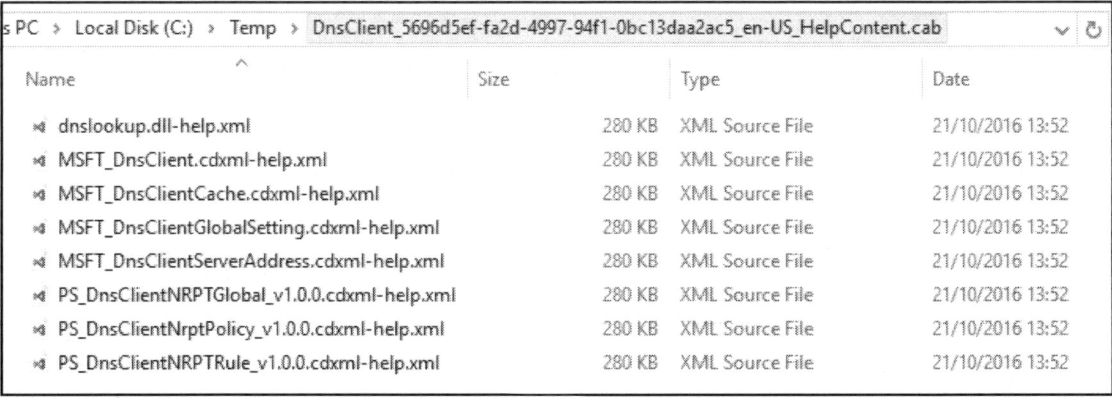

Saved help content can be copied over to another computer and imported using `Update-Help`. This technique is very useful for computers that do not have internet access as it means help content can be made available.

Update-Help

Update help can perform two tasks:

- Update help files from the internet
- Import previously saved help files

To update help from the internet, `Update-Help` may be run without any parameters:

```
Update-Help
```

Administrator rights are required
Updating help for some modules will require administrative rights (run as administrator). This applies to modules stored in protected areas of the filesystem, such as those in `$PSHost` (`%SystemRoot%\System32\WindowsPowerShell\v1.0`) or under `Program Files`.

When updating help information from the internet, by default, `Update-Help` will not download help content more than once every `24 hours`. This restriction is documented in the `help` command and may be seen in action using the `Verbose` switch:

```
PS> Update-Help -Module DnsClient -Verbose
VERBOSE: Help was not updated for the module DnsClient, because the Update-
Help command was run on this computer within the last 24 hours.
To update help again, add the Force parameter to your command.
```

As described in the message, using the `Force` switch parameter will ignore the time restriction.

Importing help from a set of saved files uses the `SourcePath` parameter:

```
Update-Help -SourcePath C:\temp
```

The following error message may be generated when attempting to import help from another culture:

```
PS> Update-Help -SourcePath C:\Temp -Module DnsClient
Update-Help : Failed to update Help for the module(s) 'DnsClient' with
UIculture(s) {en-GB} :
Unable to retrieve the HelpInfo XML file for UI culture en-GB. Make sure
the HelpInfoUri property in the module manifest is valid or check your
network connection and then try the command again.
At line:1 char:1
+ Update-Help -SourcePath C:\Temp -Module DnsClient -Verbose -Force
+ ~~~~~~~~~~~~~~~~~~~~~~~~~~~~~~~~~~~~~~~~~~~~~~~~~~~~~~~~~~~~~~~~
    + CategoryInfo          : ResourceUnavailable: (:) [Update-Help],
Exception
    + FullyQualifiedErrorId :
UnableToRetrieveHelpInfoXml,Microsoft.PowerShell.Commands.UpdateHelpCommand
```

The culture of the computer in question is set to `en-GB` (`Get-UICulture`) but the help files are for `en-US`.

It is possible to work around this problem with the `UICulture` parameter for `Update-Help`, as follows:

```
Update-Help -SourcePath C:\Temp -Module DnsClient -UICulture en-US
```

About help files

About documents describe features of a language or concepts that apply to more than one command. These items do not fit in help for individual commands.

The list of help files may be viewed by running `Get-Help` with the category as `HelpFile`, as demonstrated in the following code:

```
PS> Get-Help -Category HelpFile
```

These files cover a huge variety of topics from aliases to modules to WMI:

```
Name                                    Category Synopsis
----                                    -------- --------
about_Aliases HelpFile                  SHORT    DESCRIPTION
about_Arithmetic_Operators HelpFile     SHORT    DESCRIPTION
about_Arrays HelpFile                   SHORT    DESCRIPTION
about_Assignment_Operators HelpFile     SHORT    DESCRIPTION
about_Automatic_Variables HelpFile      SHORT    DESCRIPTION
about_Break HelpFile                    SHORT    DESCRIPTION
about_Classes HelpFile                  SHORT    DESCRIPTION
about_Command_Precedence HelpFile       SHORT    DESCRIPTION
about_Command_Syntax HelpFile           SHORT    DESCRIPTION
about_Comment_Based_Help HelpFile       SHORT    DESCRIPTION
about_CommonParameters HelpFile         SHORT    DESCRIPTION
about_Comparison_Operators HelpFile     SHORT    DESCRIPTION
about_Continue HelpFile                 SHORT    DESCRIPTION
about_Core_Commands HelpFile            SHORT    DESCRIPTION
about_Data_Sections HelpFile            SHORT    DESCRIPTION
...
```

Command naming and discovery

Commands in PowerShell are formed around verb and noun pairs in the form verb-noun.

This feature is useful when finding commands; it allows you to make educated guesses such that there is little need to memorize long lists of commands.

Verbs

The list of verbs is maintained by Microsoft. This formal approach to naming commands greatly assists discovery.

Verbs are words such as `Add`, `Get`, `Set`, and `New`. In addition to these, we have `ConvertFrom` and `ConvertTo`.

The list of verbs is available within PowerShell, as follows:

```
Get-Verb
```

Each verb has a group, such as data, life cycle, or security. Complementary actions such as encryption and decryption tend to use verbs in the same group; for example, the verb protect may be used to encrypt something and the verb unprotect may be used to decrypt.

A detailed list of verbs, along with use cases, is available on MSDN:

`https://msdn.microsoft.com/en-us/library/ms714428(v=vs.85).aspx`

Nouns

The noun provides a very short description of the object the command is expecting to act on.

The noun part may be a single word, as is the case with `Get-Process`, `New-Item`, or `Get-Help` or more than one word, as seen with `Get-ChildItem`, `Invoke-WebRequest`, or `Send-MailMessage`.

Finding commands

The verb-noun pairing can make it a lot easier to find commands (without resorting to search engines).

For example, if we want to list firewall rules and we already know of the `NetSecurity` module, we can run the following command that shows the `Get` commands in that module:

```
PS> Get-Command Get-*Firewall* -Module NetSecurity

CommandType Name                                Version Source
----------- ----                                ------- ------
Function    Get-NetFirewallAddressFilter        2.0.0.0 NetSecurity
Function    Get-NetFirewallApplicationFilter    2.0.0.0 NetSecurity
Function    Get-NetFirewallInterfaceFilter      2.0.0.0 NetSecurity
Function    Get-NetFirewallInterfaceTypeFilter 2.0.0.0 NetSecurity
Function    Get-NetFirewallPortFilter           2.0.0.0 NetSecurity
Function    Get-NetFirewallProfile              2.0.0.0 NetSecurity
Function    Get-NetFirewallRule                 2.0.0.0 NetSecurity
Function    Get-NetFirewallSecurityFilter       2.0.0.0 NetSecurity
Function    Get-NetFirewallServiceFilter        2.0.0.0 NetSecurity
Function    Get-NetFirewallSetting              2.0.0.0 NetSecurity
```

From the previous list, `Get-NetFirewallRule` closely matches the requirement (to see a list of firewall rules) and should be explored.

Taking a broader approach, if the module was not known, we might still be able to guess by searching for commands containing specific nouns, for example, commands to get existing items that mention a firewall:

```
Get-Command Get-*Firewall*
```

Once a potential command has been found, `Get-Help` can be used to assess whether or not the command is suitable.

Aliases

An alias in PowerShell is an alternate name for a command. A command may have more than one alias.

The list of aliases may be viewed using `Get-Alias`, as shown in the following example:

```
PS> Get-Alias

CommandType Name
----------- ----
Alias       % -> ForEach-Object
Alias       ? -> Where-Object
Alias       ac -> Add-Content
Alias       asnp -> Add-PSSnapin
Alias       cat -> Get-Content
Alias       cd -> Set-Location
```

`Get-Alias` may be used to find the command behind an alias:

```
Get-Alias dir
```

It can also be used to find the aliases for a command name:

```
Get-Alias -Definition Get-ChildItem
```

Examples of aliases that are frequently used in examples on the internet include the following:

- `%` for `ForEach-Object`
- `?` for `Where-Object`
- `cd` for `Set-Location`
- `gc` or `cat` for `Get-Content`
- `ls` or `dir` for `Get-ChildItem`
- `man` for `help` (and then `Get-Help`)

An alias does not change how a command is used. There is no practical difference between the following two following commands:

```
cd $env:TEMP
Set-Location $env:TEMP
```

New aliases are created with the `New-Alias` command; for example, we might choose to create an alias named `grep` for `Select-String`:

```
New-Alias grep -Value Select-String
```

Each alias exists until the PowerShell session is closed.

More information is available about aliases in the help file that may be viewed using the following command:

```
Get-Help about_Aliases
```

Parameters and parameter sets

As seen while looking at syntax in `Get-Help`, commands accept a mixture of parameters.

Parameters

When viewing help for a command, we can see many different approaches to different parameters.

Optional parameters

Optional parameters are surrounded by square brackets. This denotes an optional parameter that requires a value (when used):

```
SYNTAX
    Get-Process [-ComputerName <String[]>] ...
```

In this case, if a value for a parameter is to be specified, the name of the parameter must also be specified, as shown in the following example:

```
Get-Process -ComputerName somecomputer
```

Optional positional parameters

It is not uncommon to see an optional positional parameter as the first parameter:

```
SYNTAX
    Get-Process [[-Name] <String[]>] ...
```

In this example, we may use either of the following:

```
Get-Process -Name powershell
Get-Process powershell
```

Mandatory parameters

A mandatory parameter must always be supplied and is written as follows:

```
SYNTAX
    Get-ADUser -Filter <string> ...
```

In this case, the `Filter` parameter must be written and it must be given a value. For example, to supply a `Filter` for the command, the `Filter` parameter must be explicitly written:

```
Get-ADUser -Filter { sAMAccountName -eq "SomeName" }
```

As the parameter, name (`Filter`) must always be supplied.

Mandatory positional parameters

Parameters that are mandatory and accept values based on position are written as follows:

```
SYNTAX
    Get-ADUser [-Identity] <ADUser> ...
```

In this case, the `Identity` parameter name is optional but the value is not. The command may be used as described by either of the following examples:

```
Get-ADUser -Identity useridentity
Get-ADUser useridentity
```

In both cases, the supplied value fills the `Identity` parameter.

A command with more than one mandatory positional parameter may appear as follows:

```
SYNTAX
    Add-Member [-NotePropertyName] <String> [-NotePropertyValue]
    <Object> ...
```

In this case, the command may be called as follows:

```
Add-Member -NotePropertyName Name -NotePropertyValue "value"
Add-Member -NotePropertyValue "value" -NotePropertyName Name
Add-Member Name -NotePropertyValue "value"
Add-Member Name "value"
```

Switch parameters

Switch parameters have no arguments (values); the presence of a switch parameter is sufficient; for example, `Recurse` is a switch parameter for `Get-ChildItem`:

```
SYNTAX
    Get-ChildItem ... [-Recurse] ...
```

As with the other types of parameters, optional use is denoted by square brackets.

Switch parameters, by default, are `false` (not set). If a switch parameter is `true` (set) by default, it is possible to set the value to `false` using the notation, as shown in the following code:

```
Get-ChildItem -Recurse:$false
```

In the case of `Get-ChildItem`, this does nothing; this technique is most widely used with the `Confirm` switch parameter discussed later in this chapter.

Common parameters

When looking at the syntax, you will see that most commands end with a `CommonParameters` item:

```
SYNTAX
    Get-Process ... [<CommonParameters>]
```

These common parameters are documented inside PowerShell:

```
Get-Help about_CommonParameters
```

These parameters let you control some of the standardized functionality PowerShell provides, such as verbose output and actions to take when errors occur.

For example, `Stop-Process` does not explicitly state that it has a `Verbose` parameter, but as `Verbose` is a common parameter, it may be used. This can be seen if `notepad` is started and immediately stopped:

```
PS> Start-Process notepad -Verbose -PassThru | Stop-Process -Verbose
VERBOSE: Performing the operation "Stop-Process" on target "notepad
(5592)".
```

Not so verbose:
Just because a command supports a set of common parameters does not mean it must use them; for example, `Get-Process` supports the `verbose` parameter, yet it does not write any verbose output.

Parameter values

Value types of arguments (the type of value expected by a parameter) are enclosed in angular brackets, as shown in the following example:

```
<string>
<string[]>
```

If a value is in the `<string>` form, a single value is expected. If the value is in the `<string[]>` form, an array (or list) of values is expected.

For example, `Get-CimInstance` accepts a single value only for the `ClassName` parameter:

```
SYNTAX
    Get-CimInstance [-ClassName] <String> ...
```

The command may be called the same as the following:

```
Get-CimInstance -ClassName Win32_OperatingSystem
```

In comparison, `Get-Process` accepts multiple values for the `Name` parameter:

```
SYNTAX
    Get-Process [[-Name] <String[]>] ...
```

`Get-Process` may be called the same as the following:

```
Get-Process -Name powershell, explorer, smss
```

Parameter sets

Many of the commands in PowerShell have more than one parameter set. This was seen while looking at the syntax section of help; for example, `Stop-Process` has three parameter sets:

```
SYNTAX
    Stop-Process [-Id] <Int32[]> [-Confirm] [-Force] [-PassThru]
[-WhatIf] [<CommonParameters>]
    Stop-Process [-InputObject] <Process[]> [-Confirm] [-Force]
[-PassThru] [-WhatIf] [<CommonParameters>]
    Stop-Process [-Confirm] [-Force] -Name <String[]> [-PassThru]
[-WhatIf] [<CommonParameters>]
```

Each parameter set must have one or more parameters unique to that set. This allows each set to be distinguished from the other. In the previous example, `Id`, `InputObject`, and `Name` are used as differentiators.

The first parameter set expects a process ID, and this ID may be supplied with the parameter name or based on position; for example, both of these commands close the current PowerShell console:

```
Stop-Process -Id $PID
Stop-Process $PID
```

The second parameter set needs a value for `InputObject`. Again, this may be supplied as a positional parameter. In this case, it will be distinguished based on its type:

```
$process = Start-Process notepad -PassThru
Stop-Process -InputObject $process
Stop-Process $process
$process | Stop-Process
```

Pipeline input:
`Get-Help` should help show which parameters accept pipeline input and examples are likely to show how.
If `Get-Help` is incomplete, `Get-Command` can be used to explore parameters:
`(Get-Command Stop-Process).Parameters.InputObject.Attributes`

Confirm, WhatIf, and Force

The Confirm, WhatIf, and Force parameters are used with commands that make changes (to files, variables, data, and so on). These parameters are often used with commands that use the verbs Set or Remove, but the parameters are not limited to specific verbs.

Confirm and WhatIf have associated preference variables. Preference variables have an about file, which may be viewed using the following command:

```
Get-Help about_Preference_Variables
```

The Force parameter is not one of the common parameters, but it is often seen in commands which might otherwise prompt for confirmation. There is no fixed use of the Force parameter. The effect of using Force is a choice a command developer must make. The Help documentation should state the effect of using Force, as is the case with the Remove-Item command in the following example:

```
Get-Help Remove-Item -Parameter Force
```

Confirm parameter

The Confirm parameter causes a command to prompt before an action is taken; for example, the Confirm parameter forces Remove-Item to prompt when a file is to be removed:

```
PS> Set-Location $env:TEMP
New-Item IMadeThisUp.txt -Force
Remove-Item .\IMadeThisUp.txt -Confirm
Confirm
Are you sure you want to perform this action?
Performing the operation "Remove File" on target
"C:\Users\whoami\AppData\Local\Temp\IMadeThisUp.txt".
[Y] Yes [A] Yes to All [N] No [L] No to All [S] Suspend [?] Help (default
is "Y"):
```

We have seen that a confirmation prompt may be forcefully requested in the previous example. In a similar manner, confirmation prompts may be suppressed; for example, the value of the Confirm parameter may be explicitly set to false, as shown in the following code:

```
Remove-Item .\IMadeThisUp.txt -Confirm:$false
```

There is more than one way of prompting:
There are two ways of requesting confirmation in PowerShell: `Confirm` and the associated `ConfirmPreference`; the variable only acts against one of these.
Using the parameter or changing the variable will not suppress all prompts. For example, `Remove-Item` will always prompt if you attempt to delete a directory that is not empty without supplying the `Recurse` parameter.

This technique is useful for commands that prompt by default; for example, `Clear-RecycleBin` will prompt by default:

```
PS> Clear-RecycleBin
Confirm
Are you sure you want to perform this action?
Performing the operation "Clear-RecycleBin" on target " All of the contents
of the Recycle Bin".
[Y] Yes [A] Yes to All [N] No [L] No to All [S] Suspend [?] Help (default
is "Y"):
```

Setting the `Confirm` parameter to `false` for `Clear-RecycleBin` will bypass the prompt and immediately empty the recycle bin:

```
Clear-RecycleBin -Confirm:$false
```

Finding commands with a specific impact:
The following snippet will return a list of all commands that state they have a high impact:

```
Get-Command -CommandType Cmdlet, Function | Where-Object
{ (New-Object
System.Management.Automation.CommandMetadata($_)).Confirm
Impact -eq 'High' }
```

ConfirmPreference

If the `Confirm` parameter is not set, whether or not a prompt is shown is determined by PowerShell. The value of the `ConfirmPreference` variable is compared with the stated impact of a command.

By default, the value of `ConfirmPreference` is `High`, as shown in the following code:

```
PS> $ConfirmPreference
High
```

By default, commands have a medium impact.

Finding ConfirmImpact:
In scripts and functions, the `ConfirmImpact` setting is part of the `CmdletBinding` attribute:
`[CmdletBinding(ConfirmImpact = 'High')]`
If `CmdletBinding` or `ConfirmImpact` are not present, the impact is medium.
The impact of a function or `cmdlet` may be viewed using the `ConfirmImpact` property of a command's metadata:

```
New-Object
System.Management.Automation.CommandMetadata(Get-Command
Remove-Item)
```

`ConfirmPreference` has four possible values:

- `High` : Prompts when command impact is `High` (default)
- `Medium` : Prompts when command impact is `Medium` or `High`
- `Low` : Prompts when command impact is `Low`, `Medium`, or `High`
- `None` : Never prompts

A new value may be set by assigning it in the console; for example, it can be set to `Low`:

```
$ConfirmPreference = 'Low'
```

ConfirmPreference and the Confirm parameter:
While `ConfirmPreference` may be set to `None` to suppress confirmation prompts, confirmation may still be explicitly requested. Let's look at an example:

```
$ConfirmPreference = 'None'
New-Item NewFile.txt -Confirm
```

As the `Confirm` parameter is supplied, the `ConfirmPreference` value within the scope of the command (`New-Item`) is `Low`, and therefore the prompt displays.

WhatIf parameter

The `WhatIf` parameter replaces the confirmation prompt with a simple statement that should state what would have been done using `Remove-Item` as an example again:

```
PS> Set-Location $env:TEMP
New-Item IMadeThisUp.txt -Force
Remove-Item .\IMadeThisUp.txt -WhatIf
Confirm
Are you sure you want to perform this action?
What If: Performing the operation "Remove File" on target
"C:\Users\whoami\AppData\Local\Temp\IMadeThisUp.txt".
```

If both `Confirm` and `WhatIf` are used with a command, `WhatIf` takes precedence.

`WhatIf` may be unset on a per-command basis by supplying a value of `false` in the same manner as the `Confirm` parameter. Let's look at the following example:

```
'Some message' | Out-File $env:TEMP\test.txt -WhatIf:$false
```

The previous technique can be useful if a file (such as a log file) should be written to irrespective of whether `WhatIf` is being used or not.

WhatIfPreference

The `WhatIfpreference` variable holds a Boolean (`true` or `false`) value and has a default value of `false`.

If the preference variable is set to `true`, all commands that support `WhatIf` will act as if the parameter is explicitly set. A new value may be set for the variable as shown in the following code:

```
$WhatIfPreference = $true
```

The `WhatIf` preference variable takes precedence over the `Confirm` parameter. For example, the `WhatIf` dialog will be shown when running the following `New-Item`, the `Confirm` prompt will not:

```
$WhatIfPreference = $true
New-Item NewFile.txt -Confirm
```

Force parameter

The `Force` parameter has a different purpose.

With the `Force` parameter, `New-Item` will overwrite any existing file with the same path. When used with `Remove-Item`, the `Force` parameter allows removal of files with `Hidden` or `System` attributes. The error generated when attempting to delete a `Hidden` file is shown in the following code:

```
PS> Set-Location $env:TEMP
New-Item IMadeThisUp.txt -Force
Set-ItemProperty .\IMadeThisUp.txt -Name Attributes -Value Hidden
Remove-Item IMadeThisUp.txt
Remove-Item : Cannot remove item
C:\Users\whoami\AppData\Local\Temp\IMadeThisUp.txt: You do not have
sufficient access rights to perform this operation.
At line:1 char:1
+ Remove-Item .\IMadeThisUp.txt
+ ~~~~~~~~~~~~~~~~~~~~~~~~~~~~~
    + CategoryInfo : PermissionDenied:
(C:\Users\uktpcd...IMadeThisUp.txt:FileInfo) [Remove-Item], IOException
    + FullyQualifiedErrorId :
RemoveFileSystemItemUnAuthorizedAccess,Microsoft.PowerShell.Commands.Remove
ItemCommand
```

Adding the `Force` parameter allows the operation to continue without the error message:

```
PS> Set-Location $env:TEMP
New-Item IMadeThisUp.txt -Force
Set-ItemProperty .\IMadeThisUp.txt -Name Attributes -Value Hidden
Remove-Item IMadeThisUp.txt -Force
```

Providers

Providers in PowerShell present access to data that is not normally easily accessible. There are providers for the filesystem, registry, certificate store, and so on. Each provider arranges data so that it resembles a filesystem.

A longer description of `Providers` may be seen by viewing the `about` file:

```
Get-Help about_Providers
```

The list of providers available in the current PowerShell session may be viewed by running `Get-PSProvider`, as shown in the following example:

```
PS> Get-PSProvider
Name            Capabilities                            Drives
----            ------------                            ------
Registry        ShouldProcess, Transactions             {HKLM, HKCU}
Alias           ShouldProcess                           {Alias}
Environment     ShouldProcess                           {Env}
FileSystem      Filter, ShouldProcess, Credentials {C, D}
Function        ShouldProcess                           {Function}
Variable        ShouldProcess                           {Variable}
Certificate     ShouldProcess                           {Cert}
WSMan           Credentials                             {WSMan}
```

Each of the previous providers has a help file associated with it. These can be accessed using the following code:

```
Get-Help -Name <ProviderName> -Category Provider
```

For example, the help file for the certificate provider may be viewed by running the following code:

```
Get-Help -Name Certificate -Category Provider
```

A list of all help files for providers may be seen by running the following code:

```
Get-Help -Category Provider
```

Drives using providers

The output from `Get-PSProvider` shows that each provider has one or more drives associated with it.

You can, alternatively, see the list of drives (and the associated provider) using `Get-PSDrive`, as shown in the following code:

```
PS> Get-PSDrive

Name      Used (GB) Free (GB) Provider        Root
----      --------- --------- --------        ----
Alias                         Alias
C 89.13       89.13    111.64 FileSystem      C:\
Cert                          Certificate     \
D              0.45     21.86 FileSystem      D:\
Env                           Environment
```

```
Function                    Function
HKCU                        Registry       HKEY_CURRENT_USER
HKLM                        Registry       HKEY_LOCAL_MACHINE
Variable                    Variable
WSManWSMan
```

As providers are presented as a filesystem, accessing a provider is similar to working with a drive. Let's look at the following example:

```
PS C:\> Set-Location Cert:\LocalMachine\Root

PS Cert:\LocalMachine\Root> Get-ChildItem

    Directory: Microsoft.PowerShell.Security\Certificate::LocalMachine\Root


Thumbprint                                Subject
----------                                -------
CDD4EEAE6000AC7F40C3802C171E30148030C072 CN=Microsoft Root Certif...
BE36A4562FB2EE05DBB3D32323ADF445084ED656 CN=Thawte Timestamping C...
A43489159A520F0D93D032CCAF37E7FE20A8B419 CN=Microsoft Root Author...
```

A similar approach may be taken to access the registry. By default, drives are available for the current user (HKCU) and local machine (HKLM) hives. Accessing `HKEY_USERS` is possible by adding a new drive with the following command:

```
New-PSDrive HKU -PSProvider Registry -Root HKEY_USERS
```

After running the command, a new drive may be used:

```
PS C:\> Get-ChildItem HKU:


    Hive: HKEY_USERS


Name                           Property
----                           --------
.DEFAULT
S-1-5-19
S-1-5-20
```

Running HKCU: or Cert: does not change the drive:
Running `C:` or `D:` in the PowerShell console changes to a new drive letter. This is possible because `C:` is a function that calls `Set-Location`:

```
(Get-Command C:).Definition
```

Every letter of the alphabet (A to Z) has a predefined function (`Get-Command*:`) but the other drives (for example, Cert, HKCU, and so on) do not. `Set-Location` (or its alias `cd`) must be used to switch into these drives.

Using providers

As seen previously, providers may be accessed in the same way as the filesystem. Commands we might traditionally think of as filesystem commands (such as `Get-ChildItem`, `New` and `Remove-Item`, `Get` and `Set-Acl`, and `Get` and `Set-ItemProperty`) can work with data presented by a provider.

The list of parameters for the filesystem commands changes depending on the provider. The affected parameters are detailed in the help files for individual providers.

If we look at the `FileSystem` provider help file (`Get-Help FileSystem`), we can see that `Get-ChildItem` has a `File` switch parameter that can be used to filter files only:

```
-File <System.Management.Automation.SwitchParameter>
   Gets files.
   The File parameter was introduced in Windows
   PowerShell 3.0.
   To get only files, use the File parameter and omit
   the
   Directory parameter. To exclude files, use the
   Directory
   parameter and omit the File parameter, or use the
   Attributes parameter.
   Cmdlets Supported: Get-ChildItem
```

Let's look at the following example:

```
Set-Location C:
Get-ChildItem -File
```

Looking at the `Certificate provider` help file (`Get-Help Certificate`), a different set of parameters is available. For example, this excerpt shows the `ExpiringInDays` parameter for `Get-ChildItem`:

```
-ExpiringInDays <System.Int32>
   Gets certificates that are expiring in or before
   the specified number of days. Enter an integer. A
   value of 0 (zero) gets certificates that have
   expired.
   This parameter is valid in all subdirectories of
   the Certificate provider, but it is effective only
   on certificates.
   This parameter was introduced in Windows
   PowerShell 3.0.
   Cmdlets Supported: Get-ChildItem
```

The previous parameter may be used to find the `Root` certificates expiring in the next two years, as shown in the following example:

```
Set-Location Cert:\LocalMachine\Root
Get-ChildItem -ExpiringInDays 730
```

The parameters discussed in each help file are only valid inside a drive based on the provider in question, that is, `ExpiringInDays`. The previous example will work if the current location is a part of `Certificate provider`. Attempting to run the command from the `C:` drive (under the `FileSystem` provider) results in an error as demonstrated in the following code:

```
PS C:\> Get-ChildItem -Path Cert:\LocalMachine\Root -ExpiringInDays 730
Get-ChildItem : A parameter cannot be found that matches parameter name
'ExpiringInDays'.
At line:1 char:45
+ Get-ChildItem -Path Cert:\LocalMachine\Root -ExpiringInDays 730
+ ~~~~~~~~~~~~~~~
    + CategoryInfo : InvalidArgument: (:) [Get-ChildItem],
ParameterBindingException
    + FullyQualifiedErrorId :
NamedParameterNotFound,Microsoft.PowerShell.Commands.GetChildItemCommand
```

Summary

In this chapter, we explored the help system built into PowerShell. We took a brief look at syntax, examples, and parameters. We also looked at how help content may be moved between computers.

Command naming and discovery introduced how we might use the verb-noun pairing to discover commands that can be used. Aliases were introduced briefly.

Parameters and parameter sets were explored as well as different types of parameters.

Finally, we looked at providers and how they are used.

In `Chapter 3`, *Modules and Snap-Ins*, we will explore modules and snap-ins.

3
Modules and Snap-Ins

Modules and snap-ins are packaged collections of commands that may be loaded inside PowerShell.

In this chapter, we will cover the following topics:

- What are modules?
- What is the PS Gallery?
- The `Get-Module` command
- The `Import-Module` command
- The `Remove-Module` command
- The `Find-Module` command
- The `Install-Module` command
- The `Save-Module` command
- What is a snap-in?
- Using snap-ins

What is a module?

Modules were introduced with the release of PowerShell version 2.0. Modules represented a significant step forward over snap-ins. Unlike snap-ins, modules do not have to be formally installed or registered for use with PowerShell.

It is most common to find a module that targets a specific system or focuses on a small set of related operations. For example, the `Microsoft.PowerShell.LocalAccounts` module contains commands for interacting with the local account database (users and groups).

A module may be binary, script, dynamic, or manifest:

- **Binary module**: This is written in a language, such as C# or VB.NET, and then compiled into a library (DLL)
- **Script module**: This is a collection of functions written in the PowerShell language. The commands typically reside in a script module file (PSM1)
- **Dynamic module**: This does not have files associated with it. This is created using the `New-Module` command. The following command creates a very simple dynamic module that adds the `Get-Number` command:

```
New-Module -Name TestModule -ScriptBlock {
    function Get-Number { return 1 }
}
```

A manifest module combines different items to make a single consistent module. For example, a manifest may be used to create a single module out of a DLL containing `cmdlets` and a script containing functions. For example, `Microsoft.PowerShell.Utility` is a manifest module that combines a binary and script module.

A manifest module may also be used to build commands based on WMI classes. The `cmdlets-over-objects` feature was added with PowerShell 3, an XML file with a `cdxml` extension (`Cmdlet` definition XML). For example, the `Defender` module creates commands based on WMI classes in `ROOT/Microsoft/Windows/Defender namespace`.

The manifest module file serves a number of purposes, as follows:

- Describing the files that should be loaded (such as a script module file, a binary library, and a `cmdlet` definition XML file)
- Listing any dependencies the module may have (such as other modules, .NET libraries, or other DLL files)
- Listing the commands that should be exported (made available to the end user)
- Recording information about the author or the project

When loading a module with a manifest, PowerShell will try and load any listed dependencies. If a module fails to load because of a dependency, the commands written as part of the module will not be imported.

What is the PowerShell Gallery?

The PowerShell Gallery is a repository and distribution platform for scripts, modules, and **Desired State Configuration** (**DSC**) resources that have been written by Microsoft or other users of PowerShell.

In February 2016, Microsoft made the PowerShell Gallery public.

The PowerShell Gallery has parallels in other scripting languages, as shown in the following examples:

- Perl has `cpan.org`
- Python has PyPI
- Ruby has RubyGems

Support for the gallery is included by default in PowerShell 5. For PowerShell 3 and 4, PowerShellGet (via the `PackageManagement PowerShell` modules preview package) must be installed:

`https://www.microsoft.com/en-us/download/details.aspx?id=51451`

The PowerShell Gallery may be searched using `https://www.powershellgallery.com`:

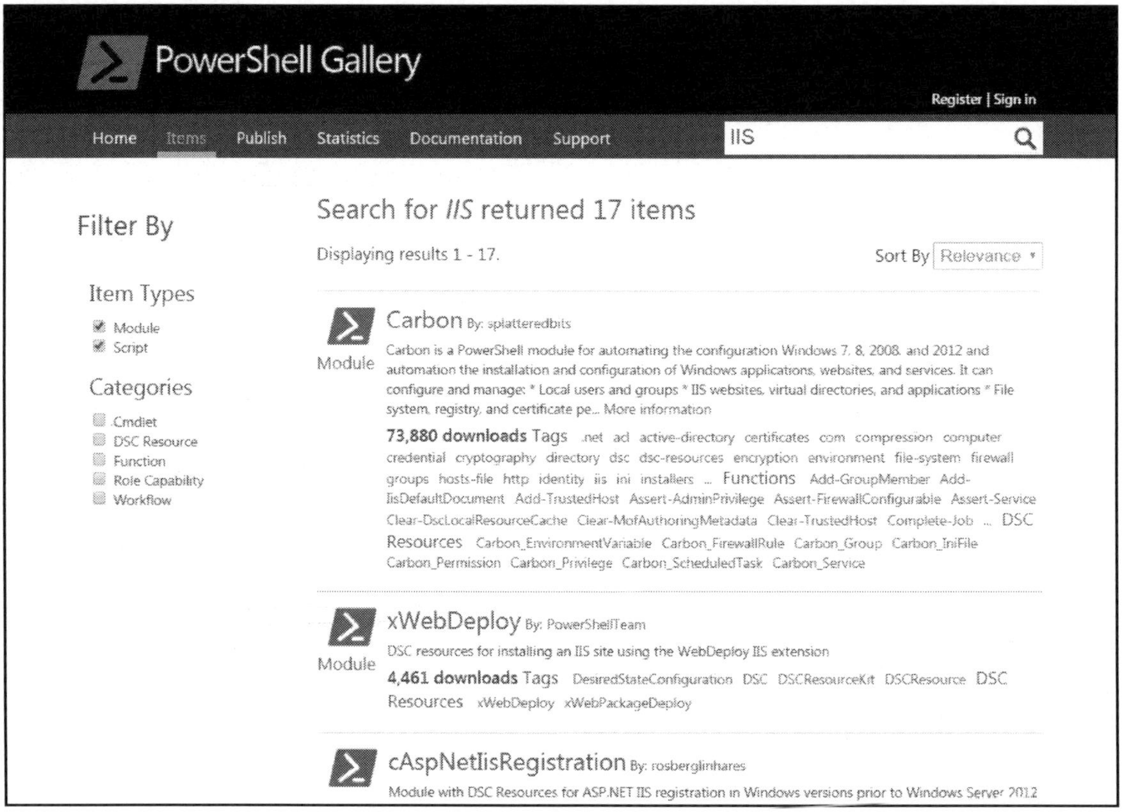

PowerShell Gallery

Register | Sign in

Home Items Publish Statistics Documentation Support IIS

Filter By

Item Types

Module
Script

Categories

Cmdlet
DSC Resource
Function
Role Capability
Workflow

Search for *IIS* returned 17 items

Displaying results 1 - 17.

Sort By Relevance

Carbon By: splatteredbits

Module

Carbon is a PowerShell module for automating the configuration Windows 7, 8, 2008, and 2012 and automation the installation and configuration of Windows applications, websites, and services. It can configure and manage: * Local users and groups * IIS websites, virtual directories, and applications * File system, registry, and certificate pe... More information

73,880 downloads Tags .net ad active-directory certificates com compression computer credential cryptography directory dsc dsc-resources encryption environment file-system firewall groups hosts-file http identity iis ini installers ... Functions Add-GroupMember Add-IisDefaultDocument Add-TrustedHost Assert-AdminPrivilege Assert-FirewallConfigurable Assert-Service Clear-DscLocalResourceCache Clear-MofAuthoringMetadata Clear-TrustedHost Complete-Job ... DSC Resources Carbon_EnvironmentVariable Carbon_FirewallRule Carbon_Group Carbon_IniFile Carbon_Permission Carbon_Privilege Carbon_ScheduledTask Carbon_Service

xWebDeploy By: PowerShellTeam

Module

DSC resources for installing an IIS site using the WebDeploy IIS extension

4,461 downloads Tags DesiredStateConfiguration DSC DSCResourceKit DSCResource DSC Resources xWebDeploy xWebPackageDeploy

cAspNetIisRegistration By: rosberglinhares

Module with DSC Resources for ASP.NET IIS registration in Windows versions prior to Windows Server 2012

Private PowerShell Gallery:
An internal version of the PowerShell Gallery may be configured based on the NuGet Gallery project:
`https://github.com/NuGet/NuGetGallery`
Once available, the repository may be registered using `Register-PSRepository`. See the following article for further details:
`https://blogs.msdn.microsoft.com/powershell/2014/05/20/setting-up-an-internal-powershellget-repository/`.

The Get-Module command

The Microsoft Windows operating system, especially the most recent versions, comes with a wide variety of modules preinstalled. These, as well as any other modules that have been installed, can be viewed using the `Get-Module` command.

By default, `Get-Module` shows modules that have been imported (either automatically or using `Import-Module`); for example, if the command is run from PowerShell ISE, it will show that the `ISE` module has been loaded:

```
PS> Get-Module

ModuleType Version Name                               ExportedCommands
---------- ------- ----                               ----------------
Script     1.0.0.0 ISE                                {Get-
                                                      IseSnippet...}
Manifest   3.1.0.0 Microsoft.PowerShell.Management {Add-
                                                      Computer...}
Manifest   3.1.0.0 Microsoft.PowerShell.Utility       {Add-Member...}
```

The `ListAvailable` parameter shows a complete list of modules:

```
Get-Module -ListAvailable
```

Modules are listed here if they are found under any of the paths in the `%PSMODULEPATH%` environment variable. The variable contains the following paths:

```
PS> $env:PSModulePath -split ';'
C:\Users\whoami\Documents\WindowsPowerShell\Modules
C:\WINDOWS\system32\WindowsPowerShell\v1.0\Modules\
C:\Program Files\WindowsPowerShell\Modules\
```

Additional paths to search may be added to the `%PSMODULEPATH%` variable if required.

Modules may exist in more than one location. `Get-Module` (and `Import-Module`) will consider each path in order so that if a matching module is found, the search stops (even if a newer version exists in a different directory).

Merging environment variables:
The `%PSModulePath%` environment variable is made up of user-level and machine-level settings. The value held in `$env:PSMODULEPATH` is the result of merging the two values (values from user followed by values from the machine).

`Get-Module` can show each instance of a module regardless of the path using the `All` parameter:

```
Get-Module <ModuleName> -All -ListAvailable
```

The Import-Module command

PowerShell 3 and more will attempt to automatically load modules if a command from that module is used and the module is under one of the paths in the `%PSMODULEPATH%` environment variable.

For example, if PowerShell is started and the `PSDesiredStateConfiguration` module is not imported, running the `Get-DscResource` command will cause the module to be imported. This is shown in the following example:

```
PS> Get-Module PSDesiredStateConfiguration

PS> Get-DscResource

PS> Get-Module PSDesiredStateConfiguration

ModuleType Version Name                          ExportedCommands
---------- ------- ----                          ----------------
Manifest   1.1     PSDesiredStateConfiguration ...
```

In the previous example, the first time `Get-Module` is executed, the `PSDesiredStateConfiguration` module has not yet been loaded. After running `Get-DscResource`, a command from the `PSDesiredStateConfiguration` module, the module is loaded and the command is immediately executed. Once loaded, the module is visible when running `Get-Module`.

Modules in PowerShell may be explicitly imported using the `Import-Module` command. Modules may be imported using a name or with a full path, as shown by the following example:

```
Import-Module -Name PSWorkflow
Import-Module -Name
C:\Windows\System32\WindowsPowerShell\v1.0\Modules\PSWorkflow\PSWorkflow.ps
d1
```

Once a module has been imported, the commands within the module may be listed using `Get-Command` as follows:

```
Get-Command -Module PSWorkflow
```

Modules, Get-Command, and autoloading:
As the commands exported by a module can only be identified by importing the module, the previous command will trigger automatic import.

Modules installed in PowerShell 5 are placed in a folder named after the module version. This allows multiple versions of the same module to coexist, as shown in the following example:

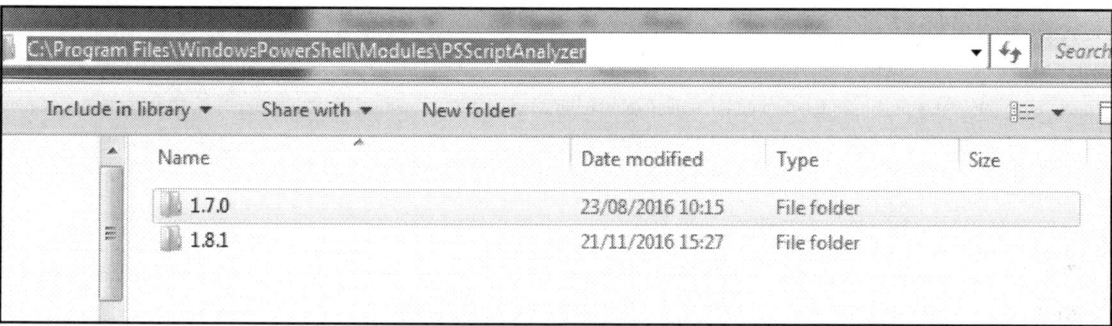

Version 1.8.1 of `PSScriptAnalyzer` will be imported by default as it is the highest version number. It is possible to import a specific version of a module using the `MinimumVersion` and `MaximumVersion` parameters:

```
Import-Module PSScriptAnalyzer -MaxmimumVersion 1.7.0
```

The Remove-Module command

The `Remove-Module` command attempts to remove a previously imported module from the current session.

For binary modules or manifest modules that incorporate a DLL, commands are removed from PowerShell but DLLs are not unloaded.

`Remove-Module` does not remove or delete the files that make up a module from a computer.

The Find-Module command

The `Find-Module` command allows you to search the PowerShell Gallery or any other registered repository for modules.

Modules can be identified by name, as shown in the following example:

```
Find-Module Carbon
Find-Module -Name Carbon
Find-Module -Name Azure*
```

If the name is not sufficient for the search, the `Filter` parameter may be used. Supplying a value for the `Filter` parameter is equivalent to using the search field in the PowerShell Gallery that expands the search to include tags:

```
Find-Module -Filter IIS
```

The Install-Module command

The `Install-Module` command installs or updates modules from the PowerShell Gallery or any other configured repository. By default, `Install-Module` adds modules to the path for `AllUsers`, `C:\Program Files\WindowsPowerShell\Modules`.

Access rights
Installing a module under the `AllUsers` scope requires a user account control administrator token (run as administrator).

For example, the `posh-git` module may be installed using either of the following two commands:

```
Find-Module posh-git | Install-Module
Install-Module posh-git
```

Modules may be installed under a user-specific path (`$home\Documents\WindowsPowerShell\Modules`) using the `Scope` parameter:

```
Find-Module carbon -Scope CurrentUser
```

If the most recent version of a module is already installed, the command ends without providing feedback. If a newer version is available that will be automatically installed alongside the original (in a folder named after the version if using PowerShell 5.0).

Reinstallation of an existing version can be forced with the following command:

```
Install-Module posh-git -Force
```

The `Install-Module` command does not provide an option to install modules under the `$PSHOME` (`%SystemRoot%\System32\WindowsPowerShell\v1.0`) directory. The `$PSHOME` path is reserved for modules created by Microsoft that are deployed with the **Windows Management Framework** (**WMF**) or the Windows operating system.

The Save-Module command

The `Save-Module` command downloads the module from the PowerShell Gallery to a given path without installing it. For example, the following command downloads the `Carbon` module into a `Modules` directory in the root of the `C:` drive:

```
Save-Module -Name Carbon -Path C:\Modules
```

`Save-Module` will do the following:

- Always download the module and overwrite any previously saved version in the specified path
- Ignore installed or other saved versions

What is a snap-in?

A snap-in was the precursor to a module. It was the mechanism available to extend the set of commands in PowerShell 1.0. The `Cmdlet` implementation inside a snap-in is similar to a binary module (written in a language such as C#). A snap-in contains a specialized class that holds the fields where were moved into the module manifest with PowerShell 2.0.

Snap-ins must be installed or registered before they can be used. This can be done using `installutil`, which is part of the .NET framework package. Many vendors (including Microsoft) took to releasing **Microsoft Installer** (**MSI**) packages to simplify the snap-in installation.

Modules have, for the most part, made snap-ins obsolete. Manifest modules accompanied by a binary module offer the same performance benefits without the installation or registration overhead.

The list of snap-ins may be viewed using the following command:

```
Get-PSSnapIn -Registered
```

If the `Registered` parameter is excluded, `Get-PSSnapIn` will show the snap-ins that have been imported into the current PowerShell session.

Microsoft.PowerShell.Core:
The core commands loaded for PowerShell are a part of the snap-in written into the `System.Management.Automation` library. This snap-in does not appear in the list of registered snap-ins.
Registered snap-ins are read from `HKLM:\Software\Microsoft\PowerShell\1\PowerShellSnapIns`.
If a computer does not have any registered snap-ins, the registry path may not exist.
The snap-in list is generated by looping through all commands and reading the `PSSnapIn` property in a manner similar to the following command:

```
(Get-Command).PSSnapIn.Name | Select-Object -Unique
```

Using snap-ins

PowerShell will not automatically load commands from a snap-in. All snap-ins, except `Microsoft.PowerShell.Core`, must be explicitly imported using the `Add-PSSnapIn` command:

```
Add-PSSnapIn WDeploySnapin3.0
```

Once a snap-in has been installed (registered) and added, `Get-Command` may be used to list the commands:

```
Get-Command -Module WDeploySnapin3.0
```

Summary

In this chapter, we looked at modules and snap-ins. Both modules and snap-ins may be used to extend the set of commands available in PowerShell.

Snap-ins are rarely used these days in favor of modules, as modules are more flexible and simpler to work with.

The PowerShell Gallery is a valuable source of modules published by Microsoft and others.

In `Chapter 4`, *Working with Objects in PowerShell,* we will dive into objects in PowerShell.

4 Working with Objects in PowerShell

Everything we do in PowerShell revolves around working with objects. Objects, in PowerShell, may have properties or methods (or both).

It is difficult to describe an object without resorting to: an object is a representation of a thing or item of data. We might use an analogy to attempt to give meaning to the term.

This book is an object.

The book has properties which describe physical characteristics, such as the number of pages, the weight, or size. It has metadata (information about data) properties that describe the author, the publisher, the table of contents, and so on.

The book might also have methods. A method affects the change on the state of an object. For example, there might be methods to open or close the book or methods to jump to different chapters. A method might also convert an object into a different form. For example, there might be a method to copy a page, or even destructive methods such as one to split the book.

PowerShell has a variety of commands that allow us to work with sets (or collections) of objects in a pipeline.

In this chapter, we are going to cover the following topics:

- Pipelines
- Members
- Enumerating and filtering
- Selecting and sorting
- Grouping and measuring
- Comparing
- Importing, exporting, and converting

Pipelines

The pipeline is one of the most prominent features of PowerShell. The pipeline is used to send output from one command (standard out or `StdOut`) into another command (standard in or `StdIn`).

Standard output

The term standard output is used because there are different kinds of output. Each of these different forms of output is referred to as a stream.

When assigning the output of a command to a variable, the values are taken from the standard output (the output stream) of a command. For example, the following command assigns the data from the standard output to a variable:

```
$stdout = Get-CimInstance Win32_ComputerSystem
```

Non-standard output

In PowerShell there are other output streams; these include error (`Write-Error`), information (`Write-Information`, introduced in PowerShell 5), warning (`Write-Warning`), and `Verbose` (`Write-Verbose`). PowerShell also has `Write-Host`, which displays information to the PowerShell host (the console, or PowerShell ISE). Each of these has a stream of its own.

For example, if the `Verbose` switch is added to the preceding command, more information is shown. This extra information is not held in the variable, it is sent to a different stream:

```
PS> $stdout = Get-CimInstance Win32_ComputerSystem -Verbose
$stdout
VERBOSE: Perform operation 'Enumerate CimInstances' with following
parameters, ''namespaceName' = root\cimv2,'className' =
Win32_ComputerSystem'.
VERBOSE: Operation 'Enumerate CimInstances' complete.
Name  PrimaryOwnerName Domain      TotalPhysicalMemory Model
----  ---------------- ------      ------------------- -----
TITAN Chris            WORKGROUP   17076875264         All Series
```

The object pipeline

Languages such as Batch scripting (on Windows) or Bash scripting (ordinarily on Linux or Unix) use a pipeline to pass text between commands. It is up to the next command to figure out what the text means.

PowerShell, on the other hand, sends objects from one command to another.

The pipe (`|`) symbol is used to send the standard output between commands.

In the following example, the output of `Get-Process` is sent to the `Where-object` command, which applies a filter. The filter restricts the list of processes to those that are using more than `50MB` of memory:

```
Get-Process | Where-Object WorkingSet -gt 50MB
```

Members

At the beginning of this chapter, the idea of properties and methods was introduced. These are part of a set of items collectively known as members. These are with which we interact with an object. A few of the more frequently used members are `NoteProperty`, `ScriptProperty`, `ScriptMethod`, and `Event`.

What are the member types?

The list of possible member types can be viewed on MSDN, which includes a short description of each member type:

`https://msdn.microsoft.com/en-us/library/system.management.automation.psmembertypes(v=vs.85).aspx`

This chapter focuses on the different property members: `Property`, `NoteProperty`, and `ScriptProperty`. They are most relevant to the commands in this chapter.

The Get-Member command

The `Get-Member` command is used to view the different members of an object. For example, it can be used to list all of the members of a process object (returned by `Get-Process`):

```
Get-Process -Id $PID | Get-Member
```

`Get-Member` offers filters using its parameters (`MemberType`, `Static`, and `View`). For example, if we wished to view only the properties of the PowerShell process, we might run the following:

```
Get-Process -Id $PID | Get-Member -MemberType Property
```

The `Static` parameter will be covered in `Chapter 8`, *Working with .NET*.

The `View` parameter is set to `all` by default. It has three additional values:

- **Base**: It shows properties which are derived from a .NET object
- **Adapted**: It shows members handled by PowerShell's **Adapted Type System (ATS)**
- **Extended**: It shows members added by PowerShell's **Extended Type System (ETS)**

Adapted and Extended Type Systems (ATS and ETS):
ATS and ETS systems make it easy to work with object frameworks other than .NET in PowerShell, for example, objects returned by ADSI, COM, WMI, or XML. Each of these frameworks is discussed later in this book. Microsoft published an article on ATS and ETS in 2011, which is still relevant today:
`https://blogs.msdn.microsoft.com/besidethepoint/2011/11/22/psobject-and-the-adapted-and-extended-type-systems-ats-and-ets/`.

Accessing properties

Properties of an object in PowerShell may be accessed by writing the property name after a period. For example, the `Name` property of the current PowerShell process may be accessed by the following:

```
$process = Get-Process -Id $PID
$process.Name
```

PowerShell also allows us to access the properties by enclosing a command in parentheses:

```
(Get-Process -Id $PID).Name
```

Properties of an object are themselves objects. For example, the `StartTime` property of a process is a `DateTime` object. We may access `DayOfWeek` property by using the following:

```
$process = Get-Process -Id $PID
$process.StartTime.DayOfWeek
```

The variable assignment step may be skipped if parentheses are used:

```
(Get-Process -Id $PID).StartTime.DayOfWeek
```

If a property name has a space, it may be accessed using a number of different notation styles. For example, a property named `"Some Name"` may be accessed by quoting the name or enclosing the name in curly braces:

```
$object = [PSCustomObject]@{ 'Some Name' = 'Value' }
$object."Some Name"
$object.'Some Name'
$object.{Some Name}
```

Using methods

As mentioned, methods effect a change in state. That may be a change to the object associated with the method, or it may take the object and convert it into something else.

Methods are called using the following notation in PowerShell:

```
<Object>.Method()
```

If a method expects to have arguments (or parameters), the notation becomes the following:

```
<Object>.Method(Argument1, Argument2)
```

When the method is called without parentheses (the brackets), PowerShell will show the overload definitions. The overload definitions are a list of the different sets of arguments that can be used with a method. For example, the `Substring` method of `System.String` has two definitions:

```
PS> 'thisString'.Substring
OverloadDefinitions
-------------------
string Substring(int startIndex)
string Substring(int startIndex, int length)
```

An example of a method that takes an object and converts it into something else is shown here. In this case, a date is converted to a string:

```
PS> $date = Get-Date "01/01/2010"
$date.ToLongDateString()
01 January 2010
```

An example of a method that changes a state might be a TCP socket. TCP connections must be opened before data can be sent over a network:

```
PS> $tcpClient = New-Object System.Net.Sockets.TcpClient
$tcpClient.Connect("127.0.0.1", 135)
```

A TCP client is created then an attempt is made to connect to the RPC endpoint mapper port (`TCP/135`) on the localhost.

The `Connect` method does not return anything (although it will throw an error if the connection fails). It affects the state of the object reflected by the `Connected` property:

```
PS> $tcpClient.Connected
True
```

The state of the object may be changed again by calling the `Close` method to disconnect:

```
PS> $tcpClient.Close()
```

An example of a method that takes arguments might be the `ToString` method on a `DateTime` object. `Get-Date` can be used to create a `DateTime` object:

```
PS> (Get-Date).ToString('u')
2016-12-08 21:18:49Z
```

In the preceding example, the letter `u` is one of the standard date and time format strings (`https://msdn.microsoft.com/en-us/library/az4se3k1(v=vs.110).aspx`) and represents a universal sortable date/time pattern. The same result may be achieved using the `Format` parameter of `Get-Date`:

```
PS> Get-Date -Format u
2016-12-08 21:19:31Z
```

The advantage the method has over the parameter is the date can be adjusted before conversion by using some of the other properties and methods:

```
(Get-Date).Date.AddDays(-1).ToString('u')
```

The result of this command will be the start of yesterday (midnight, one day before today).

Access modifiers

Depending on the type of object, properties may be read-only or read/write. These may be identified using `Get-Member` and by inspecting the access modifiers.

In the following example, the value in curly braces at the end of each line is the access modifier:

```
PS> $File = New-Item NewFile.txt -Force
$File | Get-Member -MemberType Property
TypeName: System.IO.FileInfo
Name                 MemberType Definition
----                 ---------- ----------
Attributes           Property   System.IO.FileAttributes Attributes
{get;set;}
CreationTime         Property   datetime CreationTime {get;set;}
CreationTimeUtc      Property   datetime CreationTimeUtc {get;set;}
Directory            Property   System.IO.DirectoryInfo Directory {get;}
DirectoryName        Property   string DirectoryName {get;}
Exists               Property   bool Exists {get;}
```

When the modifier is `{get;}`, the property value is read-only; attempting to change the value will result in an error:

```
PS> $File = New-Item NewFile.txt -Force
$File.Name = 'NewName'
'Name' is a ReadOnly property.
At line:1 char:1
+ $File.Name = 'NewName'
+ ~~~~~~~~~~~~~~~~~~~~~~
 + CategoryInfo : InvalidOperation: (:) [], RuntimeException
 + FullyQualifiedErrorId : PropertyAssignmentException
```

When the modifier is `{get;set;}`, the property value may be read and changed. In the preceding example, the `CreationTime` has the set access modifier: the value can be changed; in this case, it may be set to any date after January 1, 1601:

```
$File = New-Item NewFile.txt
$File.CreationTime = Get-Date -Day 1 -Month 2 -Year 1692
```

The result of the preceding command can be seen by reviewing the properties for the file, either in PowerShell or Explorer, as shown in the following screenshot:

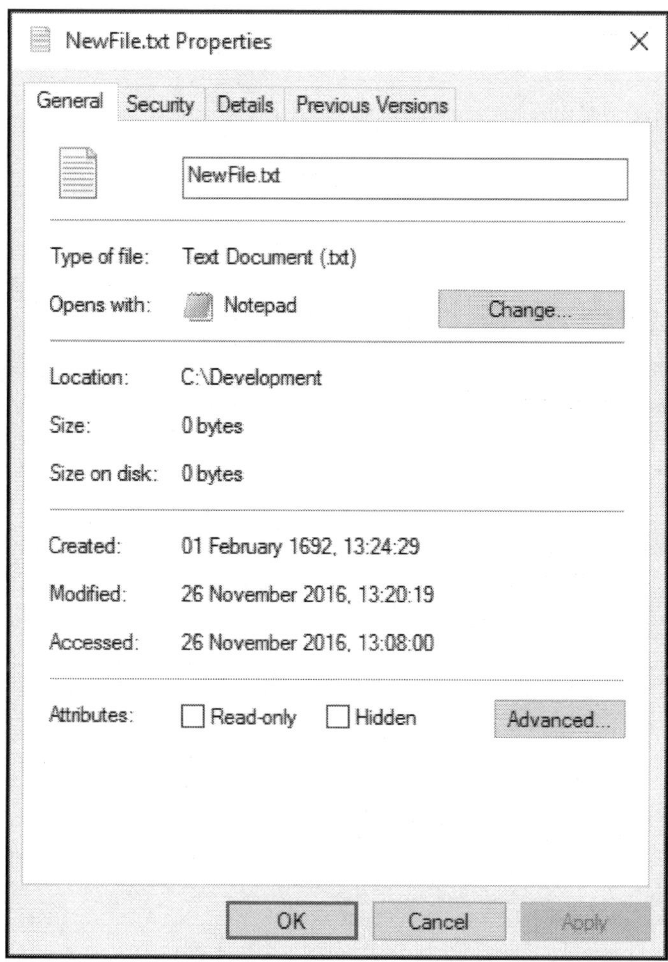

In the preceding example, the change made to `CreationTime` is passed from the object representing the file to the file itself. The object used here, based on the .NET class, `System.IO.FileInfo`, is written in such a way that it supports the change. A property may indicate that it can be changed (by supporting the set access modifier in `Get-Member`) and still not pass the change back to whatever the object represents.

The Add-Member command

`Add-Member` allows new members to be added to existing objects.

Starting with an `empty` object, it is possible to add new properties:

```
PS> $empty = New-Object Object
$empty | Add-Member -Name New -Value 'Hello world' -MemberType NoteProperty
```

Methods may be added as well. For example, a method to replace the word `world`.

Enumerating and filtering

Enumerating, or listing, the objects in a collection in PowerShell does not need a specialized command. For example, if the results of `Get-PSDrive` were assigned to a variable, enumerating the content of the variable is as simple as writing the variable name and pressing *Return*:

```
PS> $drives = Get-PSDrive
$drives
Name     Used (GB) Free (GB) Provider    Root
----     --------- --------- --------    ----
Alias                        Alias
C           319.37    611.60 FileSystem  C:\
Cert                         Certificate \
Env                          Environment
...
```

`ForEach-Object` may be used where something complex needs to be done to each object.

`Where-Object` may be used to filter results.

The ForEach-Object command

`ForEach-Object` is most often used as a loop (of sorts). For example, the following command works on each of the results from `Get-Process` in turn:

```
Get-Process | ForEach-Object {
    Write-Host $_.Name -ForegroundColor Green
}
```

In the preceding example, a special variable, `$_`, is used to represent each of the processes in turn.

`ForEach-Object` may also be used to get a single property, or execute a single method on each of the objects. For example, `ForEach-Object` may be used to return only the `Path` property when using `Get-Process`:

```
Get-Process | ForEach-Object Path
```

Where-Object command

Filtering the output from commands may be performed using `Where-Object`. For example, we might filter processes that started after 5 p.m. today:

```
Get-Process | Where-Object StartTime -gt (Get-Date 17:00:00)
```

The syntax shown in help for `Where-Object` does not quite match the syntax used here. The help text is as follows:

```
Where-Object [-Property] <String> [[-Value] <Object>] -GT ...
```

In the preceding example, we see the following:

- `StartTime` is the argument for the `Property` parameter (first argument by position)
- The comparison is greater than, as signified by the `gt` switch parameter
- The date (using the `Get-Date` command) is the argument for the `Value` parameter (second argument by position)

Based on that, the example might be written as follows:

```
Get-Process | Where-Object -Property StartTime -Value (Get-Date 17:00:00) -
gt
```

However, it is far easier to read `StartTime` is greater than `<some date>`, so most examples tend to follow that pattern.

`Where-Object` will also accept filters using the `FilterScript` parameter.

Selecting and sorting

`Select-Object` allows a subset of data to be returned when executing a command. This may be a more restrictive number of elements, or a smaller number of properties.

`Sort-Object` can be used to perform both simple and complex sorting.

The Select-Object command

`Select-Object` is most frequently used to limit values by a command. The command is extremely versatile as it enables you to do the following:

- Limit the properties returned by a command by name:

```
Get-Process | Select-Object -Property Name, Id
```

- Limit the properties returned from a command using wildcards:

```
Get-Process | Select-Object -Property Name, *Memory
```

- List everything but a few properties:

```
Get-Process | Select-Object -Property * -Exclude *Memory*
```

- Get the first few objects:

```
Get-ChildItem C:\ -Recurse | Select-Object -First 2
```

- Get the last few objects:

```
Get-ChildItem C:\ | Select-Object -Last 3
```

- Skip items at the beginning. In this example, this returns the fifth item:

```
Get-ChildItem C:\ | Select-Object -Skip 4 -First 1
```

- Skip items at the end. This example returns the third from the end:

```
Get-ChildItem C:\ | Select-Object -Skip 2 -Last 1
```

- Expand individual properties:

```
Get-ChildItem C:\ | Select-Object -ExpandProperty FullName
```

- `Select-Object` can return unique values from arrays of simple values:

```
1, 1, 1, 3, 5, 2, 2, 4 | Select-Object -Unique
```

About Get-Unique:

`Get-Unique` may also be used to create a list of unique elements. When using `Get-Unique`, a list must be sorted first, for example:

```
1, 1, 1, 3, 5, 2, 2, 4 | Sort-Object | Get-Unique
```

It can also return unique values from arrays of objects, but only if a list of properties is specified or a wildcard is used for the list of properties.

In the following example, we create an object with one property called `Number`. The value for the property is `1`, `2`, or `3`. There are two objects with a value of `1`, two with a value of `2`, and two with a value of `3`:

```
PS> (1..3 + 1..3) | ForEach-Object { [PSCustomObject]@{ Number = $_ } }

Number
------
 1
 2
 3
 1
 2
 3
```

`Select-Object` can remove the duplicates from the set in the example using the `Unique` parameter if a list of properties (or a wildcard for the properties) is set:

```
PS> (1..3 + 1..3) | ForEach-Object { [PSCustomObject]@{ Number = $_ } } |
 Select-Object -Property * -Unique

Number
------
 1
 2
 3
```

When using `Get-Member`, you may have noticed the `PropertySet` member type. `Select-Object` can display the properties within the set. In the following example, `Get-Member` is used to view property sets, and `Select-Object` is used to display the first property set (`PSConfiguration`):

```
PS> Get-Process -Id $PID | Get-Member -MemberType PropertySet
TypeName: System.Diagnostics.Process

Name            MemberType  Definition
```

```
----           ----------  ----------
PSConfiguration PropertySet PSConfiguration {Name, Id, ...
PSResources PropertySet PSResources {Name, Id, Hand...

PS> Get-Process -Id $PID | Select-Object PSConfiguration

Name              Id PriorityClass FileVersion
----              -- ------------- -----------
powershell_ise 5568         Normal 10.0.14393.103
(rs1_release_inmarket.160819-1924)
```

Select-Object is also able to make new properties. It will build a property if given a name and a means of calculating it (an expression):

```
Get-Process | Select-Object -Property Name, Id,
    @{Name='FileOwner'; Expression={ (Get-Acl $_.Path).Owner }}
```

In the preceding example, @{} is a hashtable. Hashtables are discussed in Chapter 6, *Variables, Arrays, and Hashtables.*

Select-Object can change objects:

When Select-Object is used with the Property parameter, a new object is created (based on the value Select-Object is working with). For example, the first process may be selected as shown here. The resulting object type is Process:

```
(Get-Process | Select-Object -First 1).GetType()
```

If Select-Object also requests a list of properties, the object type changes to PSCustomObject:

```
(Get-Process | Select -Property Path, Company -First
1).GetType()
```

This is important if something else is expected to use the process. For example, Stop-Process will throw an error because the object being passed is not a process, nor is there sufficient information available to determine which process must stop (either the Id or Name properties):

```
Get-Process | Select-Object -Property Path, Company -
First 1 | Stop-Process -WhatIf
```

The Sort-Object command

The `Sort-Object` command allows objects to be sorted on one or more properties.

By default, `Sort-Object` will sort numbers in ascending order:

```
PS> 5, 4, 3, 2, 1 | Sort-Object
1
2
3
4
5
```

Strings are sorted in ascending order, irrespective of uppercase or lowercase:

```
PS> 'ccc', 'BBB', 'aaa' | Sort-Object
aaa
BBB
ccc
```

When dealing with complex objects, `Sort-Object` may be used to sort based on a named property. For example, processes may be sorted based on the `Id` property:

```
Get-Process | Sort-Object -Property Id
```

Objects may be sorted on multiple properties; for example, a list of files may be sorted on `LastWriteTime` and then on `Name`:

```
Get-ChildItem C:\Windows\System32 |
    Sort-Object LastWriteTime, Name
```

In the preceding example, items are first sorted on `LastWriteTime`. Items that have the same value for `LastWriteTime` are then sorted based on `Name`.

`Sort-Object` is not limited to sorting on existing properties. A script block (a fragment of script, enclosed in curly braces) can be used to create a calculated value for sorting. For example, it is possible to order items based on a word, as shown here:

```
PS> $examResults = @(
  [PSCustomObject]@{ Exam = 'Music'; Result = 'N/A'; Mark = 0 }
  [PSCustomObject]@{ Exam = 'History'; Result = 'Fail'; Mark = 23 }
  [PSCustomObject]@{ Exam = 'Biology'; Result = 'Pass'; Mark = 78 }
  [PSCustomObject]@{ Exam = 'Physics'; Result = 'Pass'; Mark = 86 }
  [PSCustomObject]@{ Exam = 'Maths'; Result = 'Pass'; Mark = 92 }
)
$examResults | Sort-Object {
 switch ($_.Result) {
```

```
    'Pass' { 1 }
    'Fail' { 2 }
    'N/A' { 3 }
    }
}

Exam    Result Mark
----    ------ ----
Biology Pass   78
Physics Pass   86
Maths   Pass   92
History Fail   23
Music   N/A    0
```

In the preceding example, when `Sort-Object` encounters a `Pass` result, it is given the lowest numeric value (`1`). As `Sort-Object` defaults to ascending ordering, this means exams with a result of `Pass` appear first in the list. This process is repeated to give a numeric value to each of the other possible results.

As `Sort-Object` is capable of sorting on more than one property, the preceding example can be taken further to sort on `Mark` next:

```
$examResults | Sort-Object {
    switch ($_.Result) {
        'Pass' { 1 }
        'Fail' { 2 }
        'N/A'  { 3 }
    }
}, Mark
```

Adding the `Descending` parameter to `Sort-Object` will reverse the order of both fields:

```
$examResults | Sort-Object {
    switch ($_.Result) {
        'Pass' { 1 }
        'Fail' { 2 }
        'N/A'  { 3 }
    }
}, Mark -Descending
```

The ordering behavior can be made property-specific using the notation shown in the following example:

```
$examResults | Sort-Object {
    switch ($_.Result) {
        'Pass' { 1 }
        'Fail' { 2 }
```

```
            'N/A'  { 3 }
        }
    }, @{ Expression = { $_.Mark }; Descending = $true }
```

The hashtable, `@{}`, is used to describe an expression (a calculated property; in this case, the value for `Mark`) and the sorting order which is either ascending or descending.

In the preceding example, the first property, based on `Result`, is sorted in ascending order as this is the default. The second property, `Mark`, is sorted in descending order.

Grouping and measuring

`Group-Object` is a powerful utility that allows you to group objects together based on similar values.

`Measure-Object` supports a number of simple mathematical operations, such as counting the number of objects, calculating an average, calculating a sum, and so on. It also allows characters, words, or lines to be counted in text fields.

The Group-Object command

The `Group-Object` command shows a group and count for each occurrence of a value in a collection of objects.

Given the sequence of numbers shown, `Group-Object` creates a `Name` that holds the value it is grouping, a `Count` as the number of occurrences of that value, and a `Group` as the set of similar values:

```
PS> 6, 7, 7, 8, 8, 8 | Group-Object

Count  Name                       Group
-----  ----                       -----
 1     6                          {6}
 2     7                          {7, 7}
 3     8                          {8, 8, 8}
```

The `Group` property may be removed using the `NoElement` parameter, which simplifies the output from the command:

```
PS> 6, 7, 7, 8, 8, 8 | Group-Object -NoElement

Count Name
----- ----
    1 6
    2 7
    3 8
```

`Group-Object` can group based on a specific property. For example, it might be desirable to list the number of occurrences of particular files in an extensive folder structure. In the following example, the `C:\Windows\Assembly` folder contains different versions of DLLs for different versions of packages including the .NET Framework:

```
Get-ChildItem C:\Windows\Assembly -Filter *.dll -Recurse |
    Group-Object Name
```

Combining `Group-Object` with commands such as `Where-Object` and `Sort-Object` allows reports about the content of a set of data to be generated extremely quickly, for example, the top five files which appear more than once in a file tree:

```
PS> Get-ChildItem C:\Windows\Assembly -Filter *.dll -Recurse |
        Group-Object Name -NoElement |
        Where-Object Count -gt 1 |
        Sort-Object Count, Name -Descending |
        Select-Object Name, Count -First 5

Name                                                Count
----                                                -----
Microsoft.Web.Diagnostics.resources.dll             14
Microsoft.Web.Deployment.resources.dll              14
Microsoft.Web.Deployment.PowerShell.resources.dll   14
Microsoft.Web.Delegation.resources.dll              14
Microsoft.Web.PlatformInstaller.resources.dll       13
```

As was seen with `Sort-Object`, `Group-Object` can group on more than one property. For example, we might group on both a filename and the size of a file (the `Length` property of a file):

```
PS> Get-ChildItem C:\Windows\Assembly -Filter *.dll -Recurse |
         Group-Object Name, Length -NoElement |
         Where-Object Count -gt 1 |
         Sort-Object Name -Descending |
         Select-Object Name, Count -First 6
```

```
Name                                              Count
----                                              -----
WindowsBase.ni.dll, 4970496                           2
System.Xml.ni.dll, 6968320                            2
System.Windows.Interactivity.ni.dll, 121856           2
System.Windows.Forms.ni.dll, 17390080                 2
System.Web.ni.dll, 16481792                           2
System.Web.ni.dll, 13605888                           2
```

In the preceding example, we can see that `System.Web.ni.dll` appears four times (a count of `2`, twice) in the folder structure, and that each pair of files has the same size.

Like `Sort-Object`, `Group-Object` is not limited to properties that already exist. It can create calculated properties in much the same way. For example, grouping on an email domain in a list of email addresses might be useful:

```
PS> 'one@one.example', 'two@one.example', 'three@two.example' |
 Group-Object { ($_ -split '@')[1] }

Count Name                      Group
----- ----                      -----
 2    one.example               {one@one.example, two@one.example}
 1    two.example               {three@two.example}
```

In this example, the split operator is used to split on the At (`@`) character; Everything to the left is stored in index 0, everything to the right in index 1.

By default, `Group-Object` returns the collection of objects shown in each of the preceding examples. `Group-Object` is also able to return a `hashtable` using the `AsHashtable` parameter.

When using the `AsHashTable` parameter, the `AsString` parameter is normally used. The `AsString` parameter forces the key for each entry in the `hashtable` to be a string, for example:

```
PS> $hashtable = 'one', 'two', 'two' | Group-Object -AsHashtable -
AsString
$hashtable['one']

one
```

By default, `Group-Object` is case insensitive. The strings `one`, `ONE`, and `One`, are all considered equal. The `CaseSensitive` parameter forces `Group-Object` to differentiate between items where cases differs:

```
PS> 'one', 'ONE', 'One' | Group-Object -CaseSensitive

Count Name                      Group
----- ----                      -----
    1 one                       {one}
    1 ONE                       {ONE}
    1 One                       {One}
```

The Measure-Object command

When used without any parameters, `Measure-Object` will return a value for `Count`, which is the number of items passed in using the pipeline, for example:

```
PS> 1, 5, 9, 79 | Measure-Object

Count      : 4
Average    :
Sum        :
Maximum    :
Minimum    :
Property   :
```

Each of the remaining properties is empty, unless requested using their respective parameters. For example, `Sum` may be requested:

```
PS> 1, 5, 9, 79 | Measure-Object -Sum

Count       : 4
Average     :
Sum         : 94
Maximum     :
Minimum     :
Property    :
```

Adding the remaining parameters will fill in the rest of the fields (except `Property`):

```
PS> 1, 5, 9, 79 | Measure-Object -Average -Maximum -Minimum -Sum

Count         : 4
Average       : 23.5
Sum           : 94
Maximum       : 79
```

```
Minimum      : 1
Property     :
```

The value for `Property` is filled in when `Measure-Object` is asked to work against a particular property (instead of a set of numbers), for example:

```
PS> Get-Process | Measure-Object WorkingSet -Average

Count        : 135
Average      : 39449395.2
Sum          :
Maximum      :
Minimum      :
Property     : WorkingSet
```

When working with text, `Measure-Object` can count characters, words, or lines. For example, it can be used to count the number of lines, words, and characters in a text file:

```
PS> Get-Content C:\Windows\WindowsUpdate.log | Measure-Object -Line -Word -
Character

Lines Words Characters Property
----- ----- ---------- --------
    3    32        267
```

Comparing

The `Compare-Object` command allows collections of objects to be compared to one another.

`Compare-Object` must be supplied with a value for the `ReferenceObject` and `DifferenceObject` parameters, which are normally collections or arrays of objects. If both values are equal, `Compare-Object` does not return anything by default. For example, both the `Reference` and `Difference` object in the following example are identical:

```
Compare-Object -ReferenceObject 1, 2 -DifferenceObject 1, 2
```

If there are differences, `Compare-Object` will display the results, as shown here:

```
PS> Compare-Object -ReferenceObject 1, 2, 3, 4 -DifferenceObject 1, 2

InputObject SideIndicator
----------- -------------
          3 <=
          4 <=
```

This shows that the `Reference` object (the collection on the left) has the values, but the `Difference` object (the collection on the right) does not.

`Compare-Object` has a number of other parameters that may be used to change the output. The `IncludeEqual` parameter adds values which are present in both collections to the output:

```
PS> Compare-Object -ReferenceObject 1, 2, 3, 4 -DifferenceObject 1, 2 -
IncludeEqual

InputObject SideIndicator
----------- -------------
          1 ==
          2 ==
          3 <=
          4 <=
```

`ExcludeDifferent` will omit the results which differ. This parameter makes sense if `IncludeEqual` is also set; without this, the command will always return nothing.

The `PassThru` parameter is used to return the original object instead of the representation showing the differences. In the following example, it is used to select values that are common to both the reference and difference object:

```
PS> Compare-Object -ReferenceObject 1, 2, 3, 4 -DifferenceObject 1, 2 -
ExcludeDifferent -IncludeEqual -PassThru
1
2
```

`Compare-Object` is able to compare based on properties of objects as well as the simpler values in the preceding examples. This can be a single property, or a list of properties. For example, the following command compares the content of `C:\Windows\System32 with C:\Windows\SysWOW64`, returning files that have the same name and are the same size in both:

```
$reference = Get-ChildItem C:\Windows\System32 -File
$difference = Get-ChildItem C:\Windows\SysWOW64 -File
Compare-Object $reference $difference -Property Name, Length -IncludeEqual
-ExcludeDifferent
```

Importing, exporting, and converting

Getting data in and out of PowerShell is a critical part of using the language. There are a number of commands dedicated to this task by default.

The Export-Csv command

The `Export-Csv` command writes data from objects to a text file, for example:

```
Get-Process | Export-Csv processes.csv
```

By default, `Export-Csv` will write a comma-delimited file using ASCII encoding and will completely overwrite any file using the same name.

`Export-Csv` may be used to add lines to an existing file using the `Append` parameter. When the `Append` parameter is used, the input object must have each of the fields listed in the CSV header or an error will be thrown unless the `Force` parameter is used:

```
PS> Get-Process powershell | Select-Object Name, Id | Export-Csv
.\Processes.csv
Get-Process explorer | Select-Object Name | Export-Csv .\Processes.csv
-Append
Export-Csv : Cannot append CSV content to the following file:
.\Processes.csv.
The appended object does not have a property that corresponds to the
following column: Id. To continue with mismatched properties, add the -
Force parameter, and then retry the command.
At line:2 char:51
     + ... ershell_ise | Select-Object Name | Export-Csv .\Processes.csv -
Append
+ ~~~~~~~~~~~~~~~~~~~~~~~~~~~~~~~~~~~
      + CategoryInfo : InvalidData: (Id:String) [Export-Csv],
InvalidOperationException
      + FullyQualifiedErrorId :
CannotAppendCsvWithMismatchedPropertyNames,Microsoft.PowerShell.Commands.Ex
portCsvCommand
```

If the `Append` parameter is used and the input object has more fields than the CSV, the extra fields will be silently dropped when writing the CSV file. For example, the value held in `Id` will be ignored when writing the results to the existing CSV file:

```
Get-Process powershell | Select-Object Name | Export-Csv .\Processes.csv
Get-Process explorer | Select-Object Name, Id | Export-Csv .\Processes.csv
-Append
```

`Export-Csv` will write a header line to each file which details the .NET type it has just exported. If the preceding example is used, that will be the following:

```
#TYPE Selected.System.Diagnostics.Process
```

`Export-Csv` can be instructed to exclude this header using the `NoTypeInformation` parameter:

```
Get-Process | Export-Csv processes.csv -NoTypeInformation
```

`ConvertTo-Csv` is similar to `Export-Csv`, except that instead of writing content to a file, content is written as command output:

```
PS> Get-Process powershell | Select-Object Name, Id | ConvertTo-Csv
#TYPE Selected.System.Diagnostics.Process
"Name","Id"
"powershell","404"
```

Both `Export-Csv` and `ConvertTo-Csv` are limited in what they can do with arrays of objects. For example, `ConvertTo-Csv` is unable to display the values that are in an array:

```
PS> [PSCustomObject]@{
    Name = "Numbers"
    Value = 1, 2, 3, 4, 5
} | ConvertTo-Csv -NoTypeInformation
"Name","Value"
"Numbers","System.Object[]"
```

The value it writes is taken from `theToString` method, which is called on the property called `Value`, for example:

```
PS> $object = [PSCustomObject]@{
    Name = "Numbers"
    Value = 1, 2, 3, 4, 5
}
$object.Value.ToString()

System.Object[]
```

If a CSV file is expected to hold the content of an array, code must be written to convert it into a suitable format. For example, the content of the array can be written after converting it to a string:

```
PS> [PSCustomObject]@{
    Name = "Numbers"
    Value = 1, 2, 3, 4, 5
} | ForEach-Object {
```

```
    $_.Value = $_.Value -join ', '
    $_
} | ConvertTo-Csv -NoTypeInformation

"Name","Value"
"Numbers","1, 2, 3, 4, 5"
```

In the preceding example, the value of the property is joined using a comma followed by a space. The modified object (held in `$_`) is passed on to the `ConvertTo-Csv` command.

The Import-Csv command

Comma-Separated Values (**CSV**) files are plain text. Applications such as Microsoft Excel can work with CSV files without changing the file format, although the advanced features Excel has cannot be saved to a CSV file.

By default, `Import-Csv` expects input to have a header row, to be comma delimited, and to use ASCII file encoding. If any of these items are different, the `command` parameters may be used. For example, a tab may be set as the delimiter:

```
Import-Csv TabDelimitedFile.tsv -Delimiter `t
```

A tick followed by `t` (`` `t ``) is used to represent the tab character in PowerShell.

Data imported using `Import-Csv` will always be formatted as a string. If `Import-Csv` is used to read a file containing the following text, each of the numbers will be treated as a string:

```
Name,Position
Jim,35
Matt,3
Dave,5
```

Attempting to use `Sort-Object` on the imported CSV file will result in values being sorted as if they were strings, not numbers:

```
PS> Import-Csv .\positions.csv | Sort-Object Position

Name Position
---- --------
Matt 3
Jim  35
Dave 5
```

Sort-Object can be used to consider the value for Position as an integer by using a script block expression:

```
PS> Import-Csv .\positions.csv | Sort-Object { [Int]$_.Position }

Name Position
---- --------
Matt  3
Dave  5
Jim   35
```

This conversion problem exists whether the data in a CSV file is a number, or a date, or any type other than string.

ConvertFrom-Csv is similar to Import-Csv, except that content is read from PowerShell instead of a file:

```
PS> "powershell,404" | ConvertFrom-Csv -Header Name, Id

Name           Id
----           --
powershell     404
```

Export-Clixml and Import-Clixml

Export-Clixml creates representations of objects in XML files. Export-Clixml is extremely useful where type information about each property must be preserved.

For example, the following object may be exported using Export-Clixml:

```
[PSCustomObject]@{
    Number  = 1
    Decimal = 2.3
    String  = 'Hello world'
} | Export-Clixml .\object.xml
```

The resulting XML file shows the type for each of the properties it has just exported:

```
PS> Get-Content object.xml
<Objs Version="1.1.0.1"
xmlns="http://schemas.microsoft.com/powershell/2004/04">
  <Obj RefId="0">
    <TN RefId="0">
      <T>System.Management.Automation.PSCustomObject</T>
      <T>System.Object</T>
    </TN>
```

```
    <MS>
      <I32 N="Number">1</I32>
      <Db N="Decimal">2.3</Db>
      <S N="String">Hello world</S>
    </MS>
  </Obj>
</Objs>
```

`I32` is a 32-bit integer (Int32). `Db` is a double-precision floating-point number (double). `S` is a string.

With this extra information in the file, PowerShell can rebuild the object, including the different types, using `Import-Clixml` as follows:

```
$object = Import-Clixml .\object.xml
```

Once imported, the value types can be inspected using the `GetType` method:

```
PS> $object.Decimal.GetType()

IsPublic IsSerial Name                 BaseType
-------- -------- ----                 --------
True     True     Double               System.ValueType
```

Summary

In this chapter, we have explored the object pipeline, as well as objects themselves.

Many of the commands for working with objects in a pipeline were introduced. This includes the ability to filter and select from sets of objects, to sort, group, and measure.

Finally, we explored exporting, importing, and converting objects.

In `Chapter 5`, *Operators*, we will explore PowerShell's operators.

5
Operators

In programming, an operator is an object that is used to manipulate an item of data. PowerShell has a wide variety of operators; most of these will be briefly explored within this chapter.

In this chapter, we are going to cover the following topics:

- Arithmetic operators
- Assignment operators
- Comparison operators
- Regular-expression-based operators
- Binary operators
- Logical operators
- Type operators
- Redirection operators
- Other operators

Arithmetic operators

Arithmetic operators are used to perform numeric calculations. The operators available are the following:

- **Addition**: `+`
- **Subtraction**: `-`
- **Multiplication**: `*`
- **Division**: `/`
- **Modulus**: `%`

- **Shift left**: `-shl`
- **Shift right**: `-shr`

As well as numeric calculations, the addition operator may also be used with strings, arrays, and hashtables; the multiplication operator may also be used with strings and arrays.

Operator precedence

Mathematical operations are executed in a specific order. For example, consider the following two simple calculations:

```
3 + 2 * 2
2 * 2 + 3
```

The result of both of the preceding expressions is `7` (`2` multiplied by `2`, then add `3`).

PowerShell, and most other programming languages, will calculate elements of an expression using multiplication (`*`), division (`/`), and modulus (`%`) first. Addition (`+`) and subtraction (`-`) are calculated next.

PowerShell has two additional operators in this category, `-shl` and `-shr`. These two have the lowest precedence and are only executed once all other operations have completed. For example, the result of the following calculation will be `128`:

```
2 * 4 -shl 2 + 2
```

`2 * 4` is calculated, followed by `2 + 2`, and then `-shl` is used. The `-shl` operator is discussed in detail later in this chapter.

Expressions in parentheses are always calculated first to cater for more advanced situations. For example, the result of the following calculation is `10`:

```
(3 + 2) * 2
```

Addition and subtraction operators

The addition operator may be used to add numeric values:

```
2.71828 + 3.14159
```

It may also be used to concatenate strings:

```
'hello'  + ' ' + 'world'
```

If an attempt is made to concatenate a string with a number, the number will be converted into a string:

```
'hello number ' + 1
```

This style of operation will fail if the number is used first. PowerShell expects the entire expression to be numeric if that is how it begins:

```
PS> 1 + ' is the number I like to use'
Cannot convert value "is the number I like to use" to type "System.Int32".
Error: "Input string was not in a correct format."
At line:1 char:1
+ 1 + ' is the number I like to use'
+ ~~~~~~~~~~~~~~~~~~~~~~~~~~~~~~~~~~
    + CategoryInfo : InvalidArgument: (:) [], RuntimeException
    + FullyQualifiedErrorId : InvalidCastFromStringToInteger
```

The addition operator may be used to add single elements to an existing array. The following expression results in an array containing `1`, `2`, and `3`:

```
@(1, 2) + 3
```

Joining arrays with the addition operator is simple. Each of the following three examples creates an array and each array contains the values `1`, `2`, `3`, and `4`:

```
@(1, 2) + @(3, 4)
(1, 2) + (3, 4)
1, 2 + 3, 4
```

Hashtables may be joined in a similar manner:

```
@{key1 = 1} + @{key2 = 2}
```

The addition operation will fail if keys are duplicated as part of the addition operation:

```
PS> @{key1 = 1} + @{key1 = 2}
Item has already been added. Key in dictionary: 'key1' Key being added:
'key1'
At line:1 char:1
+ @{key1 = 1} + @{key1 = 2}
+ ~~~~~~~~~~~~~~~~~~~~~~~~~
    + CategoryInfo : OperationStopped: (:) [], ArgumentException
    + FullyQualifiedErrorId : System.ArgumentException
```

The subtraction operator may only be used for numeric expressions. The results of the following expressions are 3 and -18, respectively:

```
5 - 2
2 - 20
```

Multiplication, division, and modulus operators

The multiplication operator is able to perform simple numeric operations. For example, the result of the following expression is 5:

```
2.5 * 2
```

The multiplication operator may also be used to duplicate strings:

```
'hello' * 3
```

As with the addition operator, the multiplication operator will throw an error if a number is on the left of the expression:

```
PS> 3 * 'hello'
Cannot convert value "hello" to type "System.Int32". Error: "Input string
was not in a correct format."
At line:1 char:2
+ 3 * 'hello'
+ ~~~~~~~~~~~
    + CategoryInfo : InvalidArgument: (:) [], RuntimeException
    + FullyQualifiedErrorId : InvalidCastFromStringToInteger
```

The multiplication operator may also be used to duplicate arrays. Each of the following examples creates an array containing one, two, one, and two:

```
@('one', 'two') * 2
('one', 'two') * 2
'one', 'two' * 2
```

The division operator performs numeric division:

```
20 / 5
```

An error will be thrown if an attempt to divide by 0 is made:

```
PS> 1 / 0
Attempted to divide by zero.
At line:1 char:1
+ 1 / 0
```

```
+ ~~~~~
    + CategoryInfo : NotSpecified: (:) [], RuntimeException
    + FullyQualifiedErrorId : RuntimeException
```

The modulus operator returns the remainder of whole-number (integer) division. For example, the result of the following operation is `1`:

```
3 % 2
```

Modulus can be used for alternation:
Aside from its value to math, the modulus operator may be used to alternate; to perform an action on every second, third, fourth, and so on, iteration of a loop:
`1..100 | ForEach-Object {# Show the value of $_ at intervals of 5if ($_ % 5 -eq 0) {Write-Host $_}}`

Shift left and shift right operators

The `-shl` and `-shr` operators were introduced with PowerShell 3.0. These operators perform bit-shifting.

The possible bit values for a byte may be represented in a table:

Bit position	1	2	3	4	5	6	7	8
Bit value	128	64	32	16	8	4	2	1

For a numeric value of `78`, the following bits must be set:

Bit value	128	64	32	16	8	4	2	1
On or off	0	1	0	0	1	1	1	0

When a left shift operation is performed, every bit is moved one to the left. Say we run this expression:

```
78 -shl 1
```

The result is `156`, which may be expressed in the bit table:

Bit value	128	64	32	16	8	4	2	1
Before shift	0	1	0	0	1	1	1	0
After shift	1	0	0	1	1	1	0	0

Shifting one bit to the right will reverse the operation:

```
PS> 156 -shr 1
78
```

When converting values using left or right shifting, bits that are set and right-shifted past the rightmost bit (bit value `1`) become `0`, for example:

```
PS> 3 -shr 1

1
```

This may be described in the following table. Bits that end up in the right-most column are discarded:

Bit value	128	64	32	16	8	4	2	1	Out of range
Before shift	0	0	0	0	0	0	1	1	
After shift	0	0	0	0	0	0	0	1	1

If the numeric value is of a specific numeric type, the resulting number cannot exceed the maximum value for the type. For example, a `Byte` has a maximum value of `255`; if the value of `255` is shifted one bit to the left, the resulting value will be `254`:

```
PS> ([Byte]255) -shl 1
254
```

Shifting out of range may be shown in a table:

Bit value	Out of range	128	64	32	16	8	4	2	1
Before shift		1	1	1	1	1	1	1	1
After shift	1	1	1	1	1	1	1	1	0

If the value were capable of being larger, such as a `16` or 32-bit integer, the value would be allowed to increase as it no longer falls out of range:

```
PS> ([Int16]255) -shl 1
510
```

Bit shifting as this is easiest to demonstrate with unsigned types such as `Byte`, `UInt16`, `UInt32`, and `UInt64`. Unsigned types cannot support values lower than `0` (negative numbers).

Signed types, such as `SByte`, `Int16`, `Int32`, and `Int64`, sacrifice their highest-order bit to indicate whether the value is positive or negative. For example, this table shows the bit positions for a **Signed Byte** (**SByte**):

Bit position	1	2	3	4	5	6	7	8
Bit value	Signing	64	32	16	8	4	2	1

The preceding bit values may be used to express number between `127` and `-128`. The binary forms of `1` and `-1` are shown as an example in the following table:

Bit value	Signing	64	32	16	8	4	2	1
1	0	0	0	0	0	0	0	1
-1	1	1	1	1	1	1	1	1

For a signed type, each bit (except for signing) adds to a minimum value:

- When the signing bit is not set, add each value to `0`
- When the signing bit is set, add each value to `-128`

Applying this to left shift, if the value of `64` is shifted one bit to the left, it becomes `-128`:

```
PS> ([SByte]64) -shl 1
-128
```

The shift into the signing bit can be expressed in a table:

Bit value	Signing	64	32	16	8	4	2	1
Before shift	0	1	0	0	0	0	0	0
After shift	1	0	0	0	0	0	0	0

Shift operations such as these are common in the networking world. For example, the IP address `192.168.4.32` may be represented in a number of different ways:

- **In hexadecimal**: `C0A80420`
- **As an unsigned 32-bit integer**: `3232236576`
- **As a signed 32-bit integer**: `-1062730720`

The signed and unsigned versions of an IP address are calculated using left shift. For example, the IP address `192.168.4.32` may be written as a signed 32-bit integer (`Int32`):

```
(192 -shl 24) + (168 -shl 16) + (4 -shl 8) + 32
```

Assignment operators

Assignment operators are used to give values to variables. The assignment operators available are the following:

- **Assign**: `=`
- **Add and assign**: `+=`
- **Subtract and assign**: `-=`
- **Multiply and assign**: `*=`
- **Divide and assign**: `/=`
- **Modulus and assign**: `%=`

As with the arithmetic operators, add and assign may be used with strings, arrays, and hashtables. Multiply and assign may be used with strings and arrays.

Assign, add and assign, and subtract and assign

The assignment operator (=) is used to assign values to variables and properties, for example, assignment to a variable:

```
$variable = 'some value'
```

Or we might change the PowerShell window title by assigning a new value to its property:

```
$host.UI.RawUI.WindowTitle = 'PowerShell window'
```

The add and assign operator (+=) operates in a similar manner to the addition operator. The following example assigns the value `1` to a variable, then += is used to add `20` to that value:

```
$i = 1
$i += 20
```

The preceding example is equivalent to writing the following:

```
$i = 1
$i = $i + 20
```

The += operator may be used to concatenate strings:

```
$string = 'one'
$string += 'one'
```

As was seen with the addition operator, attempting to add a numeric value to an existing string is acceptable. Attempting to add a string to a variable containing a numeric value is `not`:

```
PS> $variable = 1
$variable += 'one'
Cannot convert value "one" to type "System.Int32". Error: "Input string was
not in a correct format."
At line:2 char:1
+ $variable += 'one'
+ ~~~~~~~~~~~~~~~~~~
    + CategoryInfo : InvalidArgument: (:) [], RuntimeException
    + FullyQualifiedErrorId : InvalidCastFromStringToInteger
```

It is possible to work around this by assigning a type to the variable:

```
[String]$string = 1
$string += 'one'
```

The += operator may be used to add single elements to an existing array:

```
$array = 1, 2
$array += 3
```

Or to add another array:

```
$array = 1, 2
$array += 3, 4
```

The += operator may be used to join together two hashtables:

```
$hashtable = @{key1 = 1}
$hashtable += @{key2 = 2}
```

As was seen using the addition operator, the operation will fail if one of the keys already exists.

The subtract and assign operator (-=) is intended for numeric operations as shown in the following examples:

```
$i = 20
$i -= 2
```

Multiply and assign, divide and assign, and modulus and assign

Numeric assignments using the multiply and assign operator may be performed using *=. The value held by the following variable `i` will be `4`:

```
$i = 2
$i *= 2
```

The multiply and assign operator may be used to duplicate a string held in a variable:

```
$string = 'one'
$string *= 2
```

The value on the right-hand side of the *= operator must be numeric or must be able to convert to a number. For example, a string containing the number `2` is acceptable:

```
$string = 'one'
$string *= '2'
```

Using a string that is unable to convert to a number results in an error as follows:

```
PS> $variable = 'one'
$variable *= 'one'

Cannot convert value "one" to type "System.Int32". Error: "Input string was
```

```
not in a correct format."
At line:2 char:1
+ $variable *= 'one'
+ ~~~~~~~~~~~~~~~~~~
    + CategoryInfo : InvalidArgument: (:) [], RuntimeException
    + FullyQualifiedErrorId : InvalidCastFromStringToInteger
```

The multiply and assign operator may be used to duplicate an array held in a variable. In the following example, the variable will hold the values `1`, `2` , `1`, and `2` after this operation:

```
$variable = 1, 2
$variable *= 2
```

The assign and divide operator is used to perform numeric operations. The variable will hold a value of `1` after the following operation:

```
$variable = 2
$variable /= 2
```

The modulus and assign operator assigns the result of the modulus operation to a variable:

```
$variable = 10
$variable %= 3
```

After the preceding operation, the variable will hold a value of `1`, the remainder when dividing `10` by `3`.

Comparison operators

PowerShell has a wide variety of comparison operators:

- **Equal to and not equal to**: `-eq` and `-ne`
- **Like and not like**: `-like` and `-notlike`
- **Greater than and greater than or equal to**: `-gt` and `-ge`
- **Less than and less than or equal to**: `-lt` and `-le`
- **Contains and not contains**: `-contains` and `-notcontains`
- **In and not in**: `-in` and `-notin`

Case-sensitivity

None of the comparison operators are case sensitive by default. Each of the comparison operators has two additional variants, one which explicitly states it is case-sensitive, and another which explicitly states it is case-insensitive.

For example, the following statement returns `true`:

```
'Trees' -eq 'trees'
```

Adding a `c` modifier in front of the operator name forces PowerShell to make a case-sensitive comparison. The following statement will return `false`:

```
'Trees' -ceq 'trees'
```

In addition to this the case-sensitive modifier, PowerShell also has an explicit case-insensitive modifier:

```
'Trees' -ieq 'trees'
```

However, as case insensitive comparison is the default, it is extremely rare to see examples of the `i` modifier.

These behavior modifiers can be applied to all of the comparison operators.

Comparison operators and arrays

When comparison operators are used with scalar values (a single item as opposed to an array), the comparison will result in `true` or `false`.

When used with an array or collection, the result of the comparison is all matching elements, for example:

```
1, $null -ne $null                  # Returns 1
1, 2, 3, 4 -ge 3                    # Returns 3, 4
'one', 'two', 'three' -like '*e*'   # Returns one and three
```

This behavior may be problematic if a comparison is used to test whether or not a variable holding an array exists. In the following example, `-eq` is used to test that a value has been assigned to a variable called `array`:

```
$array = 1, 2
if ($array -eq $null) { Write-Host 'Variable not set' }
```

This test is apparently valid as long as the array does not hold two or more null values. When two or more values are present, the condition unexpectedly returns `true`:

```
PS> $array = 1, 2, $null, $null
if ($array -eq $null) { Write-Host 'No values in array' }

No values in array
```

This happens because the result of the comparison is an array with two `null` values. If it were a single `null` value, PowerShell would flatten the array. With two values, it cannot:

```
[Boolean]@($null)              # Returns false
[Boolean]@($null, $null)       # Returns true
```

To counteract this behavior, when testing whether or not an array exists in a variable, `null` must be on the left-hand side of the expression. For example, the following `Write-Host` statement will not execute:

```
$array = 1, 2, $null, $null
if ($null -eq $array) { Write-Host 'Variable not set' }
```

Equal to and not equal to

The `-eq` (equal to) and `-ne` (not equal to) operators perform exact (and, by default, case-insensitive) comparisons. For example, the following returns `true`:

```
1 -eq 1
'string' -eq 'string'
[char]'a' -eq 'A'
$true -eq 1
$false -eq 0
```

Similarly, `-ne` (not equal) will return `true` for each of these:

```
20 -ne 100
'this' -ne 'that'
$false -ne 'false'
```

Like and not like

The `-like` and `-notlike` operators support simple wildcards. `*` matches a string of any length (zero or more) and `?` matches a single character. Each of the following examples returns `true`:

```
'The cow jumped over the moon' -like '*moon*'
'Hello world' -like '??llo w*'
'' -like '*'
'' -notlike '?*'
```

Greater than and less than

When comparing numbers, each of the operators `-ge` (greater than or equal to), `-gt` (greater than), `-le` (less than or equal to), and `-lt` (less than) are simple to use:

```
1 -ge 1         # Returns true
2 -gt 1         # Returns true
1.4 -lt 1.9     # Returns true
1.1 -le 1.1     # Returns true
```

String comparison with operators follows the generalized pattern `0123456789aAbBcCdD...` rather than basing on a character table (such as ASCII):

- Cultural variants of characters, for example, the character å, fall between `A` and `b` in the list
- Other alphabets, for example Cyrillic or Greek, come after the Roman alphabet (after `Z`)

Comparison can be culture sensitive when using commands such as `Sort-Object` with the `Culture` parameter, but comparisons are always based on `en-US` when using the operators:

```
'apples' -lt 'pears'    # Returns true
'Apples' -lt 'pears'    # Returns true
'bears' -gt 'Apples'    # Returns true
```

Or when using case-sensitive comparison:

```
'bears' -gt 'Bears'    # False, they are equal to one another
'bears' -clt 'Bears'   # True, b before B
```

Contains and in

The `-contains`, `-notcontains`, `-in`, and `-notin` operators are used to test the content of arrays.

When using `-contains` or `-notcontains`, the array is expected to be on the left-hand side of the operator:

```
1, 2 -contains 2        # Returns true
1, 2, 3 -contains 4     # Returns false
```

When using `-in` or `-notin`, the array is expected to be on the right-hand side of the operator:

```
1 -in 1, 2, 3     # Returns true
4 -in 1, 2, 3     # Returns false
```

Contains or in?
When using comparison operators, I tend to write the subject on the left, the object on the right. Comparisons to null are an exception to the rule. The subject is the variable or property I am testing; the object is the thing I test against. For example, I might set the subject to a user in Active Directory:
`$subject = Get-ADUser -Identity $env:USERNAME -Properties department, memberOf`
I use `contains` where the subject is an array, and the object is a single value:
`$subject.MemberOf -contains 'CN=Group,DC=domain,DC=example'`
I use `in` where the subject is a single value, and the object is an array:
`$subject.Department -in 'Department1', 'Department2'`

Regular-expression-based operators

Regular expressions are an advanced form of pattern matching. In PowerShell, a number of operators have direct support for regular expressions. Regular expressions themselves are covered in greater detail in `Chapter 10`, *Regular Expressions*.

The following operators use regular expressions:

- **Match**: `-match`
- **Not match**: `-notmatch`
- **Replace**: `-replace`
- **Split**: `-split`

Match and not match

The `-match` and `-notmatch` operators return `true` or `false` when testing strings:

```
'The cow jumped over the moon' -match 'cow'   # Returns true
'The       cow' -match 'The +cow'             # Returns true
```

In the preceding example, the `+` symbol is reserved; it indicates that `The` is followed by one or more spaces before `cow`.

> **Match is a comparison operator**:
> Like the other comparison operators, if match is used against an array, it returns each matching element instead of `true` or `false`. The following comparison will return the values `one` and `three`:
> `"one", "two", "three" -match 'e'`

In addition to returning a `true` or `false` value about the state of the match, a successful match will add values to a reserved variable, `$matches`. For example, the following regular expression uses a character class to indicate it should match any character from `0` to `4` repeated 0 or more times:

```
'1234567689' -match '[0-4]*'
```

Once the match has been executed, the `matches` variable (a hashtable) will be populated with the part of the string that matched the expression:

```
PS> $matches

Name                           Value
----                           -----
0                              1234
```

Regular expressions use parentheses to denote groups. Groups may be used to capture interesting elements of a string:

```
PS> 'Group one, Group two' -match 'Group (.*), Group (.*)'
True

PS> $matches

Name                           Value
----                           -----
2                              two
1                              one
0                              Group one, Group two
```

In the preceding example, the match operator is run first then the `matches` variable is displayed. The captured value `one` is held in the first group, and is accessible using either of the following statements:

```
$matches[1]
$matches.1
```

Replace

The `-replace` operator performs replacement based on a regular expression. For example, it can be used to replace several instances of the same thing:

```
PS> 'abababab' -replace 'a', 'c'
cbcbcbcb
```

In the example, `a` is the regular expression that dictates what must be replaced. `'c'` is the value any matching values should be replaced with.

This syntax can be generalized as follows:

```
<Value> -replace <Match>, <Replace-With>
```

If the `Replace-With` value is omitted, the matches will be replaced with nothing (that is, they are removed):

```
PS> 'abababab' -replace 'a'
bbbb
```

Regular expressions use parentheses to capture groups. The replace operator can use those groups. Each group may be used in the `Replace-With` argument. For example, a set of values can be reversed:

```
'value1,value2,value3' -replace '(.*),(.*),(.*)', '$3,$2,$1'
```

The tokens `$1`, `$2`, and `$3` are references to each of the groups denoted by the parentheses.

When performing this operation, the `Replace-With` argument must use single quotes to prevent PowerShell evaluating the group references as if they were variables. This problem is shown in the following example. The first attempt works as expected; the second shows an expanded PowerShell variable instead:

```
PS> $1 = $2 = $3 = 'Oops'
Write-Host ('value1,value2,value3' -replace '(.*),(.*),(.*)', '$3,$2,$1') -
ForegroundColor Green
Write-Host ('value1,value2,value3' -replace '(.*),(.*),(.*)', "$3,$2,$1") -
ForegroundColor Red

value3,value2,value1
Oops,Oops,Oops
```

Split

The `-split` operator splits a string into an array based on a regular expression.

The following example splits the string into an array containing `a`, `b`, `c`, and `d` by matching each of the numbers:

```
PS> 'a1b2c3d4' -split '[0-9]'
a
b
c
d
```

Binary operators

Binary operators are used to perform bit-level operations. Each operator returns the numeric result of the operation:

- **Binary and**: `-band`
- **Binary or**: `-bor`

- **Binary exclusive or**: `-bxor`
- **Binary not**: `-bnot`

Binary and

The result of `-band` is a number where each of the bits is set in both the value on the left and the value on the right.

In the following example, the result is `2`:

```
11 -band 6
```

This operation can be shown in a table:

Bit value		8	4	2	1
Left-hand side	11	1	0	**1**	1
Right-hand side	6	0	1	**1**	0
`-band`	2	0	0	1	0

Binary or

The result of `-bor` is a number where the bits are set in either the value on the left or right.

In the following example, the result is `15`:

```
11 -bor 12
```

This operation can be shown in a table:

Bit value		8	4	2	1
Left-hand side	11	**1**	0	**1**	**1**
Right-hand side	12	**1**	**1**	0	0
`-band`	15	1	1	1	1

Binary exclusive or

The result of -bxor is a number where the bits are set in either the value on the left, or the value on the right, but not both.

In the following example, the result is 11:

```
6 -bxor 13
```

This operation can be shown in a table:

Bit value		8	4	2	1
Left-hand side	6	0	*1*	**1**	0
Right-hand side	13	**1**	*1*	0	**1**
-band	11	1	0	1	1

The -bxor operator is useful for toggling bit values. For example, bxor might be used to toggle the AccountDisable bit of UserAccountControl in Active Directory:

```
512 -bxor 2    # Result is 514 (Disabled, 2 is set)
514 -bxor 2    # Result is 512 (Enabled, 2 is not set)
```

Binary not

The -bnot operator is applied before a numeric value; it does not use a value on the left-hand side. The result is a value comprised of all bits that are not set.

The -bnot operator works with signed and unsigned 32-bit and 64-bit integers (Int32, UInt32, Int64, and UInt64). When working with 8-bit or 16-bit integers (SByte, Byte, Int16, and UInt16), the result is always a signed 32-bit integer (Int32).

In the following example, the result is -123:

```
-bnot 122
```

As the preceding result is a 32-bit integer (`Int32`), it is difficult to show the effect in a small table. If this value were a `SByte`, the operation could be expressed in a table as follows:

Bit value		Signing	64	32	16	8	4	2	1
Before `-bnot`	122	0	1	1	1	1	0	1	0
After `-bnot`	-123	1	0	0	0	0	1	0	1

Logical operators

Logical operators are used to evaluate two or more comparisons or other operations that produce a Boolean (`true` or `false`) result.

The following logic operators are available:

- **And**: `-and`
- **Or**: `-or`
- **Exclusive or**: `-xor`
- **Not**: `-not and !`

And

The `-and` operator will return `true` if the value on the left-hand and right-hand side are both `true`.

For example, each of the following returns `true`:

```
$true -and $true
1 -lt 2 -and "string" -like 's*'
1 -eq 1 -and 2 -eq 2 -and 3 -eq 3
(Test-Path C:\Windows) -and (Test-Path 'C:\Program Files')
```

Or

The `-or` operator will return `true` if either the value on the left, or the value on the right, or both are `true`.

For example, each of the following returns `true`:

```
$true -or $true
2 -gt 1 -or "something" -ne "nothing"
1 -eq 1 -or 2 -eq 1
(Test-Path C:\Windows) -or (Test-Path D:\Windows)
```

Exclusive or

The `-xor` operator will return `true` if either the value on the left is `true`, or the value on the right is `true`, but not both.

For example, each of the following returns `true`:

```
$true -xor $false
1 -le 2 -xor 1 -eq 2
(Test-Path C:\Windows) -xor (Test-Path D:\Windows)
```

Not

The `-not (or !)` operator may be used to negate the expression which follows.

For example, each of the following returns `true`:

```
-not $false
-not (Test-Path X:\)
-not ($true -and $false)
!($true -and $false)
```

Double negatives:
The `-not` operator has an important place, but it is worth rethinking an expression if it injects a double negative. For example, the following expression will return `true`:

```
-not (1 -ne 1)
```

The preceding expression is better written using the `-eq` operator:

```
1 -eq 1
```

Type operators

The type operators are designed to work with .NET types. The following operators are available:

- **As**: `-as`
- **Is**: `-is`
- **Is not**: `-isnot`

As

The `-as` operator is used to convert a value into an object of the specified type. The operator returns `null` (without throwing an error) if the conversion cannot be completed.

For example, the operator may be used to perform the following conversions:

```
"1" -as [Int32]
'String' -as [Type]
```

The `-as` operator can be useful for testing whether or not a value can be cast to a specific type, or whether a specific type exists.

For example, the `System.Web` assembly is not imported by default and the `System.Web.HttpUtility` class does not exist. The `-as` operator may be used to test for this condition:

```
PS> if (-not ('System.Web.HttpUtility' -as [Type])) {
    Write-Host 'Adding assembly' -ForegroundColor Green
    Add-Type -Assembly System.Web
}
Adding assembly
```

Is and isnot

The `-is` and `-isnot` operators test whether or not a value is of the specified type.

For example, each of the following returns `true`:

```
'string' -is [String]
1 -is [Int32]
[String] -is [Type]
123 -isnot [String]
```

Redirection operators

In `Chapter 4`, *Working with Objects in PowerShell*, we started exploring the different output streams PowerShell utilizes.

Information from a command may be redirected using the redirection operator >. Information may be sent to another stream or a file.

For example, the output from a command can be directed to a file. The file will contain the output as it would have been displayed in the console:

```
PS> Get-Process -Id $pid > process.txt
Get-Content process.txt

Handles NPM(K)  PM(K)   WS(K) CPU(s)     Id SI  ProcessName
------- ------  -----   ----- ------     -- --  -----------
    731     57 132264 133156   1.81 11624  1  powershell_ise
```

Each of the streams in PowerShell has a number associated with it. These are shown in the following table:

Stream name	Stream number
Standard out	1
Error	2
Warning	3
Verbose	4
Debug	5
Information	6

About Write-Host:
Before PowerShell 5, the output written using the `Write-Host` command could not be captured, redirected, or assigned to a variable. In PowerShell 5, `Write-Host` has become a wrapper for `Write-Information` and is sent to the information stream.
Information written using `Write-Host` is unaffected by the `InformationPreference` variable and the `InformationAction` parameter.

Redirection to a file

Output from a specific stream may be directed by placing the stream number on the left of the redirect operator.

For example, the output written by `Write-Warning` can be directed to a file:

```
PS> function Test-Redirect{
    'This is standard out'

    Write-Warning 'This is a warning'
}
$stdOut = Test-Redirect 3> 'warnings.txt'
Get-Content 'warnings.txt'
This is a warning
```

When using the redirect operator, any file of the same name is overwritten. If information must be added to a file, the operator becomes >>:

```
$i = 1
function Test-Redirect{
    Write-Warning "Warning $i"
}
Test-Redirect 3> 'warnings.txt'   # Overwrite
$i++
Test-Redirect 3>> 'warnings.txt'  # Append
```

It is possible to redirect additional streams, for example, warnings and errors, by adding more redirect statements. The following example redirects the error and warning streams to separate files:

```
function Test-Redirect{
    'This is standard out'
    Write-Error 'This is an error'
    Write-Warning 'This is a warning'
}
Test-Redirect 3> 'warnings.txt' 2> 'errors.txt'
```

The wildcard character `*` may be used to represent all streams if all content were to be sent to a single file:

```
$verbosePreference = 'continue'
function Test-Redirect{
    'This is standard out'

    Write-Information 'This is information'
    Write-Host 'This is information as well'
```

```
    Write-Error 'This is an error'
    Write-Verbose 'This is verbose'
    Write-Warning 'This is a warning'
}
Test-Redirect *> 'alloutput.txt'
```

The preceding example starts by setting the `verbose preference` variable. Without this, the output from `Write-Verbose` will not be shown at all.

Redirecting streams to standard output

Streams can be redirected to standard output in PowerShell. The destination stream is written on the right-hand side of the redirect operator (without a space). Stream numbers on the right-hand side are prefixed with an ampersand (`&`) to distinguish the stream from a filename.

For example, the `Information` output written by the following command is sent to standard output:

```
PS> function Test-Redirect{
    'This is standard out'

    Write-Information 'This is information'
}

$stdOut = Test-Redirect 6>&1
$stdOut

This is standard out
This is information
```

It is possible to redirect additional streams, for example, warnings and errors, by adding more redirect statements. The following example redirects the error and warning streams to standard output:

```
function Test-Redirect{
    'This is standard out'
    Write-Error 'This is an error'
    Write-Warning 'This is a warning'
}
$stdOut = Test-Redirect 2>&1 3>&1
```

The wildcard character * may be used to represent all streams if all streams were to be sent to another:

```
$verbosePreference = 'continue'
function Test-Redirect{
    'This is standard out'

    Write-Information 'This is information'
    Write-Host 'This is information as well'
    Write-Error 'This is an error'
    Write-Verbose 'This is verbose'
    Write-Warning 'This is a warning'
}
$stdOut = Test-Redirect *>&1
```

The preceding example starts by setting the verbose preference variable. Without this the output from `Write-Verbose` will not be shown at all.

Only StdOut:
Each of the preceding examples shows redirection to `StdOut`. It is not possible to redirect to streams other than standard output.

Redirection to null

Redirecting output to null is a technique used to drop unwanted output. The variable `$null` takes the place of the filename:

```
Get-Process > $null
```

The preceding example redirects standard output (stream 1), to nothing. This is equivalent to using an empty filename:

```
Get-Process > ''
```

The stream number or * may be included to the left of the redirect operator. For example, warnings and errors might be redirected to `null`:

```
.\somecommand.exe 2> $null 3> $null
.\somecommand.exe *> $null
```

Other operators

PowerShell has a wide variety of operators, a few of which do not easily fall into a specific category, as discussed shortly, including the following:

- **Call**: `&`
- **Comma**: `,`
- **Format**: `-f`
- **Increment and decrement**: `++` and `--`
- **Join**: `-join`

Call

The call operator is used to execute a string or script block. For example, the call operator may be used to execute the `ipconfig` command:

```
$command = 'ipconfig'
& $command
```

Or it may be used to execute a script block:

```
$scriptBlock = { Write-Host 'Hello world' }
& $scriptBlock
```

The `call` operator accepts a list of arguments that can be passed to the command. For example, the `displaydns` parameter can be passed into the `ipconfig` command:

```
& 'ipconfig' '/displaydns'
```

Comma

The comma operator may be used to separate elements in an array, for example:

```
$array = 1, 2, 3, 4
```

If the comma operator is used before a single value, it creates an array containing one element:

```
$array = ,1
```

Format

The `-f` operator can be used to create complex formatted strings. The syntax for the format operator is inherited from .NET; MSDN has a number of advanced examples:

`https://msdn.microsoft.com/en-us/library/system.string.format(v=vs.110).aspx#Starting`

The `-f` operator uses a number in curly braces (`{<number>}`) in a string on the left of the operator to reference a value in an array on the right, for example:

```
'1: {0}, 2: {1}, 3: {2}' -f 1, 2, 3
```

The format operator is one possible way to assemble complex strings in PowerShell. In addition to this, it may be used to simplify some string operations. For example, a decimal may be converted to a percentage:

```
'The pass mark is {0:P}' -f 0.8
```

An integer may be converted to a hexadecimal string:

```
'244 in Hexadecimal is {0:X2}' -f 244
```

A number may be written as a culture-specific currency:

```
'The price is {0:C2}' -f 199
```

Reserved characters:
When using the `-f` operator, curly braces are considered reserved characters. If a curly brace is to be included in a string as a literal value, it can be escaped:

```
'The value in {{0}} is {0}' -f 1
```

Increment and decrement

The `++` and `--` operators are used to increment and decrement numeric values. The increment and decrement operators are split into pre-increment and post-increment versions.

The post-increment operators are frequently seen in `for` loops. The value for `$i` is used, and then incremented by one after use. In the case of the `for` loop, this happens after all the statements inside the loop block have executed:

```
for ($i = 0; $i -le 15; $i++) {
    Write-Host $i -ForegroundColor $i
}
```

The post-decrement reduces the value by one after use:

```
for ($i = 15; $i -ge 0; $i--) {
    Write-Host $i -ForegroundColor $i
}
```

Post-increment and post-decrement operators are often seen when iterating through an array:

```
$array = 1..15
$i = 0
while ($i -lt $array.Count) {
    # $i will increment after this statement has completed.
    Write-Host $array[$i++] -ForegroundColor $i
}
```

Pre-increment and pre-decrement are rarely seen. Instead of incrementing or decrementing a value after use, the change happens before the value is used, for example:

```
$array = 1..5
$i = 0
do {
    # $i is incremented before use, 2 will be the first printed.
    Write-Host $array[++$i]
} while ($i -lt $array.Count -1)
```

Join

The `-join` operator joins arrays using a string. In the following example, the string is split based on a comma, and then joined based on a tab (`` `t ``):

```
PS> "a,b,c,d" -split ',' -join "`t"
a b c d
```

Summary

In this chapter, we have explored many of the operators PowerShell has to offer, including operators for performing arithmetic, assignment, and comparison.

Several specialized operators that use regular expressions were introduced for matching, replacing, and splitting.

Binary, logical, and type operators were demonstrated.

Finally, a number of other significant operators were introduced, including call, format, increment and decrement, and the join operator.

In the `Chapter 6`, *Variables, Arrays, and Hashtables*, are explored in detail.

6
Variables, Arrays, and Hashtables

This chapter explores variables along with a detailed look at arrays and hashtables, as these have their own complexities.

A variable in a programming language allows you to assign a label to a piece of information or data. A variable can be used and reused in the console, script, function, or any other piece of code.

In this chapter, we are going to cover the following topics:

- Naming and creating variables
- Variable commands
- Variable scope
- Types and type conversion
- Objects assigned to variables
- Arrays
- Hashtables
- Lists, dictionaries, queues, and stacks

A variable may be of any .NET type or object instance. The variable may be a string (`"Hello World"`), an integer (42), a decimal (3.141), an array, a hashtable, a `ScriptBlock`, and so on. Everything a variable might hold is considered to be an object when used in PowerShell.

Naming and creating variables

Variables in PowerShell are preceded by the dollar symbol (`$`), for example:

```
$MyVariable
```

The name of a variable may contain numbers, letters, and underscores. For example, each of the following is a valid name:

```
$123
$x
$my_variable
$variable
$varIABle
$Path_To_File
```

Variables are frequently written in either camel case or upper-camel case (also known as pascal case). PowerShell does not enforce any naming convention, nor does it exhibit a convention in any of the automatic variables. For example:

- `$myVariable` is camel case
- `$MyVariable` is upper-camel case or pascal case

I suggest making your variable names meaningful so that when you come and visit your script again after a long break, you can identify its purpose. I recommend choosing and maintaining a consistent style in your own code.

It is possible to use more complex variable names using the following notation:

```
${My Variable}
${My-Variable}
```

The following notation, where a file path is written as the variable `name`, allows variables to be stored on the filesystem:

```
${C:\Windows\Temp\variable.txt} = "New value"
```

Inspecting the given file path shows that the variable value has been written there:

```
PS> Get-Content C:\Windows\Temp\variable.txt
New value
```

Variables do not need to be declared prior to use, nor does a variable need to be assigned a specific type, for example:

```
$itemCount = 7
$dateFormat = "ddMMyyyy"
$numbers = @(1, 9, 5, 2)
$psProcess = Get-Process -Name PowerShell
```

It is possible to assign several variables the same value in one statement. For example, this creates two variables, `i` and `j`, both with a value of `0`:

```
$i = $j = 0
```

Variable commands

A number of commands are available to interact with variables:

- `Clear-Variable`
- `Get-Variable`
- `New-Variable`
- `Remove-Variable`
- `Set-Variable`

Clear-Variable

`Clear-Variable` removes the value from any existing variable. `Clear-Variable` does not remove the variable itself. For example, the following example calls `Write-Host` twice: the first time it writes the variable value; the second time it does not write anything:

```
PS> $temporaryValue = "Some-Value"
Write-Host $temporaryValue -ForegroundColor Green

Some-Value

PS> Clear-Variable temporaryValue
Write-Host $temporaryValue -ForegroundColor Green
```

Get-Variable

`Get-Variable` provides access to any variable that has been created in the current session as well as the default (automatic) variables created by PowerShell. For further information on automatic variables, see `about_Automatic_Variables` (`Get-Help about_Automatic_Variables`).

When using the `*-Variable` commands, the `$` preceding the variable name is not considered part of the name.

Default or automatic variables often have descriptions; these may be seen by using `Get-Variable` and selecting the description:

```
Get-Variable | Select-Object Name, Description
```

New-Variable

`New-Variable` can be used to create a new variable:

```
New-Variable -Name today -Value (Get-Date)
```

This command is the equivalent of using the following:

```
$today = Get-Date
```

`New-Variable` gives more control over the created variable. For example, you may wish to create a constant, a variable which cannot be changed after creation:

```
New-Variable -Name startTime -Value (Get-Date) -Option Constant
```

Any attempt to modify the variable after creation results in an error message; this includes changing the variable value, its properties, and attempts to remove the variable, as shown here:

```
PS> $startTime = Get-Date
Cannot overwrite variable startTime because it is read-only or constant.
At line:1 char:1
+ $startTime = Get-Date
+ ~~~~~~~~~~~~~~~~~~~~~
    + CategoryInfo : WriteError: (startTime:String) [],
SessionStateUnauthorizedAccessException
    + FullyQualifiedErrorId : VariableNotWritable
```

A variable cannot be changed into a constant after creation.

Remove-Variable

As the name suggests, `Remove-Variable` destroys a variable and any data it may hold.

`Remove-Variable` is used as follows:

```
$psProcesses = Get-Process powershell
Remove-Variable psProcesses
```

If more than one variable refers to an object, the object will not be removed. For example, the following command shows the name of the first process running (`conhost.exe` in this case):

```
PS> $object1 = $object2 = Get-Process | Select-Object -First 1
Remove-Variable object1
Write-Host $object2.Name

conhost
```

Set-Variable

`Set-Variable` allows you to change the value and certain aspects of the created variable. For example, this sets the value of an existing variable:

```
$objectCount = 23
Set-Variable objectCount -Value 42
```

It is not common to see `Set-Variable` being used in this manner; it is simpler to directly assign the new value as was done when the variable was created. As with `New-Variable`, much of `Set-Variable`'s utility comes from the additional parameters it offers, as shown in the following examples.

Setting a description for a variable:

```
Set-Variable objectCount -Description 'The number of objects in the queue'
```

Making a variable `private`:

```
Set-Variable objectCount -Option Private
```

Private scope:
`Private` scope is accessible using `$private:objectCount`. `Set-Variable` may be used but is not required.

Variable scope

Variables may be declared in a number of different scopes. The scopes are:

- `Local`
- `Global`
- `Private`
- `Script`
- A numeric scope relative to the current scope

More about scopes:
The help document, `About_Scopes` (`Get-Help about_Scopes`), has more examples and detail.

By default, variables are placed in `Local` scope. Access to variables is hierarchical: a child (scopes created beneath a parent) can access variables created by the parent (or ancestors).

Local and Global scope

When creating a variable in the console (outside of functions or script blocks), the `Local` scope is `Global`. The `Global` scope can be accessed from inside a function (child) because it is a parent scope:

```
Remove-Variable thisValue -ErrorAction SilentlyContinue
$Local:thisValue = "Some value"
"From Local: $local:thisValue"          # Accessible
"From Global: $global:thisValue"        # Accessible

function Test-ThisScope {
    "From Local: $local:thisValue"      # Does not exist
    "From Global: $global:thisValue"    # Accessible
}

Test-ThisScope
```

When scopes are explicitly named as this, the source of a variable value can be reasonably clear. If the `scope` prefix is removed, PowerShell attempts to resolve the variable by searching the parent scopes:

```
Remove-Variable thisValue -ErrorAction SilentlyContinue
# This is still "local" scope
$thisValue = "Some value"

function Test-ThisScope {
    "From Local: $local:thisValue"        # Does not exist
    "From Global: $global:thisValue"      # Accessible
    "Without scope: $thisValue"           # Accessible
}

Test-ThisScope
```

The variable `thisValue` was created in the `Global` scope. As the function does not have a similarly named variable in its `Local` scope, it walks up the scope hierarchy and picks out the variable from the parent scope.

Private scope

The `Private` scope may be accessed using the `private` prefix, as follows:

```
$private:thisValue = "Some value"
```

Moving a variable into the `Private` scope will hide the variable from child scopes:

```
Remove-Variable thisValue -ErrorAction SilentlyContinue
# This is still "local" scope
$private:thisValue = "Some value"
"From global: $global:thisValue"              # Accessible

function Test-ThisScope {
    "Without scope: $thisValue"               # Not accessible
     "From private: $private:thisValue"        # Not accessible
    "From global: $global:thisValue"          # Not accessible
}

Test-ThisScope
```

If the stack depth is increased, the variable search can be made to skip a `private` variable within an intermediate function and reference the variable from an ancestor, as shown here:

```
PS> function bottom {
    $thisValue = "Bottom"
```

```
    Write-Host "Bottom: $thisValue"
    middle
}
function middle {
    # Hide thisValue from children
    $private:thisValue = "Middle" # Middle only
    Write-Host "Middle: $thisValue"
    top
}
function top {
    Write-Host "Top: $thisValue" # Original value
}
bottom

Bottom: Bottom
Middle: Middle
Top: Bottom
```

Script scope

The `Script` scope is shared across all children in a script or script module. The `Script` scope is a useful place to store variables which must be shared without exposing the variable to the `Global` scope (and therefore to anyone with access to the session).

For example, the following short script stores a version number in a script-level variable. The functions `Get-Version` and `Set-Version` both interact with the same variable:

```
# Script file: example.ps1
[Version]$Script:Version = "0.1"

function Get-Version {
    Write-Host "Version: $Version"
}

function Set-Version {
    param(
        [Version]$version
    )

    $Script:Version = $version
}

Set-Version 0.2
Write-Host (Get-Version)
```

The function `Set-Version` implements a `Local` variable in the `param` block with the same name as the `Script` scope variable. To access the `Script` scope variable `version`, the name must be prefixed with the scope.

Scope confusion:
If variables within a named scope are used, I recommend referencing the scope whenever the variable is used to make it clear where the values originate from.
In the preceding example, that means using `$Script:Version` in the `Get-Version` command.

Type and type conversion

Type conversion in PowerShell is used to switch between different types of a value. Types are written between square brackets, in which the type name must be a .NET type, or a class, or an enumeration, such as a string, an integer (`Int32`), a date (`DateTime`), and so on.

For example, a date may be changed to a string:

```
PS> [String](Get-Date)
10/27/2016 13:14:32
```

Or a string may be changed into a date:

```
PS> [DateTime]"01/01/2016"

01 January 2016 00:00:00
```

In a similar manner, variables may be given a fixed type. To assign a type to a variable, the following notation is used:

```
[String]$thisString = "some value"
[Int]$thisNumber = 2
[DateTime]$date = '01/01/2016'
```

This adds an argument type converter attribute to the variable. The presence of this converter is visible using `Get-Variable`, although the resultant type is not:

```
PS> [String]$thisString = "some value"
(Get-Variable thisString).Attributes

TransformNullOptionalParameters TypeId
------------------------------- ------
                           True
System.Management.Automation.ArgumentTypeConverterAttribute
```

Subsequent assignments made to the variable will be converted into a string. This remains so for the lifetime of the variable: until the session is closed, the variable falls out of scope, or the variable is removed with `Remove-Variable`.

Setting the variable value to `$null` does not remove the type conversion attribute. This can be seen here:

```
PS> [String]$thisString = 'A string value'
$thisString = $null
$thisString = Get-Process powershell
$thisString.GetType()


IsPublic IsSerial Name                     BaseType
-------- -------- ----                     --------
True     True     String                   System.Object
```

PowerShell's type conversion is exceptionally powerful. When converting a value, PowerShell uses the following conversions:

- Direct assignment
- Language-based conversion
- Parse conversion
- Static create conversion
- Constructor conversion
- Cast conversion
- IConvertible conversion
- IDictionary conversion
- PSObject property conversion
- `TypeConverter` conversion

More about type conversion:
The conversion process is extensive but there is documentation available.
The preceding list can be found on an MSDN blog:
`https://blogs.msdn.microsoft.com/powershell/2013/06/11/understanding-powershells-type-conversion-magic/`
Experimentation with the process is a vital part of learning.

Objects assigned to variables

So far, we have explored one-off assignments of simple value types, and while these values are considered objects, they are still (reasonably) simple objects. Once created, variables holding simple values such as integers and strings can diverge without affecting one another.

That is, the numeric value assigned to each variable is independent after creation:

```
$i = $j = 5
```

Each of the following commands increases the value held in the variable `i` by creating a new integer object (based on the original object):

```
$i = $j = 5
$i++
$i += 1
$i = $i + 1
```

If each statement is executed in turn, the variable `i` will be `8` and the variable `j` will be `5`.

When changing the value of a property on a more complex object, the change will be reflected in any variable referencing that object. Consider this example where we create a custom object and assign it to two variables:

```
$object1 = $object2 = [PSCustomObject]@{
    Name = 'First object'
 }
```

A change to a property on an object will be reflected in both variables. The action of changing a property value does not create a new copy of the object. The two variables will continue to reference the same object:

```
PS> $object1.Name = 'New name'
Write-Host $object2.Name

New name
```

The same applies when using nested objects: objects that use other objects as properties:

```
PS> $complexObject = [PSCustomObject]@{
    OuterNumber = 1
    InnerObject = [PSCustomObject]@{
        InnerNumber = 2
    }
}

$innerObject = $complexObject.InnerObject
$innerObject.InnerNumber = 5
Write-Host $complexObject.InnerObject.InnerNumber

5
```

Arrays

An array contains a set of objects of the same type. Each entry in the array is called an element and each element has an index (position). Indexing in an array starts from `0`.

Arrays are an important part of PowerShell. When the return from a command is assigned to a variable, an array will be the result if the command returns more than one object. For example, the following command will yield an array of objects:

```
$processes = Get-Process
```

Array type:
In PowerShell, arrays are, by default, given the type `System.Object[]` (an array of objects `where []` is used to signify that it is an array).

Why System.Object?
All object instances are derived from a .NET, type or class, and in .NET every object instance is derived from `System.Object` (including strings and integers). Therefore, an array of `System.Object` in PowerShell can hold just about anything.

Arrays in PowerShell (and .NET) are immutable, and the size is declared on creation and it cannot be changed. A new array must be created if an element is to be added or removed. The array operations described next are considered less efficient for large arrays because of the re-creation overhead involved in changing the array size.

We will explore creating arrays, assigning a type to the array, selecting elements, as well as adding and removing elements. We will also take a brief look at how arrays may be used to fill multiple variables, and finish off with a look at multi-dimensional arrays and jagged arrays.

Creating an array

A number of ways exist to create arrays. An empty array (containing no elements) can be created the same as the following:

```
$myArray = @()
```

An empty array of a specific size may be created using `New-Object`. Using `[]` after the name of the type denotes that it is an array, and the number following sets the array size:

```
$myArray = New-Object Object[] 10         # 10 objects
$byteArray = New-Object Byte[] 100        # 100 bytes
$ipAddresses = New-Object IPAddress[] 5   # 5 IP addresses
```

An array with a few strings in it can be created the same as this:

```
$myGreetings = "Hello world", "Hello sun", "Hello moon"
```

Or the same as this:

```
$myGreetings = @("Hello world", "Hello sun", "Hello moon")
```

An array may be spread over multiple lines in either the console or a script that may make it easier to read in a script:

```
$myGreetings = "Hello world",
               "Hello sun",
               "Hello moon"
```

You can mix values that are considered to be objects without losing anything:

```
$myThings = "Hello world", 2, 34.23, (Get-Date)
```

Arrays with a type

An array may be given a type in similar manner to a variable holding a single value. The difference is that the type name is followed by `[]` as was the case when creating an empty array of a specific size. For example, each of these is an array type, which may appear before a variable name:

```
[String[]]        # An array of strings
[UInt64[]]        # An array of unsigned 64-bit integers
[Xml[]]           # An array of XML documents
```

If a type is set for the array, more care must be taken about assigning values. If a type is declared, PowerShell will attempt to convert any value assigned to an array element to that type.

In this example, `$null` will become `0`, and `3.45` (a Double) will become `3` (normal rounding rules apply when converting integers):

```
[Int32[]]$myNumbers = 1, 2, $null, 3.45
```

The following example shows an error being thrown, as a string cannot be converted to an integer:

```
PS> [Int32[]]$myNumbers = 1, 2, $null, "A string"
Cannot convert value "A string" to type "System.Int32". Error: "Input
string was not in a correct format."
At line:1 char:1
+ [Int32[]]$myNumbers = 1, 2, $null, "A string"
+ ~~~~~~~~~~~~~~~~~~~~~~~~~~~~~~~~~~~~~~~~~~~~~
    + CategoryInfo : MetadataError: (:) [],
ArgumentTransformationMetadataException
    + FullyQualifiedErrorId : RuntimeException
```

Adding elements to an array

A single item can be added to the end of an array using the assignment by addition operator:

```
$myArray = @()
$myArray += "New value"
```

The preceding command is equivalent to the following:

```
$myArray = $myArray + "New value"
```

In the background, PowerShell creates a new array with one extra element, copies the existing array in, and then adds the value for the new element before disposing of the original array. The larger the array, the less efficient this operation becomes.

The same technique can be used to join one array to another:

```
$firstArray = 1, 2, 3
$secondArray = 4, 5, 6
$mergedArray = $firstArray + $secondArray
```

Selecting elements from an array

Individual elements from an array may be selected using an index. The index counts from `0` to the end of the array. The first and second elements are available using index `0` and `1`:

```
$myArray = 1, 2, 3, 4, 5, 6, 7, 8, 9, 10
$myArray[0]
$myArray[1]
```

In a similar manner, array elements can be accessed counting backward, from the end. The last element is available using the index `-1`, and the penultimate element with `-2`, for example:

```
$myArray[-1]
$myArray[-2]
```

Ranges of elements may be selected either going forward (starting from `0`) or going backward (starting with `-1`):

```
$myArray[2..4]
$myArray[-1..-5]
```

More than one range can be selected in a single statement:

```
$myArray[0..2 + 6..8 + -1]
```

This requires some care. The first part of the index set must be an array for the addition operation to succeed, The expression in square brackets is evaluated first, converted into a single array (of indexes) before any elements are selected from the array:

```
PS> $myArray[0 + 6..8 + -1]
Method invocation failed because [System.Object[]] does not contain a
method named 'op_Addition'.
At line:1 char:1
+ $myArray[0 + 6..8 + -1]
+ ~~~~~~~~~~~~~~~~~~~~~~~
```

```
    + CategoryInfo : InvalidOperation: (op_Addition:String) [],
RuntimeException
    + FullyQualifiedErrorId : MethodNotFound
```

Exactly the same error would be shown when running the expression within square brackets alone:

```
0..2 + 6..8 + -1
```

The following modified command shows two different ways to achieve the intended result:

```
$myArray[@(0) + 6..8 + -1]
$myArray[0..0 + 6..8 + 1]
```

Changing element values in an array

Elements within an array may be changed by assigning a new value to a specific index, for example:

```
$myArray = 1, 2, 9, 4, 5
$myArray[2] = 3
```

Values in an array may be changed within a loop:

```
$myArray = 1, 2, 3, 4, 5
for ($i = 0; $i -lt $myArray.Count; $i++) {
     $myArray[$i] = 9
}
```

Removing elements from an array

Removing elements from an array is difficult because arrays are immutable. To remove an element, a new array must be created.

It is possible to appear to remove an element by setting it to null, for example:

```
$myArray = 1, 2, 3, 4, 5
$myArray[1] = $null
$myArray
```

However, observe that the count does not decrease when a value is set to `null`:

```
PS> $myArray.Count
5
```

Loops (or pipelines) consuming the array will not skip the element with the null value (extra code is needed to guard against the `null` value):

```
$myArray | ForEach-Object { Write-Host $_ }
```

`Where-Object` may be used to remove the null value, creating a new array:

```
$myArray | Where-Object { $_ } | ForEach-Object { Write-Host $_ }
```

Depending on usage, a number of ways are available to address removal. Removal by index and removal by value are discussed next.

Removing elements by index

Removing elements based on an index requires the creation of a new array and omission of the value in the element in that index. In each of the following cases, an array with `100` elements will be used as an example; the element at index `49` (with the value of `50`) will be removed:

```
$oldArray = 1..100
```

This method uses indexes to access and add everything we want to keep:

```
$newArray = $oldArray[0..48] + $oldArray[50..99]
```

Using the .NET `Array.Copy` static method (see `Chapter 8`, *Working with .NET*):

```
$newArray = New-Object Object[] ($oldArray.Count - 1)
# Before the index
[Array]::Copy($oldArray,     # Source
              $newArray,     # Destination
              49)            # Number of elements to copy
# After the index
[Array]::Copy($oldArray,     # Source
              50,            # Copy from index of Source
              $newArray,     # Destination
              49,            # Copy to index of Destination
              50)            # Number of elements to copy
```

Using a `for` loop:

```
$newArray = for ($i = 0; $i -lt $oldArray.Count; $i++) {
    if ($i -ne 49) {
        $oldArray[$i]
    }
}
```

Removing elements by value

Removing an element with a specific value from an array can be achieved in a number of different ways.

Again, starting with an array of 100 elements:

```
$oldArray = 1..100
```

Where-Object might be used to identify and omit the element with the value 50. If 50 were to occur more than once, all instances would be omitted:

```
$newArray = $oldArray | Where-Object { $_ -ne 50 }
```

The index of the element might be identified and removed using the methods explored in removing elements by the index:

```
$index = $oldArray.IndexOf(50)
```

If the value of the variable index is -1, the value is not present in the array (0 would indicate it is the first element):

```
$index = $oldArray.IndexOf(50)
if ($index -gt -1) {
    $newArray = $oldArray[0..($index - 1)] +
        $oldArray[($index + 1)..99]
}
```

Unlike the Where-Object version, which inspects all elements, IndexOf gets the first occurrence of a value only. A complementary method, LastIndexOf, allows the last occurrence of a value to be removed.

Clearing an array

Finally, an array may be completely emptied by calling the Clear method:

```
$newArray = 1, 2, 3, 4, 5
$newArray.Clear()
```

Filling variables from arrays

It is possible to fill two (or more) variables from an array:

```
$i, $j = 1, 2
```

This is often encountered when splitting a string:

```
$firstName, $lastName = "First Last" -split " "
$firstName, $lastName = "First Last".Split(" ")
```

If the array is longer than the number of variables, all remaining elements are assigned to the last variable. For example, the variable `k` will hold `3`, `4`, and `5`:

```
$i, $j, $k = 1, 2, 3, 4, 5
```

If there are too few elements, the remaining variables will not be assigned a value. In this example, `k` will be null:

```
$i, $j, $k = 1, 2
```

Multi-dimensional and jagged arrays

Given that an array contains objects, an array can therefore also contain other arrays.

For example, an array that contains other arrays (a multi-dimensional array) might be created as follows:

```
$arrayOfArrays = @(
    @(1, 2, 3),
    @(4, 5, 6),
    @(7, 8, 9)
)
```

Be careful to ensure the comma following each of the inner arrays (except the last) is in place. If that comma is missing, the entire structure will be flattened, merging the three inner arrays.

Elements in the array are accessed by indexing into each array in turn (starting with the outermost). The element with value `2` is accessible using this notation:

```
PS> $arrayOfArrays[0][1]
2
```

This states that we wish to retrieve the first element (which is an array) and the second element of that array.

The element with the value `6` is accessible using the following:

```
PS> $arrayOfArrays[1][2]
6
```

Jagged arrays are a specific form of multi-dimensional array. An example of a jagged array follows:

```
$arrayOfArrays = @(
    @(1,  2),
    @(4,  5,  6,  7,  8,  9),
    @(10, 11, 12)
)
```

Same as the first example, it is an array containing arrays. Instead of containing inner arrays, which all share the same size (dimension), the inner arrays have no consistent size (hence they are jagged).

In this example, the element with value `9` is accessed using the following:

```
PS> $arrayOfArrays[1][5]
9
```

Hashtables

A hashtable is an associative array or an indexed array. Individual elements in the array are created with a unique key. Keys cannot be duplicated within the hashtable.

Hashtables are important in PowerShell. They are used to create custom objects, to pass parameters into commands, to create custom properties using `Select-Object`, and as the type for values assigned to parameter values of many different commands, and so on.

For finding commands that use `Hashtable` as a parameter, we use the following:
`Get-Command -ParameterType Hashtable`

This topic explores creating hashtables, selecting elements, enumerating all values in a hashtable, as well as adding and removing elements.

Creating a hashtable

An empty hashtable is created the same as the following:

```
$hashtable = @{}
```

A hashtable with a few objects looks the same as the following:

```
$hashtable = @{Key1 = "Value1"; Key2 = "Value2"}
```

Elements in a hashtable may be spread across multiple lines:

```
$hashtable = @{
    Key1 = "Value1"
    Key2 = "Value2"
}
```

Adding and changing elements to a hashtable

Elements may be explicitly added to a hashtable using the Add method:

```
$hashtable = @{}
$hashtable.Add("Key1", "Value1")
```

If the value already exists, using Add will generate an error (as shown here):

```
$hashtable.Add("Existing", "Value1")

Exception calling "Add" with "2" argument(s): "Item has already been added.
Key in dictionary: 'Existing' Key being added: 'Existing'"
At line:2 char:1
+ $hashtable.Add("Existing", "Value1")
+ ~~~~~~~~~~~~~~~~~~~~~~~~~~~~~~~~~~~~
    + CategoryInfo : NotSpecified: (:) [], MethodInvocationException
    + FullyQualifiedErrorId : ArgumentException
```

The Contains method will return true or false depending on whether or not a key is present in the hashtable. This may be used to test for a key before adding:

```
$hashtable = @{}
if (-not $hashtable.Contains("Key1")) {
    $hashtable.Add("Key1", "Value1")
}
```

Alternatively, two different ways of adding or changing elements are available:

```
$hashtable = @{ Existing = "Old" }
$hashtable["New"] = "New"                 # Add this
$hashtable["Existing"] = "Updated"        # Update this
```

Or:

```
$hashtable = @{ Existing = "Old" }
$hashtable.New = "New"                    # Add this
$hashtable.Existing = "Updated"           # Update this
```

If a value should only be changed if it exists, the `Contains` method may be used:

```
$hashtable = @{ Existing = "Old" }
 if ($hashtable.Contains("Existing")) {
     $hashtable.Existing = "New"
}
```

This may also be used to ensure a value is only added if it does not exist:

```
$hashtable = @{ Existing = "Old" }
 if (-not $hashtable.Contains("New")) {
     $hashtable.New = "New"
}
```

Keys cannot be added nor can values be changed while looping through the keys in a `hashtable` using the `Keys` property. Doing so changes the underlying structure of the `hashtable`, invalidating the iterator:

```
PS> $hashtable = @{
    Key1 = 'Value1'
    Key2 = 'Value2'
}
foreach ($key in $hashtable.Keys) {
    $hashtable[$key] = "NewValue"
}

Collection was modified; enumeration operation may not execute.
At line:5 char:10
+ foreach ($key in $hashtable.Keys) {
+ ~~~~
    + CategoryInfo : OperationStopped: (:) [], InvalidOperationException
    + FullyQualifiedErrorId : System.InvalidOperationException
```

It is possible to work around this problem by first creating an array of the keys:

```
$hashtable = @{
    Key1 = 'Value1'
    Key2 = 'Value2'
}
[Object[]]$keys = $hashtable.Keys
foreach ($key in $keys) {
    $hashtable[$key] = "NewValue"
}
```

Notice that the highlighted `keys` variable is declared as an array of objects. Earlier in this chapter, we discussed assigning objects to variables and how an assignment does not always create a new instance of an object. Using the `Object[]` type conversion forces the creation of a new object (a new array of objects) based on the values held in the `KeyCollection`. Without this step, the preceding error message would repeat.

Another approach uses the `ForEach-Object` to create a new array of the keys:

```
$hashtable = @{
    Key1 = 'Value1'
    Key2 = 'Value2'
}
$keys = $hashtable.Keys | ForEach-Object { $_ }
foreach ($key in $keys) {
    $hashtable[$key] = "NewValue"
}
```

Selecting elements from a hashtable

Individual elements may be selected by key. A number of different formats are supported for selecting elements:

```
$hashtable["Key1"]
```

Using dot notation:

```
$hashtable.Key1
```

The key is not case sensitive, but it is type sensitive and will not automatically convert. For instance, consider this hashtable:

```
$hashtable = @{1 = 'one'}
```

The value one can be selected if an integer is used as the key, but not if a string is used. That is, this works:

```
$hashtable.1
$hashtable[1]
```

While this does not:

```
$hashtable."1"
$hashtable["1"]
```

Enumerating a hashtable

A hashtable can return the information it holds in several ways. Start with hashtable:

```
$hashtable = @{
    Key1 = 'Value1'
    Key2 = 'Value2'
}
```

Keys can be returned using the Keys property of the hashtable, which returns a KeyCollection:

```
$hashtable.Keys
```

Values can be returned using the Values property, which returns a ValueCollection. The key is discarded when using the Values property:

```
$hashtable.Values
```

A simple loop can be used to retain the association between the key and value:

```
foreach ($key in $hashtable.Keys) {
    Write-Host "Key: $key    Value: $($hashtable[$key])"
}
```

Removing elements from a hashtable

Unlike arrays, removing an element from a hashtable is straightforward: an element is removed using the Remove method:

```
$hashtable = @{ Existing = "Existing" }
$hashtable.Remove("Existing")
```

If the requested key does not exist, the command does nothing (and does not throw an error).

The `Remove` method cannot be used to modify the `hashtable` while looping through the keys in a `hashtable` using the `Keys` property:

```
PS> $hashtable = @{
    Key1 = 'Value1'
    Key2 = 'Value2'
}
foreach ($key in $hashtable.Keys) {
    $hashtable.Remove($key)
}

Collection was modified; enumeration operation may not execute.
At line:5 char:10
+ foreach ($key in $hashtable.Keys) {
+ ~~~~
    + CategoryInfo : OperationStopped: (:) [], InvalidOperationException
    + FullyQualifiedErrorId : System.InvalidOperationException
```

The same method discussed in the, *Adding and changing elements in a hashtable,* may be used.

Finally, a `hashtable` may be completely emptied by calling the `Clear` method:

```
$hashtable = @{one = 1; two = 2; three = 3}
$hashtable.Clear()
```

Lists, dictionaries, queues, and stacks

Arrays and hashtables are integral to PowerShell and being able to manipulate these is critical. If these simpler structures fail to provide an efficient means to work with a set of data, there are advanced alternatives.

The following .NET collections will be discussed:

- `System.Collections.Generic.List`
- `System.Collections.Generic.Dictionary`
- `System.Collections.Generic.Queue`
- `System.Collections.Generic.Stack`

Each of these collections has detailed documentation (for .NET) on MSDN:

https://msdn.microsoft.com/en-us/library/system.collections.generic(v=vs.110).aspx

Lists

A lists is the same as an array but with a larger set of features, such as the ability to add elements without copying two arrays into a new one. The generic list, using the .NET class, `System.Collections.Generic.List`, is shown next.

The `ArrayList` is often used in examples requiring advanced array manipulation in PowerShell. However, `ArrayList` is older (.NET 2.0), less efficient (it can use more memory), and cannot be strongly typed, as will be shown when creating a generic list.

Creating a list

A generic list must have a type declared. A generic list, in this case a list of strings, is created as follows:

```
$list = New-Object System.Collections.Generic.List[String]
```

An `ArrayList` is created in a similar manner. The `ArrayList` cannot have type declared:

```
$arrayList = New-object System.Collections.ArrayList
```

Once created, the `ArrayList` may be used in much the same way as a generic list.

Adding elements to the list

`Add` can be used to add new elements to the end of the list:

```
$list.Add("David")
```

The `Insert` and `InsertRange` methods are available to add items elsewhere in the list. For example, an element may be added at the beginning:

```
$list.Insert(0, "Sarah")
$list.Insert(2, "Jane")
```

Selecting elements from the list

As with the array, elements may be selected by index:

```
$list = New-Object System.Collections.Generic.List[String]
$list.AddRange([String[]]("Tom", "Richard", "Harry"))
$list[1]    # Returns Richard
```

The generic list offers a variety of methods that may be used to find elements when the index is not known, such as the following:

```
$index = $list.FindIndex( { $args[0] -eq 'Richard' } )
```

Predicates:
In the preceding example, the `ScriptBlock` is a predicate. Arguments are passed into the `ScriptBlock` and all list items matching the query are returned.
The predicate is similar in syntax to `Where-Object`, except `$args[0]` is used to refer to the item in the list instead of the pipeline variable, `$_`.
A param block may be declared for the `ScriptBlock` to assign a more meaningful name to the argument (`$args[0]`) if desirable.

Alternatively, the `IndexOf` and `LastIndex` methods may be used. Both of these methods support additional arguments (as opposed to `Array.IndexOf`, which only supports a restrictive search for a value) to constrain the search. For example, the search may start at a specific index:

```
$list.IndexOf('Harry', 2)    # Start at index 2
$list.IndexOf('Richard', 1, 2)    # Start at index 1, and 2 elements
```

Finally, a generic list offers a `BinarySearch` (half-interval) search method. This method may dramatically cut the time to search very large, sorted, datasets when compared to a linear search.

In a binary search, the element in the middle of the list is selected, and compared to the value. If the value is larger, the first half of the list is discarded, and the element in the middle of the new, smaller, set is selected for comparison. This process repeats (always cutting the list in half) until the value is found (or it runs out of elements to test):

```
$list = New-Object System.Collections.Generic.List[Int]
$list.AddRange([Int[]](1..100000000))
# Linear and Binary are roughly comparable
Measure-Command { $list.IndexOf(24) }    # A linear search
Measure-Command { $list.BinarySearch(24) }    # A binary search
# Binary is more effective
Measure-Command { $list.IndexOf(99767859) }    # A linear search
Measure-Command { $list.BinarySearch(99767859) }    # A binary search
```

The time taken to execute a binary search remains fairly constant, regardless of the element position. The time taken to execute a linear search increases as every element must be read (in sequence).

Removing elements from the list

Elements in a list may be removed based on the index or value:

```
$list = New-Object System.Collections.Generic.List[String]
$list.AddRange([String[]]("Tom", "Richard", "Harry", "David"))
$list.RemoveAt(1)           # By Richard by index
$list.Remove("Richard")     # By Richard by value
```

All instances of a particular value may be removed using the `RemoveAll` method:

```
$list.RemoveAll( { $args[0] -eq "David" } )
```

Changing element values in a list

Elements within a list may be changed by assigning a new value to a specific index, for example:

```
$list = New-Object System.Collections.Generic.List[Int]
 $list.AddRange([Int[]](1, 2, 2, 4))
$list[2] = 3
```

Dictionaries

A dictionary, using the .NET class `System.Collections.Generic.Dictionary`, is most similar to a hashtable. The same as the hashtable, it is a form of associative array.

Unlike the hashtable, a dictionary implements a type for both the key and the value, which may make it easier to use.

Creating a dictionary

A dictionary must declare a type for the key and value when it is created. A dictionary which uses a `String` for the key and `IPAddress` for the value may be created using either of the following examples:

```
$dictionary = New-Object
System.Collections.Generic.Dictionary"[String,IPAddress]"
$dictionary = New-Object
"System.Collections.Generic.Dictionary[String,IPAddress]"
```

Adding and changing elements in a dictionary

As with the hashtable, the `Add` method may be used to add a new value to a dictionary:

```
$dictionary.Add("Computer1", "192.168.10.222")
```

If the key already exists, using `Add` will generate an error, as was the case with the hashtable.

In a dictionary, the `Contains` method behaves differently from the same method in the hashtable. When checking for the existence of a key, the `ContainsKey` method should be used:

```
if (-not $dictionary.ContainsKey("Computer2")) {
    $dictionary.Add("Computer2", "192.168.10.13")
}
```

The dictionary supports the addition of elements using dot-notation:

```
$dictionary.Computer3 = "192.168.10.134"
```

The dictionary leverages PowerShell's type conversion for both the key and the value. For example, if a numeric key is used, it will be converted into a string. If an IP address is expressed as a string, it will be converted into an `IPAddress` object.

For example, consider the addition of the following element:

```
$dictionary.Add(1, 20)
```

In this case, the key `1` is converted into a string, and the value `20` is converted to an `IPAddress`. Inspecting the element afterward shows the following:

```
PS> $dictionary."1"


Address            : 20
AddressFamily      : InterNetwork
ScopeId            :
IsIPv6Multicast    : False
IsIPv6LinkLocal    : False
IsIPv6SiteLocal    : False
IsIPv6Teredo       : False
IsIPv4MappedToIPv6 : False
IPAddressToString  : 20.0.0.0
```

Selecting elements from a dictionary

Individual elements may be selected by a key. As with the hashtable, two different notations are supported:

```
$dictionary["Computer1"]     # Key reference
$dictionary.Computer1        # Dot-notation
```

We have seen that when adding elements, types are converted. Looking back to selecting elements from a hashtable, we know the value for the key was sensitive to type. As the dictionary has a type declared for the key, it can leverage PowerShell's type conversion.

Consider a dictionary created using a number as a string for the key:

```
$dictionary = New-Object
System.Collections.Generic.Dictionary"[String,IPAddress]"
$dictionary.Add("1", "192.168.10.222")
$dictionary.Add("2", "192.168.10.13")
```

Each of the following examples works to access the value:

```
$dictionary."1"
$dictionary[1]
$dictionary["1"]
```

Enumerating a dictionary

A dictionary can return the information it holds in several ways. Start with this dictionary:

```
$dictionary = New-Object
System.Collections.Generic.Dictionary"[String,IPAddress]"
$dictionary.Add("Computer1", "192.168.10.222")
$dictionary.Add("Computer2", "192.168.10.13")
```

Keys can be returned using the `Keys` property of the dictionary, which returns a `KeyCollection`:

```
$dictionary.Keys
```

Values can be returned using the `Values` property, which returns a `ValueCollection`. The key is discarded when using the `Values` property:

```
$dictionary.Values
```

A simple loop can be used to retain the association between `key` and `value`:

```
foreach ($key in $dictionary.Keys) {
    Write-Host "Key: $key    Value: $($dictionary[$key])"
}
```

Removing elements from a dictionary

An element may be removed from a dictionary using the `Remove` method:

```
$dictionary.Remove("Computer1")
```

The `Remove` method cannot be used to modify the dictionary while looping through the keys in a dictionary using the `Keys` property.

Queues

A queue is a first-in, first-out array. Elements are added to the end of the queue and taken from the beginning.

The queue uses the .NET class `System.Collections.Generic.Queue` and must have a type set.

Creating a queue

A queue of strings may be created as follows:

```
$queue = New-Object System.Collections.Generic.Queue[String]
```

Enumerating the queue

PowerShell will display the content of a queue in the same way as it would the content of an array. It is not possible to access elements of the queue by the index. The `ToArray` method may be used to convert the queue into an array if required:

```
$queue.ToArray()
```

The preceding command returns an array of the same type as the queue. That is, if the queue is configured to hold strings, the array will be an array of strings.

The queue has a `Peek` method that allows retrieval of the next element in the queue without it being removed:

```
$queue.Peek()
```

The `Peek` method will throw an error if the queue is empty (see the, *Removing elements from the queue* section).

Adding elements to the queue

Elements are added to the end of the queue using the `Enqueue` method:

```
$queue.Enqueue("Tom")
$queue.Enqueue("Richard")
$queue.Enqueue("Harry")
```

Removing elements from the queue

Elements are removed from the end using the `Dequeue` method:

```
$queue.Dequeue()    # This returns Tom.
```

If the queue is empty and the Dequeue method is called, an error will be thrown, as shown here:

```
PS> $queue.Dequeue()
Exception calling "Dequeue" with "0" argument(s): "Queue empty."
At line:1 char:1
+ $queue.Dequeue()
+ ~~~~~~~~~~~~~~~~
    + CategoryInfo : NotSpecified: (:) [], MethodInvocationException
    + FullyQualifiedErrorId : InvalidOperationException
```

To avoid this, the Count property of the queue may be inspected, for example:

```
# Set-up the queue
$queue = New-Object System.Collections.Generic.Queue[String]
"Tom", "Richard", "Harry" | ForEach-Object {
    $queue.Enqueue($_)
}
# Dequeue until the queue is empty
while ($queue.Count -gt 0) {
    Write-Host $queue.Dequeue()
}
```

Stacks

A stack is a last-in, last-out array. Elements are added and removed from the top of the stack.

The stack uses the .NET class System.Collections.Generic.Stack and must have a type set.

Creating a stack

A stack containing strings may be created as follows:

```
$stack = New-Object System.Collections.Generic.Stack[String]
```

Enumerating the stack

PowerShell will display the content of a stack in the same way as it would the content of an array. It is not possible to index into a stack. The `ToArray()` method may be used to convert the stack into an array if required:

```
$stack.ToArray()
```

The preceding command returns an array of the same type as the stack. That is, if a stack is configured to hold strings, the array will be an array of strings.

The stack has a `Peek` method that allows retrieval of the top element from the stack without it being removed:

```
$stack.Peek()
```

The `Peek` method will throw an error if the stack is empty (see the *Removing elements from the stack* section).

Adding elements to the stack

Elements may be added to the stack using the `Push` method:

```
$stack.Push("Up the road")
$stack.Push("Over the gate")
$stack.Push("Under the bridge")
```

Removing elements from the stack

Elements may be removed from the stack using the `Pop` method:

```
$stack.Pop()     # This returns Under the bridge
```

If the stack is empty and the `Pop` method is called, an error will be thrown, as shown here:

```
PS> $stack.Pop()
Exception calling "Pop" with "0" argument(s): "Stack empty."
At line:1 char:1
+ $stack.Pop()
+ ~~~~~~~~~~~~
    + CategoryInfo : NotSpecified: (:) [], MethodInvocationException
    + FullyQualifiedErrorId : InvalidOperationException
```

To avoid this, the `Count` property of the stack may be inspected, for example:

```
# Set-up the stack
$stack = New-Object System.Collections.Generic.Stack[String]
"Up the road", "Over the gate", "Under the bridge" | ForEach-Object {
    $stack.Push($_)
}
# Pop from the stack until the stack is empty
while ($stack.Count -gt 0) {
    Write-Host $stack.Pop()
}
```

Summary

Variables can be created to hold on to information that is to be reused in a function or a script. A variable may be a simple name, or loaded from a file.

The `*-Variable` commands are available to interact with variables beyond changing the value, such as setting a description, making a variable in a specific scope, or making a variable private.

A `Variable` scope affects how variables may be accessed. Variables are created in the `Local` scope by default.

<p>Arrays are sets of objects of the same type. Arrays are immutable, and the size of an array cannot change after creation. Adding or removing elements from an array requires the creation of a new array.

Hashtables are associative arrays. An element in a hashtable is accessed using a unique key.

Lists, stacks, queues, and dictionaries are advanced collections that may be used when a particular behavior is required or if they offer a desirable performance benefit.

In the `Chapter 7`, *Branching and Looping*, we will explore branching and looping in PowerShell.

7
Branching and Looping

A branch in a script or command is created every time an `if/switch` statement or loop is added. The branch represents a different set of instructions. Branches can be conditional, such as one created by an `if` statement, or unconditional, such as a `for` loop.

As a script or command increases in complexity, the branches spread out the same as the limbs of a tree.

In this chapter, we are going to cover the following topics:

- Conditional statements
- Loops

Conditional statements

Statements or lines of code may be executed when certain conditions are met. PowerShell provides `if` and `select` statements for this purpose.

If, else, and elseif

An `if` statement is written as follows; the statements enclosed by the `if` statement will execute if the condition evaluates to `true`:

```
if (<condition>) {
    <statements>
}
```

The `else` statement is optional and will trigger if all previous conditions evaluate to `false`:

```
if (<first-condition>) {
    <first-statements>
} else {
    <second-statements>
}
```

The `elseif` statement allows conditions to be stacked:

```
if (<first-condition>) {
    <first-statements>
} elseif (<second-condition>) {
    <second-statements>
} elseif (<last-condition>) {
     <last-statements>
}
```

The `else` statement may be added after any number of `elseif` statements.

Execution of a block of conditions stops as soon as a single condition evaluates to `true`. For example, both the first and second condition would evaluate to `true` as shown following, but only the first will execute:

```
$value = 1
if ($value -eq 1) {
    Write-Host 'value is 1'
 } elseif ($value -lt 10) {
     Write-Host 'value is less than 10'
}
```

Implicit Boolean:
An implicit Boolean is a condition which can evaluate as `true` (is considered to be something) without using a comparison operator which would explicitly return `true` or `false`. For example, the number `1` will evaluate as `true`:

```
$value = 1
if ($value) {
Write-Host 'Implicit true'
}
```

In the previous example, the statement executes because casting the value `1` to Boolean results in `true`. If the variable were set to `0`, the condition would evaluate to `false`.
Each of the following will evaluate to `true` as they are considered to be something when used in this manner:

```
[Boolean]1
[Boolean]-1
[Boolean]2016
[Boolean]"Hello world"
```

Each of the following will evaluate to `false` as each is considered to be nothing:

```
[Boolean]0
[Boolean]""
[Boolean]$null
```

Assignment within if statements

An `if` statement can include an assignment step as follows:

```
if ($i = 1) {
    Write-Host "Implicit true. The variable i is $i"
}
```

This is most commonly used when testing for the existence of a value in a variable, for example:

```
if ($interface = Get-NetAdapter | Where-Object Status -eq 'Up') {
    Write-Host "$($interface.Name) is up"
 }
```

In the previous example, the statement to the right of the assignment operator (=) is executed, assigned to the variable `$interface`, then the value in the variable is treated as an implicit Boolean.

Switch

A switch statement uses the following generalized notation:

```
switch [-regex|-wildcard][-casesensitive] (<value>) {
    <condition> { <statements> }
    <condition> { <statements> }
}
```

The `casesensitive` parameter applies when testing conditions against a string value.

The switch command can also be used to work on the content of a file using the following notation:

```
switch [-regex|-wildcard][-casesensitive] -File <Name> {
    <condition> { <statements> }
    <condition> { <statements> }
}
```

The `File` parameter can be used to select from a text file (line by line).

The `switch` statement differs from conditions written using `if-elseif` in one important respect. The switch statement will not stop testing conditions unless the `break` keyword is used, for example:

```
$value = 1
switch ($value) {
    1 { Write-Host 'value is 1' }
    1 { Write-Host 'value is still 1' }
}
```

Using `break`, as shown following, will exit the `switch` statement after a match:

```
$value = 1
switch ($value) {
    1 { Write-Host 'value is 1'; break }
    1 { Write-Host 'value is still 1' }
}
```

The `default` keyword provides the same functionality as the `else` statement when using `if`, for example:

```
$value = 2
switch ($value) {
    1       { Write-Host 'value is 1' }
    default { Write-Host 'No conditions matched' }
}
```

A switch statement can test more than one value at once; however, break applies to the entire statement, not just a single value. For example, without break, both of the following `Write-Host` statements execute:

```
switch (1, 2) {
     1 { Write-Host 'Equals 1' }
    2 { Write-Host 'Equals 2' }
}
```

If the `break` keyword is included as shown following, only the first executes:

```
switch (1, 2) {
    1 { Write-Host 'Equals 1'; break }
    2 { Write-Host 'Equals 2' }
}
```

Wildcard and Regex

The `wildcard` and `regex` parameters are used when matching strings. The `wildcard` parameter allows use of the characters `?` (any single character) and `*` (any character, repeated `0` or more times) in a condition, for example:

```
switch -Wildcard ('cat') {
     'c*'  { Write-Host 'The word begins with c' }
    '???' { Write-Host 'The word is 3 characters long' }
    '*t'  { Write-Host 'The word ends with t' }
}
```

The `regex` parameter allows the use of regular expressions to perform comparisons (`Chapter 10`, *Regular Expressions*, will explain this syntax in greater detail), for example:

```
switch -Regex ('cat') {
     '^c'       { Write-Host 'The word begins with c' }
    '[a-z]{3}' { Write-Host 'The word is 3 characters long' }
    't$'       { Write-Host 'The word ends with t' }
}
```

Expressions

Switch allows expressions (a `ScriptBlock`) to be used in place of a simpler condition. The result of the expression should be an explicit `true` or `false`, or an implicit Boolean, for example:

```
switch (Get-Date) {
     { $_ -is [DateTime] } { Write-Host 'This is a DateTime type' }
    { $_.Year -ge 2017 }  { Write-Host 'It is 2017 or later' }
}
```

Loops

Loops may be used to iterate through collections, performing an operation against each element in the collection; or to repeat an operation (or series of operations) until a condition is met.

Foreach

The `foreach` loop executes against each element of a collection using the following notation:

```
foreach (<element> in <collection>) {
    <body-statements>
}
```

For example, the `foreach` loop may be used to iterate through each of the processes returned by `Get-Process`:

```
foreach ($process in Get-Process) {
    Write-Host $process.Name
}
```

If the collection is `$null` or empty, the body of the loop will not execute.

For

The `for` loop is typically used to step through a collection using the following notation:

```
for (<intial>; <exit condition>; <repeat>){
    <body-statements>
 }
```

`Initial` represents the state of a variable before the first iteration of the loop. This is normally used to initialize a counter for the loop.

The exit condition must be `true` as long as the loop is executing.

`Repeat` is executed after each iteration of the body and is often used to increment a counter.

The `for` loop is most often used to iterate through a collection, for example:

```
$processes = Get-Process
for ($i = 0; $i -lt $processes.Count; $i++) {
    Write-Host $processes[$i].Name
 }
```

The `for` loop provides a significant degree of control over the loop and is useful where the step needs to be something other than simple ascending order. For example, the `repeat` may be used to execute the body for every third element:

```
for ($i = 0; $i -lt $processes.Count; $i += 3) {
    Write-Host $processes[$i].Name
 }
```

The loop parameters may also be used to reverse the direction of the loop, for example:

```
for ($i = $processes.Count - 1; $i -ge 0; $i--) {
    Write-Host $processes[$i].Name
 }
```

Do until and do while

`do until` and `do while` each execute the body of the loop at least once as the condition test is at the end of the loop statement. Loops based on `do until` will exit when the condition evaluates to `true`; loops based on do while will exit when the condition evaluates to `false`.

Do loops are written using the following notation:

```
do {
    <body-statements>
} <until | while> (<condition>)
```

`do until` is suited to exit conditions which are expected to be positive. For example, a script might wait for a computer to respond to ping:

```
do {
    Write-Host "Waiting for boot"
    Start-Sleep -Seconds 5
} until (Test-Connection 'SomeComputer' -Quiet -Count 1)
```

The `do while` loop is more suitable for exit conditions which are negative. For example, a loop might wait for a remote computer to stop responding to ping:

```
do {
    Write-Host "Waiting for shutdown"
    Start-Sleep -Seconds 5
} while (Test-Connection 'SomeComputer' -Quiet -Count 1)
```

While

As the condition for a `while` loop comes first, the body of the loop will only execute if the condition evaluates to `true`:

```
while (<condition>) {
    <body-statements>
}
```

For example, a `while` loop may be used to wait for something to happen. For example, it might be used to wait for a path to exist:

```
while (-not (Test-Path $env:TEMP\test.txt -PathType Leaf)) {
    Start-Sleep -Seconds 10
}
```

Break and continue

Break can be used to end a loop early. The loop in the following example would continue to `20`; break is used to stop the loop at `10`:

```
for ($i = 0; $i -lt 20; $i += 2) {
     Write-Host $i
    if ($i -eq 10) {
         break    # Stop this loop
    }
}
```

Break acts on the loop it is nested inside. In the following example, the inner loop breaks early when the variable `i` is less than or equal to `2`:

```
PS> $i = 1 # Initial state for i
while ($i -le 3) {
Write-Host "i: $i"
$k = 1 # Reset k
while ($k -lt 5) {
Write-Host " k: $k"
$k++ # Increment k
if ($i -le 2 -and $k -ge 3) {
break
}
}
$i++ # Increment i
}
i: 1
k: 1
k: 2
i: 2
k: 1
k: 2
i: 3
k: 1
k: 2
k: 3
k: 4
```

The `continue` keyword may be used to move on to the next iteration of a loop immediately. For example, the following loop executes a subset of the loop body when the value of the variable `i` is less than `2`:

```
for ($i = 0; $i -le 5; $i++) {
    Write-Host $i
    if ($i -lt 2) {
        continue    # Continue to the next iteration
    }
    Write-Host "Remainder when $i is divided by 2 is $($i % 2)"
}
```

Summary

In this chapter, we have explored `if` and `switch` statements.

Each of the different loops, `foreach`, `for`, `do until`, `do while`, and `while`, has been introduced.

In the `Chapter 8`, *Working with .NET*, we will explore working with the .NET Framework.

8

Working with .NET

PowerShell is written in and built on the .NET Framework. Much of the .NET Framework can be used directly, and doing so adds a tremendous amount of flexibility; it removes many of the borders the language might otherwise have.

The idea of working with objects was introduced in `Chapter 4`, *Working with Objects in Powershell*, and this chapter extends on that, moving from objects created by commands to objects created from .NET classes. Many of the chapters which follow make extensive use of .NET, simply because it is the foundation of PowerShell.

It is important to understand that the .NET Framework is vast; it is not possible to cover everything about the .NET Framework in a single chapter. This chapter aims to show how the .NET Framework may be used within PowerShell based on the MSDN reference.

What can you do with .NET?
What would you like to do?
I enjoy implementing network protocols in PowerShell. To do this, I use several branches of .NET which specialize in network operations, such as creating sockets, sending and receiving bytes, reading and converting streams of bytes, and so on.
Classes implemented in .NET will come up again and again as different areas of the language are explored. From building strings and working with Active Directory to writing graphical interfaces and working with web services, everything needs a little .NET.

In this chapter, we are going to cover the following topics:

- Assemblies
- Namespaces
- Types
- Classes
- Constructors
- Properties and methods
- Static properties
- Static methods
- Non-public classes
- Type accelerators
- Using keyword

Assemblies

.NET objects are implemented within assemblies. An assembly may be static (based on a file) or dynamic (created in memory).

Many of the classes we might commonly use exist in DLL files stored in `%SystemRoot%\Assembly`. The list of currently loaded assemblies in a PowerShell session may be viewed using the following statement:

```
[System.AppDomain]::CurrentDomain.GetAssemblies()
```

Once an assembly, and the types it contains, has been loaded into a session, it cannot be unloaded without completely restarting the session.

Much of PowerShell is implemented in the `System.Management.Automation` DLL; details of this can be shown using the following statement:

```
[System.Management.Automation.PowerShell].Assembly
```

In this statement, the type PowerShell is chosen to get the assembly. Any other type in the same assembly is able to show the same information. The PowerShell type could be replaced with another in the previous command, for example:

```
[System.Management.Automation.PSCredential].Assembly
[System.Management.Automation.PSObject].Assembly
```

Namespaces

A namespace is used to organize classes into a hierarchy, often to group types with related functionalities.

In PowerShell, the `System` namespace is implicit.

The `System.AppDomain` type was used previously; this command, used when introducing assemblies, can be shortened:

```
[AppDomain]::CurrentDomain.GetAssemblies()
```

The same applies to types with longer names, such as `System.Management.Automation.PowerShell`:

```
[Management.Automation.PowerShell].Assembly
```

Types

A type is used to represent the generalized functionality of an object. Using this book as an example again, this book may have a number of types, including:

- `PowerShellBook`
- `TextBook`
- `Book`

Each of these types describes the general functionality of the object. The type does not say how a book came to be, nor whether it will do anything (on its own) to help create one.

In PowerShell, types are written between square brackets. The `[System.AppDomain]` and `[System.Management.Automation.PowerShell]` statements used when discussing previous assemblies are types.

Type descriptions are objects in PowerShell:
`[System.AppDomain]` denotes a type, but the syntax used to denote the type is itself an object.
It has properties and methods and a type of its own (`RuntimeType`), which can be seen by running the following command:
`[System.AppDomain].GetType()`

To an extent, the terms type and class are synonymous. A class is used to define a type, but it is not the only way. Another way is what is known as a **structure** (**struct**), which is used to define value types such as integers (`Int32`, `Int64`, and so on).

A type cannot be used to create an object instance all on its own.

Classes

A class is a set of instructions that dictate how a specific instance of an object is to be created. A class is, in a sense, a recipe.

In the case of this book, a class includes details of authoring, editorial processes, and publication steps. These steps are, hopefully, invisible to anyone reading this book; they are part of the internal implementation of the class. Following these steps will produce an instance of the `PowerShellBook` object.

It is often necessary to look up the instructions for using a class in the .NET class library on MSDN:

```
https://msdn.microsoft.com/en-us/library/mt472912(v=vs.110).aspx
```

The starting point for creating an instance of an object is often what is known as a `Constructor`.

Constructors

The class `System.Text.StringBuilder` can be used to build complex strings. The `StringBuilder` class has a number of constructors which can be viewed on the MSDN class library, as shown in the following screenshot:

Constructors

	Name	Description
	StringBuilder()	Initializes a new instance of the StringBuilder class.
	StringBuilder(Int32)	Initializes a new instance of the StringBuilder class using the specified capacity.
	StringBuilder(Int32, Int32)	Initializes a new instance of the StringBuilder class that starts with a specified capacity and can grow to a specified maximum.
	StringBuilder(String)	Initializes a new instance of the StringBuilder class using the specified string.
	StringBuilder(String, Int32)	Initializes a new instance of the StringBuilder class using the specified string and capacity.
	StringBuilder(String, Int32, Int32, Int32)	Initializes a new instance of the StringBuilder class from the specified substring and capacity.

PowerShell is also able to show the list of constructors. However, PowerShell cannot show the descriptive text. This may be useful as a reminder if the general functionality is already known. In PowerShell 5.0, the following syntax may be used to list the constructors:

```
PS> [System.Text.StringBuilder]::new
OverloadDefinitions
-------------------
System.Text.StringBuilder new()
System.Text.StringBuilder new(int capacity)
System.Text.StringBuilder new(string value)
System.Text.StringBuilder new(string value, int capacity)
System.Text.StringBuilder new(string value, int startIndex, int length, int
capacity)
System.Text.StringBuilder new(int capacity, int maxCapacity)
```

For older versions of PowerShell, a longer, less descriptive alternative is available:

```
PS> [System.Text.StringBuilder].GetConstructors() |
ForEach-Object { $_.ToString() }
Void .ctor()
Void .ctor(Int32)
Void .ctor(System.String)
Void .ctor(System.String, Int32)
Void .ctor(System.String, Int32, Int32, Int32)
Void .ctor(Int32, Int32)
```

Both MSDN and PowerShell show that there are six possible constructors for `StringBuilder`. Both show that the first of those does not expect any arguments.

Calling constructors

In PowerShell 5.0 and higher, an object instance may be created using the `new` static method:

```
$stringBuilder = [System.Text.StringBuilder]::new()
```

For earlier versions of PowerShell, the object instance may be created using:

```
$stringBuilder = New-Object System.Text.StringBuilder
```

PowerShell has added the static method (discussed later in this chapter); it can be used if required, but it is not documented on the MSDN page for `StringBuilder`.

Once an instance of `StringBuilder` has been created, it can be viewed:

```
PS> $stringBuilder = New-Object System.Text.StringBuilder
$stringBuilder

Capacity MaxCapacity Length
-------- ----------- ------
      16 2147483647       0
```

The `StringBuilder` object has a number of other constructors. These are used to adjust the initial state of the instance.

Calling constructors with lists of arguments

Arguments may be passed to the class constructor using a number of different approaches.

Using `New-Object` and the `ArgumentList` parameter, passing a single argument will use the second constructor in the list on MSDN (and in PowerShell):

```
PS> New-Object -TypeName System.Text.StringBuilder -ArgumentList 10
Capacity MaxCapacity Length
-------- ----------- ------
      10  2147483647      0
```

Alternatively, the following two approaches may be used:

```
New-Object System.Text.StringBuilder(10)
[System.Text.StringBuilder]::new(10)
```

PowerShell decides which constructor to use based on the numbers and types of the arguments.

In the previous examples, one argument is passed; there are two possible constructors which accept a single argument. One of these expects a value of type `Int32`, the other a `String`.

If a string is passed, a `StringBuilder` with an initial value for the string will be created. The following example creates a `StringBuilder` object instance containing the specified string `('Hello world')`:

```
PS> $stringBuilder = New-Object System.Text.StringBuilder('Hello world')
$stringBuilder.ToString()
Hello world
```

Attempting to pass in a values of other types in may result expected behavior. For example, an argument of `$true` creates a `StringBuilder` with a capacity set to `1`. The value for `$true` is treated as an `Int32` value:

```
PS> New-Object System.Text.StringBuilder($true)
Capacity MaxCapacity Length
-------- ----------- ------
       1 2147483647       0
```

If the value for the argument does not match any of the possible constructors, an error will be thrown:

```
PS> New-Object System.Text.StringBuilder((Get-Date))
New-Object : Cannot convert argument "0", with value: "23/01/2017
15:26:59", for "StringBuilder" to type "System.Int32": "Cannot convert
value "23/01/2017 15:26:59" to type
"System.Int32". Error: "Invalid cast from 'DateTime' to 'Int32'.""
At line:1 char:1
+ New-Object System.Text.StringBuilder((Get-Date))
+ ~~~~~~~~~~~~~~~~~~~~~~~~~~~~~~~~~~~~~~~~~~~~~~~~
+ CategoryInfo : InvalidOperation: (:) [New-Object], MethodException
+ FullyQualifiedErrorId :
ConstructorInvokedThrowException,Microsoft.PowerShell.Commands.NewObjectCom
mand
```

Arguments as an array

Arguments for constructors can be passed in as an array. Each of the following may be used to create an instance of a `StringBuilder` object:

```
$argumentList = 'Initial value', 50
$stringBuilder = New-Object System.Text.StringBuilder -ArgumentList
$argumentList
$stringBuilder = New-Object System.Text.StringBuilder($argumentList)
```

Attempting to pass in a list of arguments using the `new` method will produce a different result; the initial string will be filled with both values:

```
PS> $argumentList = 'Initial value', 50
$stringBuilder = [System.Text.StringBuilder]::new($argumentList)
Write-Host $stringBuilder.ToString() -ForegroundColor Green
$stringBuilder
Initial value 50
Capacity MaxCapacity Length
-------- ----------- ------
      16  2147483647     16
```

An array may be passed in using `new`, by using a slightly different approach:

```
$stringBuilder = [System.Text.StringBuilder]::new.Invoke($argumentList)
Write-Host $stringBuilder.ToString() -ForegroundColor Green
$stringBuilder
Initial value
Capacity MaxCapacity Length
-------- ----------- ------
      50  2147483647     13
```

The ability to push arguments into an array presents a complication when an argument is an array. For example, the `MemoryStream (System.IO.MemoryStream)` class has a number of constructors; two of these expect an array of bytes, as shown in the following screenshot:

	MemoryStream(Byte[])	Initializes a new non-resizable instance of the MemoryStream class based on the specified byte array.
	MemoryStream(Byte[], Boolean)	Initializes a new non-resizable instance of the MemoryStream class based on the specified byte array with the CanWrite property set as specified.

The first of these only expects an array (of bytes) as input. The following example shows an error generated when attempting to pass in the array:

```
PS> [Byte[]]$bytes = 97, 98, 99
$memoryStream = New-Object System.IO.MemoryStream($bytes)
New-Object : Exception calling ".ctor" with "3" argument(s): "Offset and
length were out of bounds for the array or count is greater than the number
of elements from index to the end of the source collection."
At line:2 char:17
+ $memoryStream = New-Object System.IO.MemoryStream($bytes)
+ ~~~~~~~~~~~~~~~~~~~~~~~~~~~~~~~~~~~~~~~~~
+ CategoryInfo : InvalidOperation: (:) [New-Object],
MethodInvocationException
+ FullyQualifiedErrorId :
ConstructorInvokedThrowException,Microsoft.PowerShell.Commands.NewObjectCom
mand
```

PowerShell is treating each byte as an individual argument for the constructor, rather than passing all of the values into the intended constructor.

The `new` static method does not suffer from this problem:

```
[Byte[]]$bytes = 97, 98, 99
$memoryStream = [System.IO.MemoryStream]::new($bytes)
```

To work around the problem in earlier versions of PowerShell, the unary comma operator may be used as follows:

```
$memoryStream = New-Object System.IO.MemoryStream(,$bytes)
```

Using the comma operator prevents PowerShell from expanding the array into a set of arguments. The array held in bytes is wrapped in another array which contains a single element. When PowerShell executes this, the wrapper is discarded, and the inner-array (bytes) is passed without further expansion.

Properties and methods

In `Chapter 4`, *Working with Objects in Powershell,* the idea of using properties and methods was introduced. `Get-Member` was used to list each of these.

Properties for objects derived from .NET classes, such as those for the `System.Text.StringBuilder` class, are documented on MSDN:

Properties

	Name	Description
	Capacity	Gets or sets the maximum number of characters that can be contained in the memory allocated by the current instance.
	Chars[Int32]	Gets or sets the character at the specified character position in this instance.
	Length	Gets or sets the length of the current StringBuilder object.
	MaxCapacity	Gets the maximum capacity of this instance.

Similarly, methods are described in detail, often with examples of usage (in C#, VB, F#, and so on):

Methods

	Name	Description
	Append(Boolean)	Appends the string representation of a specified Boolean value to this instance.
	Append(Byte)	Appends the string representation of a specified 8-bit unsigned integer to this instance.
	Append(Char)	Appends the string representation of a specified Char object to this instance.
	Append(Char*, Int32)	Appends an array of Unicode characters starting at a specified address to this instance.
	Append(Char, Int32)	Appends a specified number of copies of the string

These methods may be used as long as the argument lists can be satisfied. The 4th item on the list is difficult to leverage in PowerShell, as `Char*` represents a pointer to an array of `Unicode` characters. A pointer is a reference to a location in memory, something not often seen in PowerShell and beyond the scope of this chapter.

Static properties

Properties require an instance of a type to be created before they can be accessed. Static properties, on the other hand, do not.

A static property is a piece of data; in some cases this includes constant values, associated with class definitions which can be retrieved without creating an object instance.

MSDN shows static properties using an `S` symbol in the left-most column. For example, the `System.Text.Encoding` class has a number of static properties denoting different text encoding types, shown in the following screenshot:

Properties

	Name	Description
S	ASCII	Gets an encoding for the ASCII (7-bit) character set.
S	BigEndianUnicode	Gets an encoding for the UTF-16 format that uses the big endian byte order.
	BodyName	When overridden in a derived class, gets a name for the current encoding that can be used with mail agent body tags.
	CodePage	When overridden in a derived class, gets the code page identifier of the current Encoding.
	DecoderFallback	Gets or sets the DecoderFallback object for the current Encoding object.
S	Default	Gets an encoding for the operating system's current ANSI code page.

PowerShell is also able to list the static properties for a type (or class) using `Get-Member` with the `Static` switch:

```
PS> [System.Text.Encoding] | Get-Member -MemberType Property -Static
TypeName: System.Text.Encoding
Name              MemberType Definition
```

```
----                ---------- ----------
ASCII               Property   static System.Text.Encoding ASCII {get;}
BigEndianUnicode Property   static System.Text.Encoding BigEndianUnicode
{get;}
Default             Property   static System.Text.Encoding Default {get;}
Unicode             Property   static System.Text.Encoding Unicode {get;}
UTF32               Property   static System.Text.Encoding UTF32 {get;}
UTF7                Property   static System.Text.Encoding UTF7 {get;}
UTF8                Property   static System.Text.Encoding UTF8 {get;}
```

These static properties are accessed using the following generalized notation:

```
[<TypeName>]::<PropertyName>
```

In the case of `System.Text.Encoding`, the `ASCII` property is accessible using the following:

```
[System.Text.Encoding]::ASCII
```

A variable may be used to represent either the type or the property name:

```
$type = [System.Text.Encoding]
$propertyName = 'ASCII'
$type::$propertyName
```

Fields are often used as part of the internal implementation of a class (or structure). Fields are not often accessible outside of a class.

The `Int32` structure exposes two static fields holding the maximum and minimum possible values the type can hold:

Fields

	Name	Description
	MaxValue	Represents the largest possible value of an Int32. This field is constant.
	MinValue	Represents the smallest possible value of Int32. This field is constant.

PowerShell does not distinguish between fields and properties. The following statements show the values of each static field in turn:

```
[Int32]::MaxValue
[Int32]::MinValue
```

Static methods

As static properties, static method do not require that an instance of a class is created.

MSDN shows static methods using an `S` symbol in the left-most column. For example, the `System.Net.NetworkInformation.NetworkInterface` class has a number of static methods. The first of these is shown in the following screenshot:

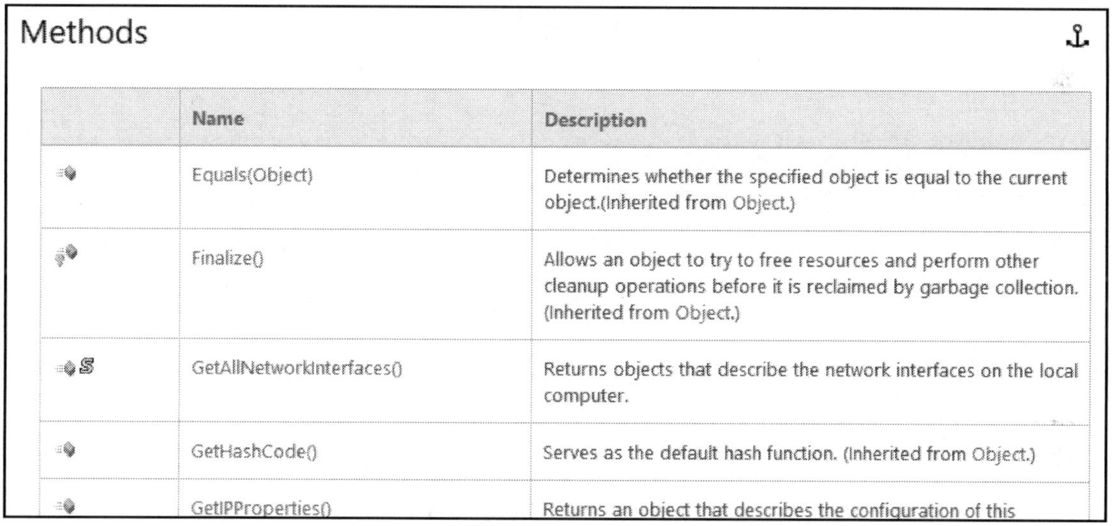

Methods

	Name	Description
	Equals(Object)	Determines whether the specified object is equal to the current object.(Inherited from Object.)
	Finalize()	Allows an object to try to free resources and perform other cleanup operations before it is reclaimed by garbage collection. (Inherited from Object.)
S	GetAllNetworkInterfaces()	Returns objects that describe the network interfaces on the local computer.
	GetHashCode()	Serves as the default hash function. (Inherited from Object.)
	GetIPProperties()	Returns an object that describes the configuration of this

PowerShell is also able to list these methods using `Get-Member` with the `Static` switch:

```
PS> [System.Net.NetworkInformation.NetworkInterface] | Get-Member -
MemberType Method -Static
TypeName: System.Net.NetworkInformation.NetworkInterface
Name                     MemberType Definition
----                     ---------- ----------
Equals                   Method     static bool Equals(System.Object objA,
System.Object objB)
GetAllNetworkInterfaces Method     static
System.Net.NetworkInformation.NetworkInterface[] GetAllNetworkInterfaces()
GetIsNetworkAvailable    Method     static bool GetIsNetworkAvailable()
```

```
ReferenceEquals          Method     static bool
ReferenceEquals(System.Object objA, System.Object objB)
```

Static methods are accessed using the following generalized notation:

```
[<TypeName>]::<MethodName>(<ArgumentList>)
```

As the `GetAllNetworkInterfaces` method does not require arguments, it may be called as follows:

```
[System.Net.NetworkInformation.NetworkInterface]::GetAllNetworkInterfaces()
```

The parentheses at the end of the statement must be included to tell PowerShell that this is a method.

As was seen with static properties, both the `type` and `method` may be assigned to variables:

```
$type = [System.Net.NetworkInformation.NetworkInterface]
$methodName = 'GetAllNetworkInterfaces'
$type::$methodName()
```

The parentheses are not part of the method name.

Static methods often require arguments. The `System.IO.Path` class has many static methods that require arguments, as shown in the following screenshot:

Methods

	Name	Description
S	ChangeExtension(String, String)	Changes the extension of a path string.
S	Combine(String, String)	Combines two strings into a path.
S	Combine(String, String, String)	Combines three strings into a path.
S	Combine(String, String, String, String)	Combines four strings into a path.
S	Combine(String[])	Combines an array of strings into a path.
S	GetDirectoryName(String)	Returns the directory information for the specified path string.
S	GetExtension(String)	Returns the extension of the specified path string.

Arguments are passed in as a comma separated list. For example, the `ChangeExtension` method may be used, as follows:

```
[System.IO.Path]::ChangeExtension("C:\none.exe", "bak")
```

An array containing a list of arguments cannot be directly supplied. For example:

```
$argumentList = "C:\none.exe", "bak"
[System.IO.Path]::ChangeExtension($argumentList)
```

If a list of arguments is to be supplied from a variable, the `method` object must be invoked:

```
$argumentList = "C:\none.exe", "bak"
[System.IO.Path]::ChangeExtension.Invoke($argumentList)
```

The `method` object (because everything is an object) is accessed by omitting the parentheses that normally follow the name of the method:

```
PS> [System.IO.Path]::ChangeExtension
OverloadDefinitions
-------------------
static string ChangeExtension(string path, string extension)
```

Non-public classes

.NET classes come with a number of access modifiers. Each of these affords a different level of protection and visibility.

Instances of a public class may be created using `New-Object` (with an appropriate list of arguments), or the `new` static method via the constructors, as shown previously.

Private and internal (non-public) classes are not directly accessible; they are placed out of sight by the developer of the class. They are often part of an implementation of a program or command and are not expected to be directly accessed.

In some cases, the decision to hide something away appears to be counterproductive. One example of this is the `TypeAccelerators` class.

The type derived from the class may be accessed using the following notation:

```
PS> [System.Management.Automation.PowerShell].Assembly.GetType(
'System.Management.Automation.TypeAccelerators')
IsPublic IsSerial Name              BaseType
-------- -------- ----              --------
False    False    TypeAccelerators System.Object
```

Type accelerators

A type accelerator is an alias for a type name. At the beginning of this chapter the `System.Management.Automation.PowerShell` type was used. This type has an accelerator available. The accelerator allows the following notation to be used:

```
[PowerShell].Assembly
```

Another commonly used example is the `ADSI` accelerator. This represents the type `System.DirectoryServices.DirectoryEntry`. The following two commands are equivalent:

```
[System.DirectoryServices.DirectoryEntry]"WinNT://$env:COMPUTERNAME"
[ADSI]"WinNT://$env:COMPUTERNAME"
```

Getting the list of type accelerators is not quite as easy as it should be. An instance of the `TypeAccelerators` type is required first. Once that has been retrieved, a static property called `Get` will retrieve the list; the first few results are shown following:

```
$type =
[PowerShell].Assembly.GetType('System.Management.Automation.TypeAccelerator
s')
$type::Get
```

New accelerators may be added; for example, an accelerator for the `TypeAccelerators` class would make life easier. To do this, an accelerator with the name `Accelerators` is added, using the `TypeAccelerators` type as the object it references:

```
$type =
[PowerShell].Assembly.GetType('System.Management.Automation.TypeAccelerator
s')
$type::Add('Accelerators', $type)
```

Once the new accelerator has been added, the previous operations can be simplified. Getting the list of accelerators is now as follows:

```
[Accelerators]::Get
```

New accelerators may be added using the following:

```
[Accelerators]::Add('<Name>', [<TypeName>])
```

Using

The using keyword was introduced with PowerShell 5.0. The using keyword may be used in a script, a module, or in the console.

The using keyword does a number of different things. It can import and declare:

- Assemblies
- Modules
- Namespaces

In the context of working with .NET, assemblies and namespaces are of interest.

Future plans for the using command look to include aliasing as well as support for type and command objects. For example, we might expect the following to work in the future:

```
using namespace NetInfo = System.Net.NetworkInformation
```

This statement will fail with a `not supported` error at this time.

Using assemblies

If an assembly is listed in the using statement for a script, it will be loaded. For example, the `System.Windows.Forms` may be loaded:

```
using assembly 'System.Windows.Forms, Version=4.0.0.0, Culture=neutral,
PublicKeyToken=b77a5c561934e089'
```

`Add-Type` is able to do much the same thing:

```
Add-Type -AssemblyName 'System.Windows.Forms, Version=4.0.0.0,
Culture=neutral, PublicKeyToken=b77a5c561934e089'
```

If a specific version is not required, the shorter name for the assembly may be used:

```
using assembly System.Windows.Forms
```

The using `assembly` command will load assemblies from a specific path if one is supplied:

```
using assembly 'C:\SomeDir\someAssembly.dll'
```

PowerShell allows the `using assembly` statement any number of times in a script (one or more assemblies can be loaded in a single script).

Using namespaces

Many of the examples used in this chapter have involved typing the full namespace path to get to a class name. This requirement can be eased with the using keyword.

For example, if a script does a lot of work with the `System.Net.NetworkInformation` class, the requirement to type the namespace every time can be removed. This allows the `System.Net.NetworkInformation.NetworkInterface` class to be used with a much shorter type name:

```
using namespace System.Net.NetworkInformation
```

With this statement in place, classes can be used without the long namespace:

```
[NetworkInterface]::GetAllNetworkInterfaces()
```

If the namespace is present within an assembly which is not loaded by default, the `using assembly` command should be added first. For example, if a script is to work with the `Windows Presentation Framework`, the following might be useful:

```
# Load the the Windows Presentation Framework
using assembly PresentationFramework
# Use the System.Windows namespace
using namespace System.Windows

$window = New-Object Window
$window.Height = 100
$window.Width = 150
# Create a System.Windows.Controls.Button object
$button = New-Object Controls.Button
$button.Content = 'Close'
$button.Add_Click( { $window.Close() } )
$window.Content = $button
$window.ShowDialog()
```

PowerShell only allows one `using namespace` statement in the console. The last used is valid. In a script, more than one `using namespace` statement may be declared.

Summary

In this chapter, we have explored assemblies, namespaces, types, and classes before delving into the creation of objects from a class.

Static properties and static methods were introduced, which may be used without creating an instance of a class.

Non-public classes were introduced before working with type accelerators.

The using keyword was introduced, with a peek at its possible future direction.

This chapter brings part one of this book to an end. In part two, we will explore working with data in PowerShell, starting with data parsing and manipulation.

9
Data Parsing and Manipulation

Access to the .NET framework means PowerShell comes with a wide variety of ways to work with simple data types, such as strings and numbers.

In this chapter, we are going to cover the following topics:

- String manipulation
- Converting strings
- Number manipulation
- Converting strings to numeric values
- Date and time manipulation

String manipulation

The .NET type `System.String` offers a wide array of methods for manipulating or inspecting strings. The following methods are case sensitive, but are in many cases faster alternatives to using regular expressions if the time it takes for a script to run is important.

Working with data held in strings is an important part of any scripting language.

Indexing into strings

In PowerShell, it is possible to index into a string the same way as selecting elements from an array. For example:

```
$myString = 'abcdefghijklmnopqrstuvwxyz'
$myString[0]      # This is a (the first character in the string)
$myString[-1]     # This is z (the last character in the string)
```

String methods and arrays

In PowerShell, some string methods can be called on an array. The method will be executed against each of the elements in the array. For example, the `trim` method is used against each of the strings:

```
('azzz', 'bzzz', 'czzz').Trim('z')
```

The `split` method is also capable of acting against an array:

```
('a,b', 'c,d').Split(',')
```

This remains `true` as long as the `array` object does not have a conflicting method or property. For example, the `Insert` method cannot be used as an `array` object has a version of its own.

Properties and methods of array elements:
The feature demonstrated here has broader scope than methods, and it applies to more than string objects.
In the case of strings, the methods that can be used can be viewed as follows:

```
$arrayMembers = (Get-Member -InputObject @() -MemberType
Property, Method).Name
'string' | Get-Member -MemberType Property, Method |
Where-Object { $_.Name -notin $arrayMembers }
```

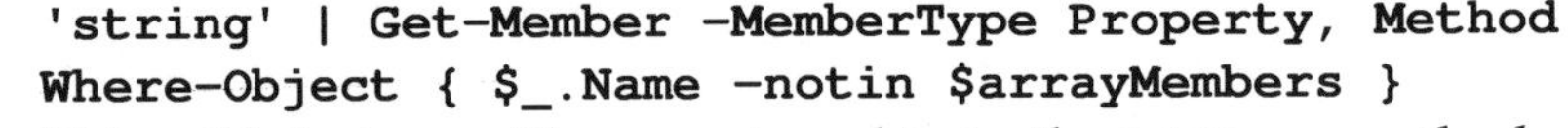

Using this feature with `DateTime` objects, the `AddDays` method may be called on each element in an array:

```
((Get-Date '01/01/2017'), (Get-Date
'01/02/2017')).AddDays(5)
```

Or the `DayOfWeek` property may be accessed on each element in the array:

```
((Get-Date '01/01/2017'), (Get-Date
'01/02/2017')).DayOfWeek
```

A similar `Get-Member` command reveals the list of properties and methods that may be used in this manner:

```
Get-Date | Get-Member -MemberType Property, Method |
Where-Object { $_.Name -notin $arrayMembers }
```

Substring

The `Substring` method selects part of a string. `Substring` can select everything after a specific index:

```
$myString = 'abcdefghijklmnopqrstuvwxyz'
$myString.Substring(20)    # Start at index 20. Returns 'uvwxyz'
```

Or it can select a specific number of characters from a starting point:

```
$myString = 'abcdefghijklmnopqrstuvwxyz'
$myString.Substring(3, 4) # Start at index 3, get 4 characters.
```

The index starts at `0`, counting from the beginning of the string.

Split

The `split` method has a relative in PowerShell, the `-split` operator. The `-split` operator expects a regular expression, the split method for a string expects an array of characters by default:

```
$myString = 'Surname,GivenName'
$myString.Split(',')
```

When splitting the following string based on a comma, the resulting array will have three elements. The first element is `Surname`, the last is `GivenName`. The second element in the array (index `1`) is blank:

```
$string = 'Surname,,GivenName'
$array = $string.Split(',')
$array.Count     # This is 3
$array[1]        # This is empty
```

This blank value may be discarded by setting the `StringSplitOptions` argument of the `Split` method:

```
$string = 'Surname,,GivenName'
$array = $string.Split(',', [StringSplitOptions]::RemoveEmptyEntries)
$array.Count     # This is 2
```

When using the `Split` method in this manner, individual variables may be filled from each value:

```
$surname, $givenName = $string.Split(',',
[StringSplitOptions]::RemoveEmptyEntries)
```

The `Split` method is powerful, but care is required using its different arguments, each of the different sets of arguments is as follows:

```
PS> 'string'.Split

OverloadDefinitions
-------------------
string[] Split(Params char[] separator)
string[] Split(char[] separator, int count)
string[] Split(char[] separator, System.StringSplitOptions options)
string[] Split(char[] separator, int count, System.StringSplitOptions
options)
string[] Split(string[] separator, System.StringSplitOptions options)
string[] Split(string[] separator, int count, System.StringSplitOptions
options)
```

PowerShell can create a character array from an array of strings (provided each string is no more than one character long), or a string. Both of the following statements will result in an array of characters (`char[]`):

```
[char[]]$characters = [string[]]('a', 'b', 'c')
[char[]]$characters = 'abc'
```

When the `Split` method is used as follows, the separator is any (and all) of the characters in the string. The result of the following expression is an array of five elements (`one`, `<empty>`, `two`, `<empty>`, and `three`):

```
$string = 'one||two||three'
$string.Split('||')
```

To split using a string (instead of an array of characters), PowerShell must be forced to use this overload definition:

```
string[] Split(string[] separator, System.StringSplitOptions options)
```

This can be achieved with the following cumbersome syntax:

```
$string = 'one||two||three'
$string.Split([String[]]'||', [StringSplitOptions]::None)
```

Replace

The `Replace` method will substitute one `string` value for another:

```
$string = 'This is the first example'
$string.Replace('first', 'second')
```

PowerShell also has a replace operator. The replace operator uses a regular expression to describe the value that should be replaced.

Regular expressions (discussed in `Chapter 10`, *Regular Expressions*) may be more difficult to work with in some cases, especially when replacing characters that are reserved in regular expressions (such as the period character, `.`):

```
$string = 'Begin the begin.'
$string -replace 'begin.', 'story, please.'
$string.Replace('begin.', 'story, please.')
```

In these cases, the `Replace` method may be easier to work with.

Trim, TrimStart, and TrimEnd

The `Trim` method, by default, removes all white space (spaces, tabs, and line breaks) from the beginning and end of a string. For example:

```
$string = "
    This string has leading and trailing white space      "
$string.Trim()
```

The `TrimStart` and `TrimEnd` methods limit their operation to either the start or end of the string.

Each of the methods accepts a list of characters to trim. For example:

```
$string = '*__This string is surrounded by clutter.--#'
$string.Trim('*_-#')
```

The `Trim` method does not remove a string from the end of another. The string supplied in the previous example (`'*_-#'`) is treated as an array. This can be seen in the definition of the method:

```
PS> 'string'.Trim

OverloadDefinitions
-------------------
string Trim(Params char[] trimChars)
string Trim()
```

A failure to appreciate this can lead to unexpected behavior. The domain name in the following example ends with the suffix `'.uk.net'`, the goal is to trim the suffix from the end of the string:

```
$string = 'magnet.uk.net'
$string.TrimEnd('.uk.net')
```

As `'.uk.net'` is treated as an array of characters, the result of this expression is shorter than may be expected if the argument were a string:

```
PS> $string = 'magnet.uk.net'
$string.Trim('.uk.net')

mag
```

Insert and Remove

The `Insert` method is able to add one string into another. This method expects an index from the beginning of the string, counting from `0`, and a string to insert:

```
$string = 'The letter of the alphabet is a'
$string.Insert(4, 'first ')  # Insert this before "letter", include a
trailing space
```

The `Remove` method removes characters from a string based on a start position and the length of the string to remove:

```
$string = 'This is is an example'
$string.Remove(4, 3)
```

The previous statement removes the first instance of `is`, including the trailing space.

IndexOf and LastIndexOf

The `IndexOf` and `LastIndexOf` may be used to locate a character or string within a string. `IndexOf` finds the first occurrence of a string, `LastIndexOf` finds the last occurrence of the string. In both cases, the zero-based index of the start of the string is returned. If the character, or string, is not present, the two methods will return `-1`:

```
$string = 'abcdefedcba'
$string.IndexOf('b')     # Returns 1
$string.LastIndexOf('b') # Returns 9
$string.IndexOf('ed')    # Returns 6
```

As `-1` is used to indicate that the value is absent, the method is not suitable for statements based on an implicit Boolean. The index `0`, a valid position, is considered to be `false`. The following example correctly handles the return value from `IndexOf` in a conditional statement:

```
$string  = 'abcdef'
if ($string.IndexOf('a') -gt -1) {
     'The string contains an a'
}
```

The scope of the `IndexOf` and `LastIndexOf` methods can be limited using the start index and count arguments.

Methods that are able to locate a position within a string are useful when combined with other string methods:

```
PS> $string = 'First,Second,Third'
$string.Substring(
    $string.IndexOf(',') + 1, # startIndex (6)
    $string.LastIndexOf(',') - $string.IndexOf(',') - 1 # length (6)
)

Second
```

PadLeft and PadRight

The `PadLeft` and `PadRight` options endeavor to make a string up to a maximum length. Both `PadLeft` and `PadRight` take the same arguments as follows:

```
PS> ''.PadRight
''.PadLeft

OverloadDefinitions
-------------------
string PadRight(int totalWidth)
string PadRight(int totalWidth, char paddingChar)
string PadLeft(int totalWidth)
string PadLeft(int totalWidth, char paddingChar)
```

Each method attempts to make a string up to the total width. If the string is already equal to, or longer than the total width, it will not be changed. Unless another is supplied, the padding character is a space.

The following example pads the right-hand side of strings using `'.'` as the padding character argument:

```
PS> ('one', 'two', 'three').PadRight(10, '.')

one.......
two.......
three.....
```

Padding a string on the left, in effect, right justifies the string:

```
PS> ('one', 'two', 'three').PadLeft(10, '.')

.......one
.......two
.....three
```

ToUpper, ToLower, and ToTitleCase

`ToUpper` converts any lowercase characters in a string to uppercase. `ToLower` converts any uppercase characters in a string to lowercase:

```
'aBc'.ToUpper()     # Returns ABC
'AbC'.ToLower()     # Returns abc
```

Considering that the methods discussed here are case sensitive, converting a string to a known case may be an important first step. For example:

```
$string = 'AbN'
$string = $string.ToLower()
$string = $string.Replace('n', 'c')
```

The `ToTitleCase` is not a method of the `String` object. It is a method of the `System.Globalization.TextInfo` class. The `ToTitleCase` method performs limited culture-specific capitalization of words:

```
PS> (Get-Culture).TextInfo.ToTitleCase('some title')
Some Title
```

As this is not a static method, the `TextInfo` object must be created first. This object cannot be directly created. `TextInfo` can be obtained via the `System.Globalization.CultureInfo` object, this object is returned by the `Get-Culture` command.

The same `TextInfo` object may also be accessed using the `host` automatic variable:

```
$host.CurrentCulture.TextInfo.ToTitleCase('another title')
```

The `ToTitleCase` method will not convert words that are entirely uppercase. Uppercase words are considered to be acronyms.

Contains, StartsWith, and EndsWith

Each of the methods `Contains`, `StartsWith`, and `EndsWith`, will return `true` or `false` depending on whether or not the string contains the specified string.

`Contains` returns `true` if the value is found within the `subject` string:

```
$string = 'I am the subject'
$string.Contains('the')    # Returns $true
```

`StartsWith` and `EndsWith` return `true` if the subject string starts or ends with the specified value:

```
$string = 'abc'
$string.StartsWith('ab')
$string.EndsWith('bc')
```

Chaining methods

As many of the string methods return a string, it is entirely possible to chain methods together. For example, each of the following methods return a string, so another method can be added to the end:

```
'     ONe*?    '.Trim().TrimEnd('?*').ToLower().Replace('o', 'O')
```

This ability to `chain` methods is not in any way unique to strings.

Converting strings

PowerShell has a variety of commands that can convert strings. These are explained in the following sections.

Working with Base64

`Base64` is a transport encoding that is used to represent binary data and therefore any (relatively simple) data type.

`Base64` is particularly useful when storing complex strings in files, or in text-based transport protocols such as SMTP.

The .NET class `System.Convert` contains static methods that can be used to work with `base64`:

- `ToBase64String`
- `FromBase64String`

Two further methods exist to work with character arrays, these are not discussed here.

The `ToBase64String` method takes an array of bytes and converts it into a string. For example, a simple byte array may be converted:

```
PS> [Byte[]]$bytes = 97, 98, 99, 100, 101
[Convert]::ToBase64String($bytes)

YWJjZGU=
```

A more meaningful byte sequence can be made from a few words by getting the byte values for each character:

```
PS> $bytes = [System.Text.Encoding]::ASCII.GetBytes('Hello world')
[Convert]::ToBase64String($bytes)

SGVsbG8gd29ybGQ=
```

The text encoding type used here is ASCII (1 byte per character), UTF16 text encoding will result in a longer `Base64` string as each character is stored in two bytes:

```
PS> $bytes = [System.Text.Encoding]::Unicode.GetBytes('Hello world')
[Convert]::ToBase64String($bytes)

SABlAGwAbABvACAAdwBvAHIAbABkAA==
```

Converting from a `base64` string to a sequence of bytes, then to a string may be achieved as follows:

```
PS> $base64String = 'YWJjZGU='
$bytes = [Convert]::FromBase64String($base64String)
[System.Text.Encoding]::ASCII.GetString($bytes)

abcde
```

`Base64` may be a handy format for storing items such as keys (normally a set of bytes) for use with the `ConvertTo-SecureString` command. For example:

```
# Create a 16-byte key
[Byte[]]$key = 1..16 | ForEach-Object { Get-Random -Minimum 0 -Maximum 256
}
# Convert the key to a string and save it in a file
[Convert]::ToBase64String($key) | Out-File 'KeepThisSafe.txt'

# Create a secure string (from plain text) to encrypt
$secure = ConvertTo-SecureString -String 'Secure text' -AsPlainText -Force
# Encrypt the password using the key (from the file)
$encrypted = ConvertFrom-SecureString -SecureString $secure -Key
([Convert]::FromBase64String((Get-Content .\KeepThisSafe.txt)))
# Decrypt the password using the same key
$secure = ConvertTo-SecureString -String $encrypted -Key
([Convert]::FromBase64String((Get-Content .\KeepThisSafe.txt)))
# Show the original password
(New-Object PSCredential('.', $secure)).GetNetworkCredential().Password
```

How Base64 works

Base64 has 64 possible values between 0 and 63. Each value (an index) has a character associated with it. The characters, in order, are A to Z, then a to z, then 0 to 9, and finally + and /. The = character is used as a padding character.

The base64 index 9 is the character J, index 56 is the character 4, and so on. We can have PowerShell make this array for us:

```
[char[]]$base64Characters = [int][char]'A'..[int][char]'Z' +
                            [int][char]'a'..[int][char]'z' +
                            [int][char]'0'..[int][char]'9'
$base64Characters += '+', '/'
```

The following process is used to convert the ASCII string He to base64.

Convert the characters to bytes:

ASCII	H	e
Code	72	101

PowerShell can convert characters to ASCII values using the following:

```
[int][char]'H'
[int][char]'e'
```

To illustrate the process, the two values are converted into bits:

```
01001000 01100101
```

The Convert class can perform this step in PowerShell:

```
[Convert]::ToString([int][char]'H', 2).PadLeft(8, '0')
[Convert]::ToString([int][char]'e', 2).PadLeft(8, '0')
```

Base64 uses a six-bit boundary (instead of eight), that gives three distinct indexes:

```
010010 = 2 + 16 = 18
000110 = 2 + 4  = 6
010100 = 4 + 16 = 20   # Padded on the right to make 6 bits
```

These indexes have base64 characters associated with them, S, G, and U in turn.

The `base64` string now needs padding until it fits into a sequence of bytes (is divisible by 8). The entire process, including the padding, is shown following:

ASCII	H								e								*<nothing>*							
Code	72								101								*<nothing>*							
Bits	0	1	0	0	1	0	0	0	0	1	1	0	0	1	0	1	0	0	0	0	0	0	0	0
Index	18						6						20						*<padding>*					
Character	S						G						U						=					

The process can be implemented in PowerShell, even if it is slower than `Convert.ToBase64String`. In this example, the bits are treated as a string:

```
function ConvertTo-Base64 {
    param(
        [string]$String
    )

    # Generate the base64 character set
    [char[]]$base64Characters = [int][char]'A'..[int][char]'Z' +
                                [int][char]'a'..[int][char]'z' +
                                [int][char]'0'..[int][char]'9'
    $base64Characters += '+', '/'

    [String]$bits = $string.ToCharArray() | ForEach-Object {
        [Convert]::ToString([int][char]$_, 2).PadLeft(8, '0')
    }
    $bits = $bits -replace ' '
    $base64String = ''
    # Get the 6-bit fragments and convert each to an index
    for ($i = 0; $i -lt $bits.Length; $i += 6) {
        # Get the bits for the index
        if ($bits.Length - $i -lt 6) {
            # If fewer than 6 characters remain, get all of them
            $indexBits = $bits.Substring($i, $bits.Length - $i)
        } else {
            # Get 6 characters
            $indexBits = $bits.Substring($i, 6)
        }
```

```
            # Pad the right so the 6-bit value is correctly padded
            # then pad the left so it can be converted to a byte
            $indexBits = $indexBits.PadRight(6, '0').PadLeft(8, '0')
            # Convert the bit string to a byte
            $index = [Convert]::ToByte($indexBits, 2)
            # Get the base64 character
            $base64String += $base64Characters[$index]
        }
        # Pad the base64 string until length is divisible by 6 and 8
        $length = $bits.Length
        while ($length % 8 -ne 0 -or $length % 6 -ne 0) {
            if ($length % 6 -eq 0) {
                # Add the padding character
                $base64String += '='
            }
            $length++
        }

        return $base64String
    }
```

Working with CSV

`ConvertTo-Csv` turns objects in PowerShell into CSV (comma-separated values) strings:

```
PS> Get-Process -Id $pid | Select-Object Name, Id, Path | ConvertTo-Csv
#TYPE Selected.System.Diagnostics.Process
"Name","Id","Path"
"powershell_ise","9956","C:\WINDOWS\System32\WindowsPowerShell\v1.0\powersh
ell_ise.exe"
```

`ConvertFrom-Csv` turns `CSV` formatted strings into objects. For example:

```
"David,0123456789,28" | ConvertFrom-Csv -Header Name, Phone, Age
```

As `ConvertFrom-Csv` is specifically written to read CSV formatted data, it will discard quotes surrounding strings, but will allow fields to spread across lines and so on. For example:

```
'David,0123456789,28,"1 Some street,
A Lane"' | ConvertFrom-Csv -Header Name, Phone, Age, Address |
Format-Table -Wrap
```

If the Header parameter is not defined, the first line ConvertFrom-Csv reads is expected to be a header. If there is only one line of data nothing will be returned:

```
'Name,Age', 'David,28' | ConvertFrom-Csv
```

Export-Csv and Import-Csv complement these two commands by writing and reading information to a file instead:

```
Get-Process -Id $pid | Select-Object Name, Id, Path | Export-Csv
'somefile.csv'
Import-Csv somefile.csv
```

Convert-String

The Convert-String command may be used to simplify some string conversion operations. The conversion is performed based on an example that must be supplied. For example, Convert-String can generate account names from a list of users:

```
'Michael Caine', 'Benny Hill', 'Raf Vallone' | Convert-String -Example
'Michael Caine=MCaine'
```

The example parameter uses the generalized syntax:

```
<Before>=<After>
```

This example text does not have to be one of the set being converted, for example, the following will work:

```
'Michael Caine', 'Benny Hill', 'Raf Vallone' | Convert-String -Example
'First Second=FSecond'
```

The following alternate syntax is also supported:

```
'Michael Caine', 'Benny Hill', 'Raf Vallone' | Convert-String -Example @{
    Before = 'First Second'
    After = 'FSecond'
}
```

The Convert-String command is not without its limitations. After may only include strings, or partial strings, from Before along with a sub-set of punctuation characters. Characters that are not permitted in After include @, $, ~, `, and !. Because of these limitations, Convert-String cannot, for example, build an email address for each user in the list in a single step.

ConvertFrom-String

`ConvertFrom-String` has two different styles of operation. The first behaves much as `ConvertFrom-Csv` except that it does not discard characters that make up the CSV format. In the following example, the quote characters surrounding the first name are preserved:

```
PS> '"bob",tim,geoff' | ConvertFrom-String -Delimiter ',' -PropertyNames
name1, name2, name3

name1 name2 name3
----- ----- -----
"bob" tim   geoff
```

The default `Delimiter` (if the parameter is not supplied) is a space. The second operating mode of `ConvertFrom-String` is far more complex. A template must be defined for each element of data that is to be pushed into a property.

The following example uses `ConvertFrom-String` to convert the output from the `tasklist` command to an object:

```
$template = '{Task*:{ImageName:System Idle Process} {[Int]PID:0}
{SessionName:Services} {Session:0} {Memory:24 K}}'
tasklist |
    Select-Object -Skip 3 |
    ConvertFrom-String -TemplateContent $template |
    Select-Object -ExpandProperty Task
```

The `Task*` element denotes the start of a data record. It allows each of the remaining fields to be grouped together under a single object.

The `ConvertFrom-String` command is good at dealing with well formatted data that is already divided correctly. In the case of the `tasklist` command, the end of a single task (or data record) is denoted by a line break.

Number manipulation

Basic mathematical operation in PowerShell makes use of the operators discussed in `Chapter 5`, *Operators*.

Formatting numbers using the format operators are introduced along with a number of features:

```
'{0:x}' -f 24244        # Lower-case hexadecimal. Returns 5eb4
'{0:X}' -f 24244        # Upper-case hexadecimal. Returns 5EB4
'{0:P}' -f 0.28232      # Percentage. Returns 28.23%
'{0:N2}' -f 32583.122   # Culture specific number format.
                        # 2 decimal places.
                        # Returns 32,583.12 (for en-GB)
```

The format operator is powerful, but it has one major shortcoming: It returns a string. It is great for when you want to display a number to a user, but will prevent sorting or work with the numeric form.

Large byte values

PowerShell provides operators for working with bytes. These operators are as follows:

- **nKB**: Kilobytes ($n * 1024^1$)
- **nMB**: Megabytes ($n * 1024^2$)
- **nGB**: Gigabytes ($n * 1024^3$)
- **nTB**: Terabytes ($n * 1024^4$)
- **nPB**: Petabytes ($n * 1024^5$)

These operators can be used to represent large values:

```
PS> 22.5GB
24159191040
```

The operators may also be used to convert large byte values to shorter values. For example, a shorter value might be added to a message using the format operator:

```
PS> '{0:F} TB available' -f (123156235234522 / 1TB)
112.01 TB available
```

Power-of-10

PowerShell uses the `e` operator to represent a scientific notation (`power-of-10, "* 10`^{n}`"`) that can be used to represent very large numbers. The exponent can be either positive or negative:

```
2e2     # Returns 200 (2 * 102)
2e-1    # Returns 0.2 (2 * 10-1)
```

Hexadecimal

Hexadecimal formats are accessible in PowerShell without any significant work. PowerShell will return the decimal form of any given hexadecimal number. The hexadecimal number should be prefixed with `0x`:

```
PS> 0x5eb4

24244
```

Using System.Math

While PowerShell itself comes with reasonably basic mathematical operators, the .NET class `System.Math` has a far wider variety.

The `Round` static method can be used to round up to a fixed number of decimal places. In the following example, the value is rounded to two decimal places:

```
[Math]::Round(2.123456789, 2)
```

The `Ceiling` and `Floor` methods are used when performing whole-number rounding:

```
[Math]::Ceiling(2.1234)     # Returns 3
[Math]::Floor(2.9876)       # Returns 2
```

The `Abs` converts a positive or negative integer to a positive integer (multiplies by `-1` if the value is negative):

```
[Math]::Abs(-45748)
```

Numbers may be raised to a power:

```
[Math]::Pow(2, 8) # Returns 256 (28)
```

A square root can be calculated:

```
[Math]::Sqrt(9)     # Returns 3
```

The `System.Math` class contains static properties for mathematical constants:

```
[Math]::pi     # π, 3.14159265358979
[Math]::e      # e, 2.71828182845905
```

Methods are also available to work with log, tan, sin, cos, and so on.

Converting strings to numeric values

In most cases, strings may be cast back to numeric values. For example:

```
[Int]"2"               # String to Int32
[Decimal]"3.141"       # String to Decimal
[UInt32]10             # Int32 to UInt32
[SByte]-5              # Int32 to SByte
```

For advanced conversions, the `System.Convert` class may be used. When exploring `Base64` encoding, the `Convert.To<NumericType>` method was used. This method can take a string and convert it to a number using a specified base.

A binary, base `2`, value is converted as follows:

```
[Convert]::ToInt32('01000111110101', 2)  # Returns 4597
```

Or a hexadecimal value, base `16`:

```
[Convert]::ToInt32('FF9241', 16)   # Returns 16749121
```

Supported bases are `2` (binary), `8` (octal), `10` (denary), and `16` (hexadecimal).

Date and time manipulation

`DateTime` objects may be created in a number of ways. The `Get-Date` command is one of these. The methods on the `DateTime` type has a number of static methods that might be used, and an instance of `DateTime` has methods that might be used.

DateTime parameters

While most commands deal with dates in a culture-specific format, care must be taken when passing dates (as strings) to parameters that cast to `DateTime`.

Casting to `DateTime` does not account for a cultural bias. For example, in the UK the format `dd/MM/yyyy` is often used. Casting this format to `DateTime` will switch the format to `MM/dd/yyyy` (as used in the US):

```
$string = "11/10/2000"     # 11th October 2000
[DateTime]$string          # 10th November 2000
```

If a function is created accepting a `DateTime` as a parameter, the result may not be as expected:

```
function Test-DateTime {
    param(
        [DateTime]$Date
    )
    $Date
}
Test-DateTime -Date "11/10/2000"
```

It is possible to work around this problem using the `Get-Date` command to ensure the culture specific conversion is correctly handled:

```
Test-DateTime -Date (Get-Date "11/10/2000")
```

Parsing dates

The `Get-Date` command is the best first stop for converting strings into dates. `Get-Date` deals with a reasonable number of formats.

If, however, `Get-Date` is unable to help, the `DateTime` class has two static methods that may be used:

- `ParseExact`
- `TryParseExact`

The format strings used by these methods are documented on MSDN:

https://msdn.microsoft.com/en-us/library/8kb3ddd4(v=vs.110).aspx

The `ParseExact` method accepts one or more format strings and returns a `DateTime` object:

```
$string = '20170102-2030'  # Represents 1st February 2017, 20:30
[DateTime]::ParseExact($string, 'yyyyddMM-HHmm', (Get-Culture))
```

The culture, returned from `Get-Culture`, used previously, fills in the format provider argument.

The format string uses:

- `yyyy` to represent a four-digit year
- `dd` for a two-digit day
- `MM` for a two-digit month
- `HH` for the hours in the day (24-hour format, `hh` would have been 12-hour format)

This can be extended to account for more than one date format. In this case, two variations of the format are accepted, the second expects seconds (`ss`):

```
$strings = '20170102-2030', '20170103-0931.24'
[String[]]$formats = 'yyyyddMM-HHmm', 'yyyyddMM-HHmm.ss'
foreach ($string in $strings) {
    [DateTime]::ParseExact(
        $string,
        $formats,
        (Get-Culture),
        'None'
    )
}
```

The final argument, `None`, grants greater control over the parsing process. The other possible values and the effect is documented on MSDN:

https://msdn.microsoft.com/en-us/library/91hfhz89(v=vs.110).aspx

The `TryParseExact` method has a safer failure control than `ParseExact` (which will throw an exception if it fails). The `TryParseExact` method itself returns `true` or `false` depending on whether or not it was able to parse the string. The date can be extracted using what is known as a reference. That is, a variable with the same type (`[DateTime]`) is provided as a reference; the method fills in the value of the variable via the reference:

```
$date = Get-Date     # A valid DateTime object
$string = '20170102-2030'
if ([DateTime]::TryParseExact($string,
                              'yyyyddMM-HHmm',
                              (Get-Culture),
                              'None',
                              [Ref]$date)) {
    $date
}
```

The highlighted line shows the reference to the `date` variable. The date held in this variable will be changed if `TryParseExact` succeeds.

Changing dates

A `date` object can be changed in a number of ways.

A `timespan` object can be added to or subtracted from a date:

```
(Get-Date) + (New-Timespan -Hours 6)
```

The `Date` property can be used, representing the start of the day:

```
(Get-Date).Date
```

The `Add<Interval>` methods can be used to add and subtract time, for example:

```
(Get-Date).AddDays(1) # One day from now
(Get-Date).AddDays(-1) # One day before now
```

In addition to `AddDays`, the `DateTime` object makes the following available:

```
(Get-Date).AddTicks(1)
(Get-Date).AddMilliseconds(1)
(Get-Date).AddSeconds(1)
(Get-Date).AddMinutes(1)
(Get-Date).AddHours(1)
(Get-Date).AddMonths(1)
(Get-Date).AddYears(1)
```

By default, dates returned by `Get-Date` are local (within the context of the current time zone). A date may be converted to UTC as follows:

```
(Get-Date).ToUniversalTime()
```

The `ToUniveralTime` method only changes the date if the `kind` property is set to `Local` or `Unspecified`.

The `ToLocalTime` method adjusts the date in accordance with the current (system) time zone. This operation may be performed if `kind` is `Utc` or unspecified.

A date of a specific `kind` may be created as follows, enabling appropriate use of `ToLocalTime` or `ToUniversalTime`:

```
$UtcDate = New-Object DateTime ((Get-Date).Ticks, 'Utc')
```

Dates may be converted to a string, either immediately using `Get-Date` with the `Format` parameter, or using the `ToString` method. The `Format` parameter and `ToString` method accept the same arguments.

The date strings created by the following statements are equal:

```
Get-Date -Format 'dd/MM/yyyy HH:mm'
(Get-Date).ToString('dd/MM/yyyy HH:mm')
```

The `ToString` method is useful as it means a date can be adjusted by chaining properties and methods before conversion to a string:

```
(Get-Date).ToUniversalTime().Date.AddDays(-7).ToString('dd/MM/yyyy HH:mm')
```

When storing dates, it might be considered a good practice to store dates in an unambiguous format such as a universal date time string. For example:

```
(Get-Date).ToUniversalTime().ToString('u')
```

Comparing dates

`DateTime` objects may be compared using PowerShell's comparison operators:

```
$date1 = (Get-Date).AddDays(-20)
$date2 = (Get-Date).AddDays(1)
$date2 -gt $date1
```

Dates can be compared to a string; the value on the right-hand side will be converted to a `DateTime`. As with casting with parameters, a great deal of care is required for date formats other than US.

For example, in the UK I might write the following, yet the comparison will fail. The value on the left will convert to 13th January, 2017, but the value on the right will convert to 1st December, 2017:

```
(Get-Date "13/01/2017") -gt "12/01/2017"
```

The `corrected` comparison is:

```
(Get-Date "13/01/2017") -gt "01/12/2017"
```

Summary

In this chapter, some of the methods used to work with strings were introduced. Alternate formats such as `base64` were explored along with the PowerShell commands for working with CSV formats.

Two new commands from PowerShell 5 were introduced: `Convert-String` and `ConvertFrom-String`.

Working with byte values in PowerShell was explored as well as the `power-of-10` operator.

The `System.Math` class adds a great deal of functionality, which was briefly demonstrated.

Finally, we took a brief look at working with `DateTime` objects.

In `Chapter 10`, *Regular Expressions*, we will look at regular expressions.

10
Regular Expressions

Regular expressions (**regex**) are used to perform advanced searches against the text.

For the uninitiated, anything but a trivial regular expression can be a confusing mess. To make the topic more involved, regular expressions are slightly different across different programming languages, platforms, and tools.

Given that PowerShell is built on .NET, PowerShell uses .NET style regular expressions. There are often several different ways to achieve a goal when using regular expressions.

In this chapter, we will cover the following topics:

- Regex basics
- Anchors
- Repetition
- Character classes
- Alternation
- Grouping
- Examples

Regex basics

A few basic characters can go a long way. A number of the most widely used characters and operators are introduced in this section and summarized in the following table:

<table>
<tr><th>Description</th><th>Character</th><th>Example</th></tr>
<tr><td>Literal character</td><td>Any except:
`[\^$.|?*+()`</td><td>`'a' -match 'a'`</td></tr>
<tr><td>Any single character (except carriage return, line feed, `\r`, and `\n`)</td><td>`.`</td><td>`'a' -match '.'`</td></tr>
<tr><td>The preceding character repeated zero or more times</td><td>`*`</td><td>`'abc' -match 'a*'`
`'abc' -match '.*'`</td></tr>
<tr><td>The preceding character repeated one or more times</td><td>`+`</td><td>`'abc' -match 'a+'`
`'abc' -match '.+'`</td></tr>
<tr><td>Escape a character's special meaning</td><td>`\`</td><td>`'*' -match '\*'`
`'\' -match '\\'`</td></tr>
<tr><td>Optional character</td><td>`?`</td><td>`'abc' -match 'ab?c'`
`'ac' -match 'ab?c'`</td></tr>
</table>

Debugging regular expressions

Regular expressions can quickly become complicated and difficult to understand. Modifying a complex regular expression is not a particularly simple undertaking.

While PowerShell indicates if there is a syntax error in a regular expression, it cannot do more than that; for example, PowerShell announces that there is a syntax error in the following expression:

```
PS> 'abc' -match '*'
parsing "*" - Quantifier {x,y} following nothing.
At line:1 char:1
+ 'abc' -match '*'
+ ~~~~~~~~~~~~~~~~
    + CategoryInfo : OperationStopped: (:) [], ArgumentException
    + FullyQualifiedErrorId : System.ArgumentException
```

Fortunately, there are a number of websites that can visualize a regular expression and lend an understanding of how it works against a string.

Debuggex is one such site; it can pick apart regular expressions, showing how each element applies to an example:

`https://www.debuggex.com/`

Debuggex uses Java regular expressions; some of the examples used in this chapter may not be compatible.

Online engines that are .NET specific but do not include visualization are as follows:

- `http://regexhero.net/tester/`
- `http://www.regexplanet.com/advanced/dotnet/index.html`

Finally, the website `http://www.regular-expressions.info` is an important learning resource that provides detailed descriptions, examples, and references.

Literal characters

The best place to begin is with the simplest of expressions: expressions that contain no special characters. These expressions contain what are known as literal characters. A literal character is anything except `[\^$.|?*+()`. Special characters must be escaped using `\` to avoid errors, for example:

```
'9*8'-match '\*'    # * is reserved
'1+5' -match '\+'    # + is reserved
```

Curly braces (`{}`) are considered literal in many contexts.

Except when...:
Curly braces become reserved characters if they enclose either a number, two numbers separated by a comma, or one number followed by a comma.
In the following two examples, `{ and }` are literal characters:
`'{string}' -match '{'`
`'{string}' -match '{string}'`
In the preceding example, the curly braces take on a special meaning. To match, the string would have to be `string` followed by `123` of the character `"g"`. We will explore `'string{123}' -match 'string{123}'`
`{}` in detail when discussing repetition.

The following statement returns `true` and fills the `matches` automatic variable with what matched. The `matches` variable is a hash table; it is only updated when something successfully `matches` when using the `match` operator:

```
PS> 'The first rule of regex club' -match 'regex'

True

PS> $matches

Name                           Value
----                           -----
0                              regex
```

If a `match` fails, the `matches` variable will continue to hold the last matching value:

```
PS> 'This match will fail' -match 'regex'

False

PS> $matches

Name                                               Value
----                                               -----
0                                                  regex
```

Any character (.)

The next step is to introduce a period, a dot (`.`). The dot matches any single character except the end of line characters. The following statement will return `true`:

```
'abcdef' -match '......'
```

As the previous expression matches any six characters anywhere in a string, it will also return `true` when a longer string is provided. There are no implied boundaries on the length of a string (only the number of characters matched):

```
'abcdefghijkl' -match '......'
```

Repetition with * and +

+ and * are two of a set of characters known as quantifiers. Quantifiers are discussed in great detail later in this chapter.

The * character can be used to repeat the preceding character zero or more times, for example:

```
'aaabc' -match 'a*'# Returns true, matches 'aaa'
```

However, zero or more means the character in question doesn't have to be present at all:

```
'bcd' -match 'a*'    # Returns true, matches nothing
```

If a character must be present in a string, the + quantifier is more appropriate:

```
'aaabc' -match 'a+'# Returns true, matches 'aaa'
'bcd' -match 'a+'    # Returns false
```

Combining * or + with . produces two very simple expressions: .* and .+. These expressions may be used as follows:

```
'Anything' -match '.*'     # 0 or more. Returns true
'' -match '.*'             # 0 or more. Returns true
'Anything' -match '.+'# 1 or more. Returns true
```

Attempting to use either * or + as a match without a preceding character will result in an error:

```
PS> '*' -match '*'
parsing "*" - Quantifier {x,y} following nothing.
At line:1 char:1
+ '*' -match '*'
+ ~~~~~~~~~~~~~~
    + CategoryInfo : OperationStopped: (:) [], ArgumentException
    + FullyQualifiedErrorId : System.ArgumentException
```

The escape character (\)

In this context, \ is an escape character, but it is perhaps more accurate to say that \ changes the behavior of the character that follows. For example, finding a string that contains the normally reserved character * may be accomplished using \:

```
'1 * 3' -match '\*'
```

In the following example, `\` is used to escape the special meaning of `\`, making it a literal character:

```
'domain\user' -match 'domain\\user'
'domain\user' -match '.*\\.*'
```

This technique may be used with `replace` to change the domain prefix:

```
'domain\user' -replace 'domain\\', 'newdomain\'
```

Using `\` alone will result in either an invalid expression or an unwanted expression. For example, the following expression is valid, but it does not act as you might expect. The `.` character is treated as a literal value because it is escaped. The following `match` will return `false`:

```
'domain\user' -match 'domain\.+'
```

The following string will be matched by the previous expression as the string contains a literal `.`:

```
'domain.user' -match 'domain\.+'
```

The `replace` operator will allow access to parts of these strings:

```
'Domain\User' -replace '.+\\'  # Everything up to and including \
```

Alternatively, it will `replace` everything after a character:

```
'Domain\User' -replace '\\.+' # Everything including and after \
```

Optional characters

The question mark character (`?`) can be used to make the preceding character optional. For example, there might be a need to look for either the singular or plural form of a certain word:

```
'There are 23 sites in the domain' -match 'sites?'
```

The regular expression will match the optional `s` if it can; the `?` character is greedy (takes as much as possible).

Non-printable characters

Regular expressions support searches for non-printable characters. The most common of these are shown in the following table:

Description	Character
Tab	`\t`
Line feed	`\n`
Carriage return	`\r`

Anchors

An anchor does not match a character; instead, it matches what comes before (or after) a character:

Description	Character	Example
Beginning of a string	`^`	`'aba' -match '^a'`
End of a string	`$`	`'cbc' -match 'c$'`
Word boundary	`\b`	`'Band and Land' -match '\band\b'`

Anchors are useful where a character, string, or word may appear elsewhere in a string and the position is critical.

For example, there might be a need to get values from the `PATH` environment variable that starts with a specific drive letter. One approach to this problem is to use the start of a string anchor, in this case, retrieving everything that starts with the `C` drive:

```
$env:PATH -split ';' | Where-Object { $_ -match '^C' }
```

Alternatively, there may be a need to get every path three or more directories deep from a set:

```
$env:PATH -split ';' | Where-Object { $_ -match '\\.+\\.+\\.+$' }
```

The word boundary matches both before and after a word. It allows a pattern to look for a specific word, rather than a string of characters that may be a word or a part of a word.

For example, if the intent is to `replace` the word `day` in this string, attempting this without the word boundary replaces too much:

```
'The first day is Monday' -replace 'day', 'night'
'Monday is the first day' -replace 'day', 'night'
```

Adding the word boundary avoids the problem without significantly increasing the complexity:

```
'The first day is Monday' -replace '\bday\b', 'night'
'Monday is the first day' -replace '\bday\b', 'night'
```

Repetition

A quantifier is used to repeat an element; three of the quantifiers have already been introduced: `*`, `+`, and `?`. The quantifiers are as follows:

Description	Character	Example
The preceding character repeated zero or more times	`*`	`'abc'-match 'a*'` `'abc'-match '.*'`
The preceding character repeated one or more times	`+`	`'abc'-match 'a+'` `'abc'-match '.+'`
Optional character	`?`	`'abc' -match 'ab?c'` `'ac' -match 'ab?c'`
A fixed number of characters	`{exactly}`	`'abbbc' -match 'ab{3}c'`

A number of characters within a range	`{min,max}`	`'abc' -match 'ab{1,3}c'`
		`'abbc' -match 'ab{1,3}c'`
		`'abbbc' -match 'ab{1,3}c'`

No less than a number of characters	`{min,}`	`'abbc' -match 'ab{2,}c'` `'abbbbbc' -match 'ab{2,}c'`

Each `*`, `+`, and `?` can be described using a curly brace notation:

- `*` is the same as `{0,}`
- `+` is the same as `{1,}`
- `?` is the same as `{0,1}`

It is extremely uncommon to find examples where the functionality of special characters is replaced with curly braces. It is equally uncommon to find examples where the quantifier `{1}` is used as it adds unnecessary complexity to an expression.

Exploring the quantifiers

Each of these different quantifiers is greedy. A greedy quantifier will grab as much as it possibly can before allowing the regex engine to move on to the next character in the expression.

In the following example, the expression has been instructed to match everything it can, ending with a `\` character. As a result, it takes everything up to the last `\` because the expression is greedy:

```
PS> 'C:\long\path\to\some\files' -match '.*\\'; $matches[0]
True
C:\long\path\to\some\
```

The repetition operators can be made lazy by adding the `?` character. A lazy expression will get as little as it can before it ends:

```
PS> 'C:\long\path\to\some\files' -match '.*?\\'; $matches[0]
True
C:\
```

A possible use of a lazy quantifier is parsing HTML. The following line describes a very simple HTML table. The goal is to get the first table's data (`td`) element:

```
<table><tr><td>Value1</td><td>Value2</td></tr></table>
```

Using a greedy quantifier will potentially take too much:

```
PS> $html = '<table><tr><td>Value1</td><td>Value2</td></tr></table>'
$html -match '<td>.+</td>'; $matches[0]
True
<td>Value1</td><td>Value2</td>
```

Using a character class is one possible way to solve this problem. The character class is used to take all characters except >, which denotes the end of the next `</td>` tag:

```
PS> $html = '<table><tr><td>Value1</td><td>Value2</td></tr></table>'
$html -match '<td>[^>]+</td>'; $matches[0]
True
<td>Value1</td>
```

Another way to solve a problem is to use a lazy quantifier:

```
PS> $html = '<table><tr><td>Value1</td><td>Value2</td></tr></table>'
$html -match '<td>.+?</td>'; $matches[0]
True
<td>Value1</td>
```

Character classes

A character class is used to match a single character to a set of possible characters. A character class is denoted using square brackets (`[ ]`).

For example, a character class may contain each of the vowels:

```
'get' -match 'g[aeiou]t'
'got' -match 'g[aeiou]'
```

Within a character class, the special or reserved characters are as follows:

- `-`: Used to define a range
- `\`: Escape character
- `^`: Negates the character class

Ranges

The hyphen is used to define a range of characters. For example, we might want to match any number repeated one or more times (using `+`):

```
'1st place' -match '[0-9]+'     # $matches[0] is "1"
'23rd place' -match '[0-9]+'    # $matches[0] is "23"
```

A range in a character class can be any range of ASCII characters, such as the following examples:

- `a-z`
- `A-K`
- `0-9`
- `1-5`
- `!-9` (`0-9` and the ASCII characters `33` to `47`)

The following returns `true` as " is character `34` and # is character `35` that is, they are within the range `!-9`:

```
PS> '"#' -match '[!-9]+'; $matches[0]
True
"#
```

The range notation allows hexadecimal numbers within strings to be identified. A hexadecimal character can be identified by a character class containing `0-9` and `a-f`:

```
PS> 'The registry value is 0xAF9B7' -match '0x[0-9a-f]+'; $matches[0]
True
0xAF9B7
```

If the comparison operator were case-sensitive, the character class may also define `A-F`:

```
'The registry value is 0xAF9B7' -cmatch '0x[0-9a-fA-F]+'
```

Alternatively, a range might be used to tentatively find an IP address in a string:

```
PS> (ipconfig) -match 'IPv4 Address.+: *[0-9]+\.[0-9]+\.[0-9]+\.[0-9]+'
   IPv4 Address. . . . . . . . . . . : 172.16.255.30
```

The range used to find the IP address here is very simple. It matches any string containing four numbers separated by a period, for example, the version number following matches:

```
'version 0.1.2.3234' -match '[0-9]+\.[0-9]+\.[0-9]+\.[0-9]+'
```

This IP address matching regular expressions will be improved as the chapter progresses.

The hyphen is not a reserved character when it is put in a position where it does not describe a range. If it is the first character (with no start to the range), it will be treated as a literal. The following split operation demonstrates this:

```
PS> 'one-two_three,four' -split '[-_,]'
one
two
three
four
```

The same output is seen when - is placed at the end (where there is no end to the range):

```
'one-two_three,four' -split '[_,-]'
```

Elsewhere in the class, the escape character may be used to remove the special meaning from the hyphen:

```
'one-two_three,four' -split '[_\-,]'
```

Negated character class

Within a character class, the caret (^) is used to negate the class. The character class `[aeiou]` matches vowels, negating it with the caret `[^aeiou]`, which matches any character except a vowel (including spaces, punctuation, tabs, and everything).

As with the hyphen, the caret is only effective if it is in the right position. In this case, it only negates the class if it is the first character. Elsewhere in the class, it is a literal character.

A negated character class is sometimes the fastest way to tackle a problem. If the list of expected characters is small, negating that list is a quick way to perform a match.

In the following example, the negated character class is used with the `replace` operator to fix a problem:

```
'Ba%by8 a12315tthe1231 k#.,154eyboard' -replace '[^a-z ]'
```

Character class subtraction

Character class subtraction is supported by .NET (and PowerShell). Character class subtraction is not commonly used at all.

Inside a character class, one character class may be subtracted from another (reducing the size of the overall set). One of the best examples of this extends to the character class containing vowels. The following matches the first vowel in a string:

```
'The lazy cat sat on the mat' -match '[aeiou]'
```

To match the first consonant, one approach can be to list all of the consonants:

```
'The lazy cat sat on the mat' -match '[b-df-hj-np-tv-z]'
```

Another approach to the problem is to take a larger character class, then subtract the vowels:

```
'The lazy cat sat on the mat' -match '[a-z-[aeiou]]'
```

Shorthand character classes

A number of shorthand character classes are available. The following table shows each of these:

Shorthand	Description	Character class
`\d`	Digit character	`[0-9]`
`\s`	White space (space, tab, carriage return, new line, and form feed)	`[ \t\r\n\f]`
`\w`	Word character	`[A-Za-z0-9_]`

Each of these shorthand classes can be negated by capitalizing the letter. `[^0-9]` may be represented using `\D`, `\S` for any character except whitespace, and `\W` for any character except a word character.

Alternation

The alternation (or) character in a regular expression is a pipe (`|`). This is used to combine several possible regular expressions. A simple example is to match a list of words:

```
'one', 'two', 'three' | Where-Object { $_ -match 'one|three' }
```

The alternation character has the lowest precedence; in the previous expression, every value is first tested against the expression to the left of the pipe and then against the expression to the right of the pipe.

The goal of the following expression is to extract strings that only contain the words `one` or `three`. Adding the start and the end of string anchors ensures that there is a boundary. However, because the left and right are treated as separate expressions, the result might not be as expected when using the following expression:

```
PS> 'one', 'one hundred', 'three', 'eighty three' |
Where-Object { $_ -match '^one|three$' }
one
one hundred
three
eighty three
```

The two expressions are evaluated as follows:

- Look for all strings that start with one
- Look for all strings that end with three

There are at least two possible solutions to this problem. The first is to add the start and end of string characters to both expressions:

```
'one', 'one hundred', 'three', 'eighty three' |
Where-Object { $_ -match '^one$|^three$' }
```

Another possible solution is to use a group:

```
'one', 'one hundred', 'three', 'eighty three' |
Where-Object { $_ -match '^(one|three)$' }
```

Grouping is discussed in detail in the following section.

Grouping

A group in a regular expression serves a number of different possible purposes:

- To denote repetition (of more than a single character)
- To restrict alternation to a part of the regular expression
- To capture a value

Repeating groups

Groups may be repeated using any of the quantifiers. The regular expression that tentatively identifies an IP address can be improved using a repeated group. The starting point for this expression is as follows:

```
[0-9]+\.[0-9]+\.[0-9]+\.[0-9]+
```

In this expression, the `[0-9]+` term followed by a literal `.` is repeated three times. Therefore, the expression can become as follows:

```
([0-9]+\.){3}[0-9]+
```

The expression itself is not very specific (it will match much more than an IP address), but it is now more concise. This example will be taken further later in this chapter.

If * is used as the quantifier for the group, it becomes optional. If faced with a set of version numbers ranging in formats from 1 to 1.2.3.4, a similar regular expression might be used:

```
[0-9]+(\.[0-9]+)*
```

The result of applying this to a number of different version strings is shown in the following code:

```
PS> 'v1', 'Ver 1.000.232.14', 'Version: 0.92', 'Version-7.92.1-alpha' |
    Where-Object { $_ -match '[0-9]+(\.[0-9]+)*' } |
    ForEach-Object { $matches[0] }
1
1.000.232.14
0.92
7.92.1
```

In the case of the last example, -alpha is ignored; if that were an interesting part of the version number, the expression would need to be modified to account for that.

Restricting alternation

Alternation is the lowest precedence operator. In a sense, it might be wise to consider it as describing an ordered list of regular expressions to test.

Placing an alternation statement in parentheses reduces the scope of the expression.

For example, it is possible to match a multi-line string using alternation:

```
PS> $string = @'
First line
second line
third line
'@

PS> if ($string -match 'First(.|\r?\n)*line') { $matches[0] }
First line
second line
third line
```

In this example, as . does not match the end of line character, using alternation allows each character to be tested against a broader set. In this case, each character is tested to see if it is any character, \r\n or \n.

A regular expression might be created to look for files with specific words or parts of words in the name:

```
Get-ChildItem -Recurse -File |
    Where-Object { $_.Name -match '(pwd|pass(word|wd)?).*\.(txt|doc)$' }
```

The expression that compares filenames looks for strings that contain `pwd`, `pass`, `password`, or `passwd` followed by anything with the extension `.txt` or `doc`.

This expression will match any of the following (and more):

```
pwd.txt
server passwords.doc
passwd.txt
my pass.doc
private password list.txt
```

Capturing values

The ability to capture values from a string is an incredibly useful feature of regular expressions.

When using the `match` operator, groups that have been captured are loaded into the `matches` variable (hashtable) in the order that they appear in the expression, for example:

```
PS> 'first second third' -match '(first) (second) (third)'; $matches
True

Name Value
---- -----
3    third
2    second
1    first
0    first second third
```

The first key, `0`, is always the string that matched the entire expression. Numbered keys are added to the hash table for each of the groups in the order that they appear. This applies to nested groups as well, counting from the leftmost `(`:

```
PS> 'first second third' -match '(first) ((second) (third))'; $matches
True

Name                           Value
----                           -----
4                              third
3                              second
2                              second third
1                              first
0                              first second third
```

When using the `replace` operator, the `matches` variable is not filled, but the contents of individual groups are available as tokens for use in `Replace-With`:

```
PS>'first second third' -replace '(first) ((second) (third))', '$1, $4, $2'
first, third, second third
```

Use single quotes when tokens are included:
As was mentioned in `Chapter 5`, *Operators*, single quotes should be used when using capture groups in `Replace-With`. Tokens in double quotes will expand as if they were PowerShell variables.

Named capture groups

Capture groups can be given names. The name must be unique within the regular expression.

The following syntax is used to name a group:

```
(?<GroupName>Expression)
```

This may be applied to the simple previous example:

```
PS> 'first second third' -match '(?<One>first) (?<Two>second)
(?<Three>third)'; $matches
True

Name                           Value
----                           -----
One                            first
Three                          third
Two                            second
0                              first second third
```

In PowerShell, this adds a pleasant additional capability. If the goal is to tear apart text and turn it into an object, one approach is as follows:

```
if ('first second third' -match '(first) (second) (third)') {
    [PSCustomObject]@{
        One   = $matches[1]
        Two   = $matches[2]
        Three = $matches[3]
    }
}
```

This produces an object that contains the result of each (unnamed) `match` group in a named property.

An alternative is to use named matches and create an object from the `matches` hash table. When using this approach, `$matches[0]` should be removed:

```
PS> if ('first second third' -match '(?<One>first) (?<Two>second)
(?<Three>third)') {
    $matches.Remove(0)
    [PSCustomObject]$matches
}

One Three Two
--- ----- ---
first third second
```

A possible disadvantage of the previous approach is that the output is not ordered as a hashtable.

Non-capturing groups

By default, every group is a capture group. A group can be marked as non-capturing using `?:` before the expression. In the following example, the third group has been marked as a non-capturing group:

```
PS> 'first second third' -match '(?<One>first) (?<Two>second) (?:third)';
$matches

True

Name                           Value
----                           -----
One                            first
Two                            second
0                              first second third
```

The outer group that previously added `second third` to the `matches` list is now excluded from the results:

```
PS> 'first second third' -match '(first) (?:(second) (third))'; $matches
True

Name                           Value
----                           -----
3                              third
2                              second
1                              first
0                              first second third
```

This technique may be useful when using `replace`; it simplifies the list of tokens available even if an expression grows in complexity:

```
PS> 'first second third' -replace '(first) (?:(second) (third))', '$1, $2,
$3'
first, second, third
```

Examples of regular expressions

The following examples walk you through creating regular expressions for a number of different formats.

MAC addresses

Media Access Control (**MAC**) is a unique identifier for network interface addresses with 6-byte fields normally written in hexadecimal.

Tools such as `ipconfig` show the value of a MAC address with each hexadecimal byte separated by a hyphen, for example, `1a-2b-3c-4d-5f-6d`.

Linux or Unix-based systems tend to separate each hexadecimal byte with `:`. This includes the Linux and Unix variants, VMWare, JunOS (Juniper network device operating system, based on FreeBSD), and so on, for example, `1a:2b:3c:4d:5f:6d`.

Cisco IOS shows a MAC address as three two-byte pairs separated by a period (`.`), for example, `1c2b.3c4d.5f6d`.

A regular expression can be created to simultaneously match all of these formats.

To match a single hexadecimal character, the following character class may be used:

```
[0-9a-f]
```

To account for the first two formats, a pair of hexadecimal characters is followed by a hyphen or a colon:

```
[0-9a-f]{2}[-:]
```

This pattern is repeated `5` times, followed by one last pair:

```
([0-9a-f]{2}[-:]){5}[0-9a-f]{2}
```

Adding the Cisco format into the mix will make the expression a little longer:

```
(([0-9a-f]{2}[-:]?){2}[-:.]){2}([0-9a-f]{2}[-:]?){2}
```

Another approach is to keep the formats separate and use the alternation operator to divide the two possibilities:

```
([0-9a-f]{2}[-:]){5}[0-9a-f]{2}|([0-9a-f]{4}\.){2}[0-9a-f]{4}
```

A small script can be written to test the regular expressions against some strings. In the following tests, the first pattern is expected to fail when testing against the Cisco IOS format:

```
$patterns = '^([0-9a-f]{2}[-:]){5}[0-9a-f]{2}$',
            '^(([0-9a-f]{2}[-:]?){2}[-:.]){2}([0-9a-f]{2}[-:]?){2}$',
            '^([0-9a-f]{2}[-:]){5}[0-9a-f]{2}|([0-9a-f]{4}\.){2}[0-9a-
f]{4}$'
$strings = '1a-2b-3c-4d-5f-6d',
           '1a:2b:3c:4d:5f:6d',
           '1c2b.3c4d.5f6d'
foreach ($pattern in $patterns) {
    Write-Host "Testing pattern: $pattern" -ForegroundColor Cyan
    foreach ($string in $strings) {
        if ($string -match $pattern) {
            Write-Host "${string}: Matches" -ForegroundColor Green
        } else {
            Write-Host "${string}: Failed" -ForegroundColor Red
        }
    }
}
```

IP addresses

Validating an IPv4 address using a regular expression is not necessarily a trivial task.

The IP address consists of four octets; each octet can be a value between 0 and 255. When using a regular expression, the values are considered to be strings, therefore the following strings must be considered:

- `[0-9]`: `0` to `9`
- `[1-9][0-9]`: `1` to `9`, then `0` to `9` (10 to 99)
- `1[0-9]{2}`: `1`, then `0` to `9`, then `0` to `9` (100 to 199)
- `2[0-4][0-9]`: `2`, then `0` to `4`, then `0` to `9` (200 to 249)
- `25[0-5]`: `2`, then `5`, then `0` to `5` (250 to 255)

Each of these is an exclusive set, so alternation is used to merge all of the previous small expressions into a single expression. This generates the following group that matches a single octet (`0` to `255`):

```
([0-9]|[1-9][0-9]|1[0-9]{2}|2[0-4][0-9]|25[0-5])
```

IP address validation contains repetition now; four octets with a period between each:

```
(([0-9]|[1-9][0-9]|1[0-9]{2}|2[0-4][0-9]|25[0-5])\.){3}([0-9]|[1-9][0-9]|1[
0-9]{2}|2[0-4][0-9]|25[0-5])
```

There are other, perhaps better, ways than such a long regex. If a string is a strong candidate for being an IP address, consider using the `TryParse` static method on the `IPAddress` type. It will handle both v4 and v6 addressing:

```
$ipAddress = [IPAddress]0 # Used as a placeholder
if ([IPAddress]::TryParse("::1", [ref]$ipAddress)) {
$ipAddress
}
```

Netstat command

The netstat command produces tab-delimited, fixed-width tables. The following example converts the active connections that list active TCP connections as well as listening TCP and UDP ports to an object.

A snippet of the output the example is intended to parse is shown in the following code:

```
PS> netstat -ano

Active Connections

  Proto Local Address Foreign Address State PID
  TCP 0.0.0.0:135 0.0.0.0:0 LISTENING 124
  TCP 0.0.0.0:445 0.0.0.0:0 LISTENING 4
  TCP 0.0.0.0:5357 0.0.0.0:0 LISTENING 4
```

When handling text such as this, a pattern based on whitespace (or not whitespace) can be used:

```
^\s*\S+\s+\S+
```

For each column, the following expression with a named group is created:

```
(?<ColumnName>\S+)\s+
```

The trailing `\s+` is omitted for the last column (`PID`):

```
^\s*(?<Protocol>\S+)\s+(?<LocalAddress>\S+)\s+(?<ForeignAddress>\S+)\s+(?<S
tate>\S+)\s+(?<PID>\d+)$
```

The expression is long but incredibly repetitive. The repetition is desirable in this case, where each column value is being pushed into a different named group.

The expression can be applied using `Where-Object`:

```
$regex =
'^\s*(?<Protocol>\S+)\s+(?<LocalAddress>\S+)\s+(?<ForeignAddress>\S+)\s+(?<
State>\S+)\s+(?<PID>\d+)$'
netstat -ano | Where-Object { $_ -match $regex } | ForEach-Object {
    $matches.Remove(0)
    [PSCustomObject]$matches
}
```

Unfortunately, the output from this command will be missing the information about UDP ports. The regular expression makes having a value in the state column mandatory. Marking this group as optional will add UDP connection information to the output:

```
(State>\S+)?
```

Inserting it back into the regular expression is as shown following:

```
$regex =
'^\s*(?<Protocol>\S+)\s+(?<LocalAddress>\S+)\s+(?<ForeignAddress>\S+)\s+(?<
State>\S+)?\s+(?<PID>\d+)$'
netstat -ano | Where-Object { $_ -match $regex } | ForEach-Object {
    $matches.Remove(0)
    [PSCustomObject]$matches
}
```

Finally, if it is desirable to return the fields in the same order as `netstat` does, `Select-Object` may be used:

```
PS>$regex =
'^\s*(?<Protocol>\S+)\s+(?<LocalAddress>\S+)\s+(?<ForeignAddress>\S+)\s+(?<
State>\S+)\s+(?<PID>\d+)$'
PS>
PS> netstat -ano | Where-Object { $_ -match $regex } | ForEach-Object {
    $matches.Remove(0)
    [PSCustomObject]$matches
} | Select-Object Protocol, LocalAddress, ForeignAddress, State, PID |
    Format-Table


Protocol LocalAddress ForeignAddress State     PID
-------- ------------ -------------- -----     ---
TCP      0.0.0.0:135  0.0.0.0:0      LISTENING 124
TCP      0.0.0.0:445  0.0.0.0:0      LISTENING 4
TCP      0.0.0.0:5357 0.0.0.0:0      LISTENING 4
```

Summary

In this chapter, we have taken a look at regular expressions and their use in PowerShell.

The *Regex basics* section introduce a number of heavily used characters. Anchors showing how the start and end of a string or a word boundary may be used to restrict the scope of an expression.

Character classes were introduced as a powerful form of alternation, providing a range of options for matching a single character. Alternation was demonstrated using different sets of expressions to be evaluated.

We looked at repetition using `"*"`, `+`, `?`, and curly braces and discussed the notion of greedy and lazy.

Grouping was introduced as a means of limiting the scope of alternation to repeat larger expressions or to capture strings.

Finally, a number of examples were included, bringing together the areas covered in this chapter to solve specific problems.

In `Chapter 11`, *Files, Folders and the Registry*, working with files, folders, and registry will be discussed.

11
Files, Folders, and the Registry

The filesystem and the registry are two of the number of providers available in PowerShell. A provider represents a data store as a filesystem.

The commands used to work with the data within a particular provider, such as the filesystem, are common to all providers.

In this chapter, we will cover the following topics:

- Working with providers
- Items
- Item properties
- Item attributes
- Permissions
- Transactions
- File catalogs

Working with providers

Each of the providers shares a common set of commands, such as `Set-Location`, `Get-Item`, and `New-Item`.

Navigating

`Set-Location`, which has the alias `cd`, is used to navigate around a provider's hierarchy; for example:

```
Set-Location \   # The root of the current drive
Set-Location Windows # A child container named Windows
Set-Location .. # Navigate up one level
Set-Location ..\.. # Navigate up two levels
Set-Location Cert: # Change to a different drive
Set-Location HKLM:\Software # Change to a specific child container under a
drive
```

`Set-Location` may only be used to switch to a container object.

The print working directory (`pwd`) variable shows the current location across all providers:

```
PS> $pwd

Path
----
HKLM:\Software\Microsoft\Windows\CurrentVersion
```

pwd and .NET:
.NET classes and methods are oblivious to PowerShell's current directory. When the following command is executed, the file will be created in the `Start in` path (if a shortcut started PowerShell):
`[System.IO.File]::WriteAllLines('file.txt', 'Some content')`
.NET constructors and methods are an ideal place to use the `pwd` variable:
`[System.IO.File]::WriteAllLines("$pwd\file.txt", 'Some content')`

Getting items

The `Get-Item` command is used to get an object represented by a path:

```
Get-Item \ # The root container
Get-Item .  # The current container
Get-Item .. # The parent container
Get-Item C:\Windows\System32\cmd.exe  # A leaf item
Get-Item Cert:\LocalMachine\Root#A container item
```

The `Get-ChildItem` command, which has the aliases of `dir` and `ls`, is used to list the children of the current item.

Both `Get-ChildItem` and `Get-Item` will not show hidden files and folders by default. The following error will be returned for a hidden item:

```
PS> Get-Item $env:USERPROFILE\AppData
Get-Item : Could not find item C:\Users\Someone\AppData.
At line:1 char:1
+ Get-Item $env:USERPROFILE\AppData
+ ~~~~~~~~~~~~~~~~~~~~~~~~~~~~~~~~~~~
    + CategoryInfo : ObjectNotFound: (C:\Users\Someone \AppData:String)
[Get-Item], IOException
    + FullyQualifiedErrorId :
ItemNotFound,Microsoft.PowerShell.Commands.GetItemCommand
```

The `Force` parameter may be added to access hidden items:

```
PS> Get-Item $env:USERPROFILE\AppData -Force

    Directory: C:\Users\Someone

Mode                LastWriteTime         Length Name
----                -------------         ------ ----
d--h--       23/09/2016     18:22                AppData
```

Drives

PowerShell will automatically create a drive for any disk with a drive letter, any existing shared drive, the `HKEY_LOCAL_MACHINE` and `HKEY_CURRENT_USER` registry hives, the certificate store, and so on.

Additional drives may be added using `New-PSDrive`; for example, a network drive can be created:

```
New-PSDrive X -PSProvider FileSystem -Root \\Server\Share
New-PSDrive HKCR -PSProvider Registry -Root HKEY_CLASSES_ROOT
```

Existing drives may be removed using `Remove-PSDrive`. PowerShell allows filesystem drives to be removed; however, this is not a destructive operation, and it only removes the reference to the drive from PowerShell.

The filesystem provider supports the use of credentials when creating a drive, allowing network shares to be mapped using specific credentials.

Items

Support for each of the `*-Item` commands varies from one provider to another. The filesystem provider supports all of the commands, while the `Registry` provider supports a smaller number.

Testing existence

The `Test-Path` command may be used to test the existence of a specific item under a drive:

```
Test-Path HKLM:\Software\Publisher
```

`Test-path` distinguishes between item types with the `PathType` parameter. The terms container and leaf are used across providers to broadly classify items.

When working with the filesystem, a container is a directory (or folder) and a leaf is a file. In the registry, a key is a container and there are no leaves. In the certificate provider, a store or store location is a container and a certificate is a leaf.

The following commands test for items of differing types:

```
Test-Path C:\Windows -PathType Container
Test-Path C:\Windows\System32\cmd.exe -PathType Leaf
```

The `Test-Path` command is often used in an `if` statement prior to creating a file or directory:

```
if (-not (Test-Path C:\Temp\NewDirectory -PathType Container)) {
    New-Item C:\Temp\NewDirectory -ItemType Directory
}
```

Get-Item, Test-Path, and pagefile.sys:
Some files in Windows are locked, to the extent where `Get-Item` and `Test-Path` are unable to correctly return results. The `pagefile.sys` file is one of these.
`Get-Item` returns an error, indicating that the file does not exist, even when the `Force` parameter is used. `Test-Path` always returns `false`. This may be considered to be a bug. To work around the problem, `Get-ChildItem` is able to get the file:
`Get-ChildItem C:\ -Filter pagefile.sys -Force`
To replace the functionality of `Test-Path`, the static method `Exists` may be used:
`[System.IO.File]::Exists('c:\pagefile.sys')`

Creating and deleting items

The `New-Item` command is able to create files, directories, and keys:

```
New-Item $env:Temp\newfile.txt -ItemType File
New-Item $env:Temp\newdirectory -ItemType Directory
New-Item HKLM:\Software\NewKey -ItemType Key
```

When creating a file using `New-Item` in PowerShell, the file is empty (0 bytes).

In PowerShell 5, `New-Item` gained the ability to create symbolic links, junctions, and hard links:

- A symbolic link is a link to another file or directory. Creating a symbolic link requires administrator privileges (run as administrator)
- A hard link is a link to another file on the same drive
- A junction is a link to another directory on any local drive. Creating a junction does not require administrative privileges

The links may be created as follows:

```
New-Item LinkName -ItemType SymbolicLink -Value \\Server\Share
New-Item LinkName.txt -ItemType HardLink -Value OriginalName.txt
New-Item LinkName -ItemType Junction -Value C:\Temp
```

Temporary files:
If a script needs a file to temporarily store data, the `New-TemporaryFile` command may be used:
`New-TemporaryFile`
This command was introduced with PowerShell 5. The earlier versions of PowerShell may use the `Path.GetTempFileName` static method:
`[System.IO.Path]::GetTempFileName()`
Both commands create an empty file. The resulting file may be used with `Set-Content`, `Out-File`, or any of the commands that write data to a file.

The `Remove-Item` command may be used to remove an existing item under a provider; for example:

```
$file = [System.IO.Path]::GetTempFileName()
Set-Content -Path $file -Value 'Temporary: 10'
Remove-Item $file
```

Providers such as filesystem and registry are reasonably flexible about removing items. When removing a directory or key with children, the `recurse` parameter should be used.

The `certificate` provider restricts the use of `Remove-Item` to certificates; certificate stores cannot be removed.

Invoking items

`Invoke-Item` (which has an alias, ii) has a number of different uses. `Invoke-Item` will open or execute an object using the default settings for that file:

```
Invoke-Item .    # Open the current directory in explorer
Invoke-Item test.ps1    # Open test.ps1 in the default editor
Invoke-Item $env:windir\system32\cmd.exe    # Open cmd
Invoke-Item Cert:# Open the certificate store MMC for the current user
```

The registry provider does not support `Invoke-Item`.

Item properties

The `Get-ItemProperty` and `Set-ItemProperty` commands allow individual properties to be modified.

Filesystem properties

When working with the filesystem provider, `Get-ItemProperty` and `Set-ItemProperty` are rarely needed. For example, `Set-ItemProperty` might be used to make a file read-only. The following example assumes that the `somefile.txt` file already exists:

```
-
```

The same property may be directly set from a file object retrieved using `Get-Item` (or `Get-ChildItem`):

```
(Get-Item 'somefile.txt').IsReadOnly = $true
```

The `IsReadOnly` flag affects the attributes of the file object, adding the `ReadOnly` flag.

Adding and removing file attributes

The attributes property of a file object is a bit field presented as a number and given an easily understandable value by the `System.IO.FileAttributes` enumeration.

Bit fields:
A bit-field is a means of exposing multiple settings that have two states (on or off binary states) using a single number.
A byte, an 8-bit value, can therefore hold eight possible settings. A 32-bit integer, 4 bytes long, can hold 32 different settings.
The following table, whose state is described by `4` bits, has four settings:
Name: `Setting4Setting3Setting2Setting1`
State: `On Off On Off`
Binary: `1 0 1 0`
Decimal: `8 4 2 1`
When settings `2` and `4` are toggled on, the value of the field is the conversion of `1010` to decimal. This value is the result of `8 -bor 4`, that is, `12`.

A number of the possible attributes are shown in the following table:

Name	Compressed	Archive	System	Hidden	Read-only
Bit value	2048	32	4	2	1

When a file is hidden and read-only, the value of the attributes property is `3 (2 + 1)`. The value `3` can be cast the `FileAttributes` type that shows the names of the individual flags:

```
PS> [System.IO.FileAttributes]3
ReadOnly, Hidden
```

While the value is numeric, the use of the enumeration means words can be used to describe each property:

```
PS> [System.IO.FileAttributes]'ReadOnly, Hidden' -eq 3
True
```

This opens up a number of possible ways to set attributes on a file.

The attributes may be replaced entirely:

```
(Get-Item 'somefile.txt').Attributes = 'ReadOnly, Hidden'
```

The attributes may be toggled:

```
$file = Get-Item 'somefile.txt'
$file.Attributes = $file.Attributes -bxor 'ReadOnly'
```

Attributes may be added:

```
$file = Get-Item 'somefile.txt'
$file.Attributes = $file.Attributes -bor 'ReadOnly'
```

The operators +, -, +=, and -= may be used, as this is a numeric operation. Addition or subtraction operations are not safe, as they do not account for existing flags. For example, if a file was already read-only and += was used to attempt to make the file read-only, the result would be a hidden file:

```
PS> $file = Get-Item 'somefile.txt'
$file.Attributes = 'ReadOnly'
$file.Attributes += 'ReadOnly'
$file.Attributes

Hidden
```

Finally, regardless of whether or not a flag is present, attributes may be written as a string:

```
$file = Get-Item 'somefile.txt'
$file.Attributes = "$($file.Attributes), ReadOnly"
```

This is a feasible approach because casting to the enumeration type will ignore any duplication:

```
PS> [System.IO.FileAttributes]'ReadOnly, Hidden, ReadOnly'
ReadOnly, Hidden
```

Registry values

`Get-ItemProperty` and `Set-ItemProperty` are most useful when manipulating registry values.

The following method may be used to get values from the registry:

```
Get-ItemProperty -Path HKCU:\Environment
Get-ItemProperty -Path HKCU:\Environment -Name Path
Get-ItemProperty -Path HKCU:\Environment -Name Path, Temp
```

Individual values may be written back to the registry under an existing key:

```
Set-ItemProperty -Path HKCU:\Environment -Name NewValue -Value 'New'
```

A value may be subsequently removed:

```
Remove-ItemProperty -Path HKCU:\Environment -Name NewValue
```

The `Set-ItemProperty` command does not directly allow the value type to be influenced. The command will do as much as it can to fit the value into the existing type. For a property with type `REG_SZ`, numbers will be converted to strings.

If a value does not already exist, a registry type will be created according to the value type:

- `Int32`: `REG_DWORD`
- `Int64`: `REG_QWORD`
- `String`: `REG_SZ`
- `String[]`: `REG_MULTI_SZ (must use "[String[]]@('value', 'value')")`
- `Byte[]`: `REG_BINARY`
- **Any other type**: `REG_SZ`

If a value of a specific type is required, the `New-ItemProperty` command should be used instead, for instance; if an expanding string must be created:

```
New-ItemProperty HKCU:\Environment -Name Expand -Value 'User: %USERNAME%' -
PropertyType ExpandString
```

`New-ItemProperty` will throw an error if a property already exists. The `Force` parameter may be used to overwrite an existing value with the same name.

Permissions

The filesystem and registry providers both support `Get-Acl` and `Set-Acl`, which allow the different access control lists to be modified.

Working with permissions in PowerShell involves a mixture of PowerShell commands and .NET objects and methods.

While some of the values and classes differ between the different providers, many of the same concepts apply.

The following snippet creates a set of files and folders in `C:\Temp`. These files and folders are used in the examples that follow:

```
New-Item C:\Temp\ACL -ItemType Directory -Force
1..5 | ForEach-Object {
New-Item C:\Temp\ACL\$_ -ItemType Directory -Force
'content' | Out-File "C:\Temp\ACL\$_\$_.txt"
New-Item C:\Temp\ACL\$_\$_ -ItemType Directory -Force
'content' | Out-File "C:\Temp\ACL\$_\$_\$_.txt"
}
```

The `Get-Acl` command is used to retrieve an existing **Access Control List** (**ACL**) for an object. `Set-Acl` is used to apply an updated `ACL` to an object.

If `Get-Acl` is used against a directory, the `ACL` type is `DirectorySecurity`; for a file, the `ACL` type is `FileSecurity`; and for a registry key, the `ACL` type is `RegistrySecurity`.

Ownership

Ownership of a file or directory may be changed using the `SetOwner` method of the `ACL` object. Changing the ownership of a file requires administrative privileges.

The owner of the `C:\Temp\ACL\1` file is the current user:

```
PS> Get-Acl C:\Temp\ACL\1 | Select-Object Owner

Owner
-----
COMPUTER\Chris
```

The owner may be changed (in this case, to the `Administrator` account) using the `SetOwner` method:

```
$acl = Get-Acl C:\Temp\ACL\1
$acl.SetOwner(
[System.Security.Principal.NTAccount]'Administrator'
)
Set-Acl C:\Temp\ACL\1 -AclObject $acl
```

This is not taking ownership:
Setting ownership when the current user already has full control is one thing. Very specific privileges are required to take ownership without existing permission:
`SeRestorePrivilege`, `SeBackupPrivilege`, and `SeTakeOwnershipPrivilege`.

Access and audit

Access lists come with two different types of access controls.

The **Discretionary Access Control List** (**DACL**) is used to grant (or deny) access to a resource. The DACL is referred to as `Access` in PowerShell.

The **System Access Control List** (**SACL**) is used to define which activities should be audited. The SACL is referred to as `Audit` in PowerShell.

Reading and setting the audit `ACL` requires administrator privileges (run as administrator). `Get-Acl` will only attempt to read the audit `ACL` if it is explicitly requested. The `Audit` switch parameter is used to request the list:

```
Get-Acl C:\Temp\ACL\1 -Audit | Format-List
```

As none of the folders created have audit ACLs at this time, the `Audit` property will be blank.

Rule protection

Access control lists, by default, inherit rules from parent container objects. Access rule protection blocks propagation of rules from a parent object.

Rule protection can be enabled for the `Access` ACL using the `SetAccessRuleProtection` method or for the `Audit` ACL using the `SetAuditRuleProtection` method.

Setting rule protection has the same effect as disabling inheritance in the GUI.

Each of the methods expects two arguments. The first argument, `isProtected`, dictates whether or not the list should be protected. The second argument, `preserveInheritance`, dictates what should be done with existing inherited entries. Inherited entries can either be copied or discarded.

In the following example, the access rule protection is enabled (inheritance is disabled) and the previously inherited rules are copied into the `ACL`:

```
$acl = Get-Acl C:\Temp\ACL\2
$acl.SetAccessRuleProtection($true, $true)
Set-Acl C:\Temp\ACL\2 -AclObject $acl
```

Copied rules will only appear on the `ACL` (as explicit rules) after `Set-Acl` has been run.

If access rule protection is subsequently re-enabled, the copied rules are not removed. The resulting `ACL` will contain both inherited and explicit versions of each of the rules. Inheritance can be re-enabled as follows:

```
$acl = Get-Acl C:\Temp\ACL\2
$acl.SetAccessRuleProtection($false, $false)
Set-Acl C:\Temp\ACL\2 -AclObject $acl
```

The access control list will have doubled in length:

```
PS> Get-PSProvider

NamePS> Get-Acl 2 | Select-Object -ExpandProperty Access |
    Select-Object FileSystemRights, IdentityReference, IsInherited

           FileSystemRights IdentityReference                  IsInherited
           ---------------- -----------------                  -----------
                 -536805376 NT AUTHORITY\Authenticated Users         False
        Modify, Synchronize NT AUTHORITY\Authenticated Users         False
                FullControl NT AUTHORITY\SYSTEM                      False
                  268435456 NT AUTHORITY\SYSTEM                      False
                  268435456 BUILTIN\Administrators                   False
                FullControl BUILTIN\Administrators                   False
ReadAndExecute, Synchronize BUILTIN\Users                            False
                FullControl BUILTIN\Administrators                    True
                  268435456 BUILTIN\Administrators                    True
                FullControl NT AUTHORITY\SYSTEM                       True
                  268435456 NT AUTHORITY\SYSTEM                       True
ReadAndExecute, Synchronize BUILTIN\Users                             True
        Modify, Synchronize NT AUTHORITY\Authenticated Users          True
                 -536805376 NT AUTHORITY\Authenticated Users          True
Capabilities                             Drives
----         ------------                ------
```

```
Registry        ShouldProcess, Transactions            {HKLM, HKCU}
Alias           ShouldProcess                          {Alias}
Environment     ShouldProcess                          {Env}
FileSystem      Filter, ShouldProcess, Credentials     {B, C, D}
Function        ShouldProcess                          {Function}
Variable        ShouldProcess                          {Variable}
```

Discarding the access rules will result in an empty `ACL`:

```
$acl = Get-Acl C:\Temp\ACL\3
$acl.SetAccessRuleProtection($true, $false)
Set-Acl C:\Temp\ACL\3 -AclObject $acl
```

Once this operation completes, any attempt to access the directory will result in access denied:

```
PS> Get-ChildItem C:\Temp\ACL\3
Get-ChildItem : Access to the path 'C:\Temp\ACL\3' is denied.
At line:1 char:1
+ Get-ChildItem C:\Temp\ACL\3
+ ~~~~~~~~~~~~~~~~~~~~~~~~~~~~
    + CategoryInfo : PermissionDenied: (C:\Temp\ACL\3:String) [Get-
ChildItem], UnauthorizedAccessException
    + FullyQualifiedErrorId :
DirUnauthorizedAccessError,Microsoft.PowerShell.Commands.GetChildItemComman
d
```

Access to the folder can be restored provided the current user has the `SeSecurityPrivilege` privilege, granted to users with administrative privileges (run as administrator). Re-enabling inheritance is the simplest method, although we might have taken the opportunity to add rules:

```
$acl = Get-Acl C:\Temp\ACL\3
$acl.SetAccessRuleProtection($false, $false)
Set-Acl C:\Temp\ACL\3 -AclObject $acl
```

In the previous example, the second argument for `SetAccessRuleProtection`, `preserveInheritance`, is set to `false`. This value has no impact; it only dictates behavior when access rule protection is enabled.

This loss of access does not apply when using the `SetAuditRuleProtection` method, as it does not describe who or what can access an object.

Inheritance and propagation flags

Inheritance and propagation flags dictate how individual access control entries are pushed down to child objects.

Inheritance flags are described by the `System.Security.AccessControl.InheritanceFlags` enumeration. The possible values are as follows:

- `None`: Objects will not inherit this access control entry
- `ContainerInherit`: Only container objects (such as directories) will inherit this entry
- `ObjectInherit`: Only leaf objects (such as files) will inherit this entry

Propagation flags are described by the `System.Security.AccessControl.PropagationFlags` enumeration. The possible values are:

- `None`: Propagation of inheritance is not changed
- `NoPropagateInherit`: Do not propagate inheritance flags
- `InheritOnly`: This entry does not apply to this object, only children

These two flag fields are used to build the `Applies to` option shown in the graphical user interface when setting security on a folder. The following table shows how each option is created:

Option	**Flags**
This folder only	• Inheritance: `None` • Propagation: `None`
This folder, subfolders, and files	• Inheritance: `ContainerInherit`, `ObjectInherit` • Propagation: `None`
This folder and subfolders	• Inheritance: `ContainerInherit` • Propagation: `None`
This folder and files	• Inheritance: `ObjectInherit` • Propagation: `None`
Subfolders only	• Inheritance: `ContainerInherit` • Propagation: `InheritOnly`

Files only	• Inheritance: `ObjectInherit` • Propagation: `InheritOnly`

The `NoPropagateInherit` propagation flag comes into play when the tick-box only applies these permissions to objects and/or containers ticked within this container. This may be used with all but in this folder, only right (where it has no effect).

Removing access control entries

Individual rules may be removed from an access control list using a number of different methods:

- `RemoveAccessRule`: Matches `IdentityReference` and `AccessMask`
- `RemoveAccessRuleAll`: Matches `IdentityReference`
- `RemoveAccessRuleSpecific`: Exact match

The access mask is a generic term used to refer to the specific rights granted (filesystem rights for a file or directory and registry rights for a registry key).

To demonstrate rule removal, explicit entries might be added to `ACL`. Enabling, then disabling, access rule protection will add new rules: the original inherited set and an explicitly set copy of the same rules.

To enable access rule protection and copy inherited rules:

```
$acl = Get-Acl C:\Temp\ACL\3
$acl.SetAccessRuleProtection($true, $true)
Set-Acl C:\Temp\ACL\3 -AclObject $acl
```

In disable protection, once committed, the inherited rules will appear alongside the copied rules:

```
$acl = Get-Acl C:\Temp\ACL\3
$acl.SetAccessRuleProtection($false, $true)
Set-Acl C:\Temp\ACL\3 -AclObject $acl
```

The rules may be viewed on ACL:

```
PS> $acl = Get-Acl C:\Temp\ACL\3
$acl.Access | Select-Object IdentityReference, FileSystemRights,
IsInherited

IdentityReference                            FileSystemRights IsInherited
-----------------                            ---------------- -----------
NT AUTHORITY\Authenticated Users                   -536805376       False
NT AUTHORITY\Authenticated Users          Modify, Synchronize       False
NT AUTHORITY\SYSTEM                               FullControl       False
NT AUTHORITY\SYSTEM                                 268435456       False
BUILTIN\Administrators                              268435456       False
BUILTIN\Administrators                            FullControl       False
BUILTIN\Users                     ReadAndExecute, Synchronize       False
BUILTIN\Administrators                            FullControl        True
BUILTIN\Administrators                              268435456        True
NT AUTHORITY\SYSTEM                               FullControl        True
NT AUTHORITY\SYSTEM                                 268435456        True
BUILTIN\Users                     ReadAndExecute, Synchronize        True
NT AUTHORITY\Authenticated Users          Modify, Synchronize        True
NT AUTHORITY\Authenticated Users                   -536805376        True
```

The following example finds each of the explicit rules and removes each from ACL:

```
$acl = Get-Acl C:\Temp\ACL\3
$acl.Access |
Where-Object { -not $_.IsInherited } |
    ForEach-Object{ $acl.RemoveAccessRuleSpecific($_) }
Set-Acl C:\Temp\ACL\3 -AclObject $acl
```

Copying lists and entries

Access lists can be copied from one object to another; for example, a template ACL might have been prepared:

```
$acl = Get-Acl C:\Temp\ACL\4
$acl.SetAccessRuleProtection($true, $true)
$acl.Access |
Where-Object IdentityReference -like '*\Authenticated Users' |
ForEach-Object { $acl.RemoveAccessRule($_) }
Set-Acl C:\Temp\ACL\4 -AclObject $acl
```

This `ACL` can be applied to another object:

```
$acl = Get-Acl C:\Temp\ACL\4
Set-Acl C:\Temp\ACL\5 -AclObject $acl
```

If `ACL` contains a mixture of inherited and explicit entries, the inherited entries will be discarded.

Access control rules may be copied in a similar manner:

```
# Get the ACE to copy
$ace = (Get-Acl C:\Temp\ACL\3).Access |
Where-Object {
$_.IdentityReference -like '*\Authenticated Users' -and
$_.FileSystemRights -eq 'Modify, Synchronize' -and
-not $_.IsInherited
}
# Get the target ACL
$acl = Get-Acl C:\Temp\ACL\5
# Add the entry
$acl.AddAccessRule($ace)
# Apply the change
Set-Acl C:\Temp\ACL\5 -AclObject $acl
```

Adding access control entries

Access control entries must be created before they can be added to an access control list.

Creating an **Access Control Entry** (**ACE**) for the filesystem or the registry and for access or audit purposes uses a set of .NET classes:

- `System.Security.AccessControl.FileSystemAccessRule`
- `System.Security.AccessControl.FileSystemAuditRule`
- `System.Security.AccessControl.RegistryAccessRule`
- `System.Security.AccessControl.RegistryAuditRule`

There are a number of different ways to use the classes; this section focuses on the most common of those.

Filesystem rights

The filesystem access control entry uses the `System.Security.AccessControl.FileSystemRights` enumeration to describe the different rights that might be granted.

PowerShell is able to list each of the names using the `GetNames` (or `GetValues`) static methods of the `Enum` type:

```
[Enum]::GetNames([System.Security.AccessControl.FileSystemRights])
```

MSDN is a better place to find the meaning of each of the different flags:

https://msdn.microsoft.com/en-us/library/system.security.accesscontrol.filesystemrights(v=vs.110).aspx

This is a bit-field, and can therefore be treated in the same way as `FileAttributes` were earlier in this chapter. The simplest way to present rights is in a comma-separated list. There is a large number of possible combinations; the graphical user interface shows a small number of these before heading into advanced. These options are shown in the following table:

GUI option	**Filesystem rights**
Full control	`FullControl`
Modify	`Modify, Synchronize`
Read and execute	`ReadAndExecute, Synchronize`
List folder contents	`ReadAndExecute, Synchronize`
Read	`Read, Synchronize`
Write	`Write, Synchronize`

The previous table shows that both read and execute and list folder contents have the same value. This is, simply put, because the access mask is the same. The difference is in the inheritance flags:

GUI option	**Inheritance flags**
Read and execute	`ContainerInherit, ObjectInherit`
List folder contents	`ContainerInherit`

In all other cases, the inheritance flags are set to `ContainerInherit, ObjectInherit`. Propagation flags are set to `None` for all examples.

Using these, a full control ACE can be created using one of the constructors for `FileSystemAccessRule`:

```
$ace = New-Object System.Security.AccessControl.FileSystemAccessRule(
    'DOMAIN\User',     # Identity reference
    'FullControl',     # FileSystemRights
    'ContainerInherit, ObjectInherit',  # InheritanceFlags
    'None',          # PropagationFlags
    'Allow'          # ACE type (allow or deny)
)
```

This `ACE` can be applied to `ACL`:

```
$acl = Get-Acl C:\Temp\ACL\5
$acl.AddAccessRule($ace)
Set-Acl C:\Temp\ACL\5 -AclObject $acl
```

Registry rights

Creating access control entries for registry keys follows exactly the same pattern as for filesystem rights. The rights are defined in the `System.Security.AccessControl.RegistryRights` enumeration.

PowerShell is able to list these rights, but the descriptions on MSDN are more useful:

`https://msdn.microsoft.com/en-us/library/system.security.accesscontrol.registryrights(v=vs.110).aspx`

A rule is created in the same way as the filesystem rule:

```
$ace = New-Object System.Security.AccessControl.RegistryAccessRule(
    'DOMAIN\User',     # Identity reference
    'FullControl',     # RegistryRights
    'ContainerInherit, ObjectInherit',  # InheritanceFlags
    'None',          # PropagationFlags
    'Allow'          # ACE type (allow or deny)
)
```

The rule can be applied to a key (in this case, a newly created key):

```
$key = New-Item HKCU:\TestKey -ItemType Key -Force
$acl = Get-Acl $key.PSPath
$acl.AddAccessRule($ace)
Set-Acl $key.PSPath -AclObject $acl
```

Transactions

A transaction allows a set of changes to be grouped together and committed at the same time.

The registry provider supports transactions, as shown in the following code:

```
PS> Get-PSProvider

Name            Capabilities                          Drives
----            ------------                          ------
Registry        ShouldProcess, Transactions           {HKLM, HKCU}
Alias           ShouldProcess                         {Alias}
Environment     ShouldProcess                         {Env}
FileSystem      Filter, ShouldProcess, Credentials    {B, C, D}
Function        ShouldProcess                         {Function}
Variable        ShouldProcess                         {Variable}
```

A transaction may be created as follows:

```
Start-Transaction
$path = 'HKCU:\TestTransaction'
New-Item $path -ItemType Key -UseTransaction
Set-ItemProperty $path -Name 'Name' -Value 'Transaction' -UseTransaction
Set-ItemProperty $path -Name 'Length' -Value 20 -UseTransaction
```

At this point, the transaction may be undone:

```
Undo-Transaction
```

Alternatively, the transaction may be committed:

```
Complete-Transaction
```

A list of the commands that support transactions may be viewed, although not all of these may be used with the registry provider:

```
Get-Command -ParameterName UseTransaction
```

File catalogs

A file catalog is a new feature with Windows PowerShell 5.1. A file catalog is a reasonably lightweight form of **File Integrity Monitoring (FIM)**. The file catalog generates and stores SHA1 hashes for each file within a folder structure and writes the result to a catalog file.

About hashing:
Hashing is a one-way process; a hash is not an encryption or encoding. A hash algorithm converts data of any length to a fixed-length value. The length of the value depends on the hashing algorithm used.

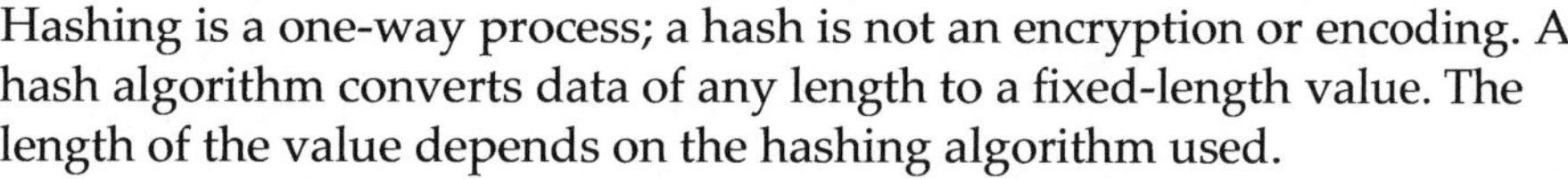

MD5 hashing is one of the more common algorithms; it produces a 128-bit hash that can be represented by a 32-character string.
SHA1 is rapidly becoming the default; it produces a 160-bit hash that can be represented by a 40-character string.
PowerShell has a `Get-FileHash` command that can be used to calculate the hash for a file.

As the catalog is the basis for determining integrity, it should be maintained in a secure location, away from the set of files being analyzed.

New-FileCatalog

The `New-FileCatalog` command is used to generate (or update) a catalog:

```
New-FileCatalog -Path <ToWatch> -CatalogFilePath <StateFile>
```

A hash can only be generated for files that are larger than 0 bytes. However, file names are recorded irrespective of the size.

The following command creates a file catalog from the files and folders created when exploring permissions:

```
New-FileCatalog -Path C:\Temp\ACL -CatalogFilePath
C:\Temp\Security\example.cat
```

If the `CatalogFilePath` was a directory instead of a file, `New-FileCatalog` would have automatically created a file named `catalog.cat`.

Test-FileCatalog

The `Test-FileCatalog` command compares the content of the catalog file to the filesystem. Hashes are re-calculated for each file.

If none of the content has changed, `Test-FileCatalog` will return `Valid`:

```
PS> Test-FileCatalog -Path C:\Temp\ACL -CatalogFilePath
C:\Temp\Security\example.cat
Valid
```

If a file is added, removed, or changed, the `Test-FileCatalog` command will return `ValidationFailed`.

At this point, the `Detailed` parameter can be used to see which file changed.

Is it faster without Detailed?
The `Detailed` parameter does not change the amount of work `Test-FileCatalog` must do. If the result is to be used, it might be better to use the `Detailed` parameter right away. This saves the CPU cycles and IO operations required to list the content of a directory and generate the hashes a second time.

The command does not provide a summary of changes; instead, it returns all files and hashes from the catalog and all files and hashes from the path being tested:

```
PS>Set-Content C:\Temp\ACL\3\3.txt -Value 'New content'
Test-FileCatalog -Path C:\Temp\ACL -CatalogFilePath
C:\Temp\Security\example.cat-Detailed


Status : ValidationFailed
HashAlgorithm : SHA1
CatalogItems : {[1\1.txt, 3B88969F774811E6A5D634832BE099EDA42B5E72],
[1\1\1.txt, 3B88969F774811E6A5D634832BE099EDA42B5E72], [2\2.txt,
                3B88969F774811E6A5D634832BE099EDA42B5E72], [2\2\2.txt,
3B88969F774811E6A5D634832BE099EDA42B5E72]...}
PathItems : {[1\1.txt, 3B88969F774811E6A5D634832BE099EDA42B5E72],
[1\1\1.txt, 3B88969F774811E6A5D634832BE099EDA42B5E72], [2\2.txt,
                3B88969F774811E6A5D634832BE099EDA42B5E72], [2\2\2.txt,
3B88969F774811E6A5D634832BE099EDA42B5E72]...}
Signature : System.Management.Automation.Signature
```

These values can be used to find changes. First, assign the result of the command to a variable:

```
$result = Test-FileCatalog -Path C:\Temp\ACL -CatalogFilePath
C:\Temp\Security\example.cat -Detailed
```

Once done, files that have been added can be listed with the following code:

```
$result.PathItems.Keys | Where-Object {
    -not $result.CatalogItems.ContainsKey($_) }
```

Files that have been removed are listed with the following code:

```
$result.CatalogItems.Keys | Where-Object {
    -not $result.PathItems.ContainsKey($_) }
```

Files that have been modified are listed with the following code:

```
$result.PathItems.Keys | Where-Object {
    $result.CatalogItems[$_] -ne $result.PathItems[$_]}
```

As the file catalog only stores hashes, the command is unable to describe exactly what has changed about a file, only that something has.

Summary

This chapter took a look at working with providers, focusing on filesystem and registry providers.

How PowerShell works with items and item properties was demonstrated.

Working with permissions in PowerShell for both the filesystem and registry was also demonstrated.

Using transactions with supported providers was demonstrated using the registry provider.

Finally, file catalogs were introduced.

`Chapter 12`, *Windows Management Instrumentation*, will explore the Windows Management Instrumentation.

12
Windows Management Instrumentation

The Windows Management Instrumentation, or WMI, was introduced as a downloadable component with Windows 95 and NT. Windows 2000 had WMI preinstalled, and it has since become a core part of the operating system.

WMI can be used to access a huge amount of information about the computer system. This includes printers, device drivers, user accounts, ODBC, and so on; there are hundreds of classes to explore.

In this chapter, we will be covering the following topics:

- Working with WMI
- CIM cmdlets
- WMI cmdlets
- Permissions

Working with WMI

The scope of WMI is vast, which makes it a fantastic resource for automating processes. WMI classes are not limited to the core operating system; it is not uncommon to find classes created after software or device drivers have been installed.

Given the scope of WMI, finding an appropriate class can be difficult. PowerShell itself is well equipped to explore the available classes.

WMI classes

PowerShell, as a shell for working with objects, presents WMI classes in a very similar manner to .NET classes or any other object. There are a number of parallels between WMI classes and .NET classes.

A WMI class is used as the recipe to create an instance of a WMI object. The WMI class defines properties and methods. The WMI class `Win32_Process` is used to gather information about running processes in a similar manner to the `Get-Process` command.

The `Win32_Process` class has properties such as `ProcessId`, `Name`, and `CommandLine`. It has a terminate method that can be used to kill a process, as well as a create static method that can be used to spawn a new process.

WMI classes reside within a WMI namespace. The default namespace is `root\cimv2`; classes such as `Win32_OperatingSystem` and `Win32_LogicalDisk` reside in this namespace.

WMI commands

PowerShell has two different sets of commands dedicated to working with WMI.

The CIM cmdlets were introduced with PowerShell 3.0. They are compatible with the **Distributed Management Task Force** (**DMTF**) standard DSP0004. A move towards compliance with open standards is critical as the Microsoft world becomes more diverse.

WMI itself is a proprietary implementation of the CIM server using the **Distributed Component Object Model** (**DCOM**), API to communicate between client and server.

Standards compliance and differences in approach aside, there are solid practical reasons to consider when choosing which to use.

The CIM cmdlets:

- Handle date conversion natively
- Have a flexible approach to networking. They use `WSMAN` for remote connections by default, but can be configured to use DCOM over RPC

The WMI cmdlets:

- Do not automatically convert dates
- Use DCOM over RPC
- Can be used for all WMI operations
- Have been superseded by the CIM cmdlets

The WMI Query Language

Before diving into the individual commands, it helps to have a grasp of the query language used for **WMI Query Language** (**WMI**) queries. Use of the query language is useful when querying classes that return multiple values.

The **WMI Query Language** (**WQL**), is used to build queries in WMI for both the CIM and WMI commands.

WQL implements a subset of **Structured Query Language** (**SQL**).

The keywords that we will look at are traditionally written in upper-case; however, WMI queries are not case-sensitive.

Both the CIM and WMI cmdlets support `Filter` and `Query` parameters, which accept WQL queries.

Understanding SELECT, WHERE, and FROM

The `SELECT`, `WHERE`, and `FROM` keywords are used with the `Query` parameter.

The generalized syntax for the `Query` parameter is as follows:

```
SELECT <Properties> FROM <WMI Class>
SELECT <Properties> FROM <WMI Class> WHERE <Condition>
```

The wildcard, `*`, may be used to request all available properties, or a list of known properties may be requested:

```
Get-CimInstance -Query "SELECT * FROM Win32_Process"
Get-CimInstance -Query "SELECT ProcessID, CommandLine FROM Win32_Process"
```

The WHERE keyword is used to filter results returned by SELECT. For example:

```
Get-CimInstance -Query "SELECT * FROM Win32_Process WHERE ProcessID=$PID"
```

Escape sequences and wildcard characters

The backslash character, \, is used to escape the meaning of characters in a WMI query. This might be used to escape a wildcard character, quotes, or itself. For example, the following WMI query uses a path; each instance of \ in the path must be escaped:

```
Get-CimInstance Win32_Process -Filter
"ExecutablePath='C:\\Windows\\Explorer.exe'"
```

About Win32_Process and the Path property:
The Path property is added to the output from the Win32_Process class by PowerShell. While it appears in the output, the property cannot be used to define a filter, nor can Path be selected using the Property parameter of either Get-CimInstance or Get-WmiObject.
Get-Member shows that it is a ScriptProperty:

```
Get-CimInstance Win32_Process -Filter "ProcessId=$pid" |
Get-Member -Name Path
Get-WmiObject Win32_Process -Filter "ProcessId=$pid" |
Get-Member -Name Path
```

WQL defines two wildcard characters that can be used with string queries:

- The % (percentage) character matches any number of characters, and is equivalent to using * in a file system path or with the -like operator
- The _ (underscore) character matches a single character and is equivalent to using ? in a filesystem path or with the -like operator

The following query filters the results of Win32_Service, including services with paths starting with a single drive letter and ending with .exe:

```
Get-CimInstance Win32_Service -Filter 'PathName LIKE "_:\\%.exe"'
```

Logic operators

Logic operators may be used with the `Filter` and `Query` parameters.

The examples in the following table are based on the following command:

```
Get-CimInstance Win32_Process -Filter "<Filter>"
```

Description	Operator	Syntax	Example
Logical and	`AND`	`<Condition1> AND <Condition2>`	`ProcessID=$pid AND Name='powershell.exe'`
Logical or	`OR`	`<Condition1> OR <Condition2>`	`ProcessID=$pid OR ProcessID=0`
Logical not	`NOT`	`NOT <Condition>`	`NOT ProcessID=$pid`

Comparison operators

Comparison operators may be used with the `Filter` and `Query` parameters.

The examples in the following table are based on the following command:

```
Get-CimInstance Win32_Process -Filter "<Filter>"
```

Description	Operator	Example
Equal to	`=`	`Name='powershell.exe' AND ProcessId=0`
Not equal to	`<>`	`Name<>'powershell.exe'`
Greater than	`>`	`WorkingSetSize>$(100MB)`
Greater than or equal to	`>=`	`WorkingSetSize>=$(100MB)`
Less than	`<`	`WorkingSetSize<$(100MB)`
Less than or equal to	`<=`	`WorkingSetSize<=$(100MB)`
Is	`IS`	`CommandLine IS NULL` `CommandLine IS NOT NULL`
Like	`LIKE`	`CommandLine LIKE '%.exe'`

Quoting values

When building a WQL query, string values must be quoted; numeric and Boolean values do not need quotes.

As the filter is also a string, this often means nesting quotes within one another. The following techniques may be used to avoid needing to use PowerShell's escape character.

For filters or queries containing fixed string values, use either of the following styles. Use single quotes outside and double quotes inside:

```
Get-CimInstance Win32_Process -Filter 'Name="powershell.exe"'
```

Alternatively, use double quotes outside and single quotes inside:

```
Get-CimInstance Win32_Process -Filter "Name='powershell.exe'"
```

For filters or queries containing PowerShell variables or subexpressions, use double quotes outside as variables within a single-quoted string that will not expand:

```
Get-CimInstance Win32_Process -Filter "ProcessId=$PID"
Get-CimInstance Win32_Process -Filter "ExecutablePath LIKE '$($pshome -
replace '\\', '\\')%'"
```

Regex recap:
The regular expression `'\\'` represents a single literal `'\'`, as the backslash is normally the escape character. Each `'\'` in the `pshome` path is replaced with `'\\'` to account for WQL using `'\'` as an escape character as well.

Finally, if a filter contains several conditions, consider using the format operator:

```
$filter = 'ExecutablePath LIKE "{0}%" AND WorkingSetSize<{1}' -f
    ($env:WinDir -replace '\\', '\\'),
    100MB
Get-CimInstance Win32_Process -Filter $filter
```

Associated classes

WMI classes often have several different associated or related classes--for example, each instance of `Win32_Process` has an associated class, `CIM_DataFile`.

Associations between two classes are expressed by a third class. In the case of `Win32_Process` and `CIM_DataFile`, the relationship is expressed by the class `CIM_ProcessExecutable`.

The relationship is defined using the antecedent and dependent properties, as shown in the following example:

```
PS> Get-CimInstance CIM_ProcessExecutable |
    Where-Object { $_.Dependent -match $PID } |
    Select-Object -First 1


Antecedent          : CIM_DataFile (Name =
"C:\WINDOWS\System32\WindowsPowerShell\v...)
Dependent           : Win32_Process (Handle = "11672")
BaseAddress         : 2340462460928
GlobalProcessCount  :
ModuleInstance      : 4000251904
ProcessCount        : 0
PSComputerName      :
```

This `CIM_ProcessExecutable` class does not need to be used directly.

WMI object path

A WMI path is required to find classes associated with an instance. The WMI object path uniquely identifies a specific instance of a WMI class.

The object path is made up of a number of components:

```
<Namespace>:<ClassName>.<KeyName>=<Value>
```

The namespace can be omitted if the class is under the default namespace, `root\cimv2`.

The `KeyName` for a given WMI class can be discovered in a number of ways. In the case of `Win32_Process`, the key name might be discovered using any of the following methods.

It can be discovered by using the CIM cmdlets:

```
(Get-CimClass Win32_Process).CimClassProperties |
    Where-Object { $_.Flags -band 'Key' }
```

It can be discovered by using the MSDN website, which provides the descriptions of each property (and method) exposed by the class:

`https://msdn.microsoft.com/en-us/library/aa394372(v=vs.85).aspx`

Having identified a key, only the value remains to be found. In the case of `Win32_Process`, the `key` (handle) has the same value as the process ID. The object path for the `Win32_Process` instance associated with a running PowerShell console is, therefore:

```
root\cimv2:Win32_Process.Handle=$PID
```

The namespace does not need to be included if it uses the default, `root\cimv2`; the object path can be shortened to:

```
Win32_Process.Handle=$PID
```

`Get-CimInstance` and `Get-WmiObject` will not retrieve an instance from an object path, but the `Wmi` type accelerator can:

```
PS> [Wmi]"Win32_Process.Handle=$PID" | Select-Object Name, Handle

Name                Handle
----                ------
powershell_ise.exe  13020
```

Using ASSOCIATORS OF

The `ASSOCIATORS OF` query may be used for any given object path. For example, using the preceding object path results in the following command:

```
Get-CimInstance -Query "ASSOCIATORS OF {Win32_Process.Handle=$PID}"
```

This query will return objects from three different classes: `Win32_LogonSession`, `Win32_ComputerSystem`, and `CIM_DataFile`.

The query can be refined to filter a specific resultant class, for example:

```
Get-CimInstance -Query "ASSOCIATORS OF {Win32_Process.Handle=$PID} WHERE
ResultClass = CIM_DATAFILE"
```

The value in the `ResultClass` condition is not quoted.

The result of this operation is a long list of files that are used by the PowerShell process. A snippet of this is shown here:

```
PS> Get-CimInstance -Query "ASSOCIATORS OF {Win32_Process.Handle=$PID}
WHERE ResultClass = CIM_DATAFILE" |
    Select-Object Name

Name
----
c:\windows\system32\windowspowershell\v1.0\powershell_ise.exe
c:\windows\system32\ntdll.dll
c:\windows\system32\mscoree.dll
c:\windows\system32\sysfer.dll
c:\windows\system32\kernel32.dll
```

CIM cmdlets

The **Common Information Model** (**CIM**), commands are:

- `Get-CimAssociatedInstance`
- `Get-CimClass`
- `Get-CimInstance`
- `Get-CimSession`
- `Invoke-CimMethod`
- `New-CimInstance`
- `New-CimSession`
- `New-CimSessionOption`
- `Register-CimIndicationEvent`
- `Remove-CimInstance`
- `Remove-CimSession`
- `Set-CimInstance`

Each of the CIM cmdlets uses either the `ComputerName` or `CimSession` parameter to target the operation at another computer.

Getting instances

The `Get-CimInstance` command is used to execute queries for instances of WMI objects. For example:

```
Get-CimInstance -ClassName Win32_OperatingSystem
Get-CimInstance -ClassName Win32_Service
Get-CimInstance -ClassName Win32_Share
```

A number of different parameters are available when using `Get-CimInstance`. The command can be used with a filter:

```
Get-CimInstance Win32_Directory -Filter "Name='C:\\Windows'"
Get-CimInstance CIM_DataFile -Filter
"Name='C:\\Windows\\System32\\cmd.exe'"
Get-CimInstance Win32_Service -Filter "State='Running'"
```

When returning large amounts of information, the `Property` parameter can be used to reduce the number of fields returned by a query:

```
Get-CimInstance Win32_UserAccount -Property Name, SID
```

The `Query` parameter can also be used, although it is rare to find a use for this that cannot be served by the individual parameters:

```
Get-CimInstance -Query "SELECT * FROM Win32_Process"
Get-CimInstance -Query "SELECT Name, SID FROM Win32_UserAccount"
```

Getting classes

The `Get-CimClass` command is used to return an instance of a WMI class:

```
PS> Get-CimClass Win32_Process

   NameSpace: ROOT/cimv2

CimClassName  CimClassMethods            CimClassProperties
------------  ---------------            ------------------
Win32_Process {Create, Terminate, Get...} {Caption, Description,
InstallDate, Name...}
```

The `Class` object describes the capabilities of that class.

By default, `Get-CimClass` lists classes from the `root\cimv2` namespace.

The `Namespace` parameter will fill using tab completion--that is, if the following partial command is entered, pressing tab repeatedly will cycle through the possible root namespaces:

```
Get-CimClass -Namespace <tab, tab, tab>
```

The child namespaces of a given namespace are listed in a `__Namespace` class instance. For example, the following command returns the namespaces under `root`:

```
Get-CimInstance __Namespace -Namespace root
```

Extending this technique, it is possible to recursively query `__Namespace` to find all of the possible namespace values. Certain WMI namespaces are only available to administrative users (run as administrator); the following function may display errors for some namespaces:

```
function Get-CimNamespace {
    param(
        $Namespace = 'root'
    )
    Get-CimInstance __Namespace -Namespace $Namespace | ForEach-Object {
        $childNamespace = Join-Path $Namespace $_.Name
        $childNamespace

        Get-CimNamespace -Namespace $childNamespace
    }
}
Get-CimNamespace
```

Calling methods

The `Invoke-CimMethod` command may be used to call a method.

The CIM class can be used to find details of the methods a class supports:

```
PS> (Get-CimClass Win32_Process).CimClassMethods

Name           ReturnType Parameters           Qualifiers
----           ---------- ----------           ----------
Create         UInt32     {CommandLine...}     {Constructor...}
Terminate      UInt32     {Reason}             {Destructor...}
GetOwner       UInt32     {Domain...}          {Implemented...}
GetOwnerSid    UInt32     {Sid}                {Implemented...}
```

The method with the `Constructor` qualifier can be used to create a new instance of `Win32_Process`.

The parameters property of a specific method can be explored to find out how to use a method:

```
PS> (Get-CimClass Win32_Process).CimClassMethods['Create'].Parameters
Name                      CimType Qualifiers
----                      ------- ----------
CommandLine                String {ID, In, MappingStrings}
CurrentDirectory           String {ID, In, MappingStrings}
ProcessStartupInformation Instance {EmbeddedInstance, ID, In,
MappingStrings}
ProcessId                  UInt32 {ID, MappingStrings, Out}
```

If an argument has the `In` qualifier, it can be passed in when creating an object. If an argument has the `Out` qualifier, it will be returned after the instance has been created. Arguments are passed in using a hashtable.

When creating a process, the `CommandLine` argument is required; the rest can be ignored until later:

```
$argumentList = @{
    CommandLine = 'notepad.exe'
}
$return = Invoke-CimMethod Win32_Process -MethodName Create -Arguments
$argumentList
```

The `return` object holds three properties in the case of `Win32_Process`:

```
PS> $return

ProcessId ReturnValue PSComputerName
--------- ----------- --------------
    15172           0
```

`PSComputerName` is blank when the request is local. The `ProcessId` is the `Out` property listed under the method parameters. `ReturnValue` indicates whether or not the operation succeeded and `0` indicates that it was successful.

A nonzero value indicates something went wrong, but the values are not translated in PowerShell. The return values are documented on the MSDN:

`https://msdn.microsoft.com/en-us/library/aa389388(v=vs.85).aspx`

The Create method used here creates a new instance. The other methods for Win32_Process act against an existing instance (an existing process).

Extending the preceding example, a process can be created and then terminated:

```
$argumentList = @{
    CommandLine = 'notepad.exe'
}
$return = Invoke-CimMethod Win32_Process -MethodName Create -Arguments
$argumentList
pause
Get-CimInstance Win32_Process -Filter "ProcessID=$($return.ProcessId)" |
    Invoke-CimMethod -MethodName Terminate
```

The pause command will wait for return to be pressed before continuing; this gives us the opportunity to show that Notepad was opened before it is terminated.

The Terminate method has an optional argument that is used as the exit code for the terminate process. This argument may be added using hashtable; in this case, a (made up) value of 5 is set as the exit code:

```
$argumentList = @{
    CommandLine = 'notepad.exe'
}
$return = Invoke-CimMethod Win32_Process -MethodName Create -Arguments
$argumentList
Get-CimInstance Win32_Process -Filter "ProcessID=$($return.ProcessId)" |
    Invoke-CimMethod -MethodName Terminate -Arguments @{Reason=5}
```

Invoke-CimMethod returns an object with a ReturnValue. A return value of 0 indicates that the command succeeded. A nonzero value indicates an error condition. The meaning of the value will depend on the WMI class.

The return values associated with the Terminate method of Win32_Process are documented on MSDN:

https://msdn.microsoft.com/en-us/library/aa393907(v=vs.85).aspx

Creating instances

The arguments for Win32_Process.Create include a ProcessStartupInformation parameter. The ProcessStartupInformation is described by a WMI class, Win32_ProcessStartup.

There are no existing instances of `Win32_ProcessStartup` (`Get-CimInstance`), and the class does not have a `Create` method (or any other constructor).

`New-CimInstance` can be used to create a class:

```
$class = Get-CimClass Win32_ProcessStartup
$startupInfo = New-CimInstance -CimClass $class -ClientOnly
```

`New-Object` can also be used:

```
$class = Get-CimClass Win32_ProcessStartup
$startupInfo = New-Object CimInstance $class
```

Properties may be set on the created instance; the effect of each property is documented on the MSDN:

`https://msdn.microsoft.com/en-us/library/aa394375(v=vs.85).aspx`

In the following example, properties are set to dictate the position and title of a `cmd.exe` window:

```
$class = Get-CimClass Win32_ProcessStartup
$startupInfo = New-CimInstance -CimClass $class -ClientOnly
$startupInfo.X = 50
$startupInfo.Y = 50
$startupInfo.Title = 'This is the window title'

$argumentList = @{
    CommandLine = 'cmd.exe'
    ProcessStartupInformation = $startupInfo
}
$returnObject = Invoke-CimMethod Win32_Process -MethodName Create -
Arguments $argumentList
```

Working with CIM sessions

As mentioned earlier in this chapter, a key feature of the CIM cmdlets is their ability to change how connections are formed and used.

The `Get-CimInstance` command has a `ComputerName` parameter, and when this is used, the command automatically creates a session to a remote system using `WSMAN`. The connection is destroyed as soon as the command completes.

While `Get-CimInstance` supports basic remote connections, it does not provide a means of authenticating a connection, nor can the protocol be changed.

The `Get-CimSession`, `New-CimSession`, `New-CimSessionOption`, and `Remove-CimSession` commands are optional commands that can be used to define the behavior of remote connections.

The `New-CimSession` command creates a connection to a remote server. For example:

```
PS> $cimSession = New-CimSession -ComputerName Remote1
$cimSession

Id            : 1
Name          : CimSession1
InstanceId    : 1cc2a889-b649-418c-94a2-f24e033883b4
ComputerName  : Remote1
Protocol      : WSMAN
```

Alongside the other parameters, `New-CimSession` has a `Credential` parameter that can be used in conjunction with `Get-Credential` to authenticate a connection.

If the remote system does not, for any reason, present access to `WSMAN`, it is possible to switch the protocol down to `DCOM` using the `New-CimSessionOption` command:

```
PS> $option = New-CimSessionOption -Protocol DCOM
$cimSession = New-CimSession -ComputerName Remote1 -SessionOption $option
$cimSession

Id            : 2
Name          : CimSession2
InstanceId    : 62b2cb56-ec84-472c-a992-4bee59ee0618
ComputerName  : Remote1
Protocol      : DCOM
```

The `New-CimSessionOption` command is not limited to protocol switching; it can affect many of the other properties of the connection, as shown in the help and the examples for the command.

Once a session has been created, it exists in memory until it is removed. The `Get-CimSession` command shows a list of connections that have been formed, and the `Remove-CimSession` command permanently removes connections.

Associated classes

The `Get-CimAssociatedClass` command replaces the use of the `ASSOCIATORS OF` query type when using the CIM cmdlets.

The following command gets the class instances associated with `Win32_NetworkAdapterConfiguration`. As the arguments for the `Get-CimInstance` command are long strings, splatting is used to pass the parameters into the command:

```
$params = @{
    ClassName = 'Win32_NetworkAdapterConfiguration'
    Filter    = 'IPEnabled=TRUE AND DHCPEnabled=TRUE'
}
Get-CimInstance @params | Get-CimAssociatedInstance
```

The following example uses `Get-CimAssociatedClass` to get the physical interface associated with the IP configuration:

```
$params = @{
    ClassName = 'Win32_NetworkAdapterConfiguration'
    Filter = 'IPEnabled=TRUE AND DHCPEnabled=TRUE'
}
Get-CimInstance @params | ForEach-Object {
    $adapter = $_ | Get-CimAssociatedInstance -ResultClassName
Win32_NetworkAdapter

     [PSCustomObject]@{
         NetConnectionID = $adapter.NetConnectionID
         Speed           = [Math]::Round($adapter.Speed / 1MB, 2)
         IPAddress       = $_.IPAddress
         IPSubnet        = $_.IPSubnet
         Index           = $_.Index
         Gateway         = $_.DefaultIPGateway
     }
}
```

The WMI cmdlets

The WMI cmdlets have been superseded by the CIM cmdlets.

The WMI commands are:

- Get-WmiObject
- Invoke-WmiMethod
- Register-WmiEvent
- Remove-WmiObject
- Set-WmiInstance

In addition to the commands, three type accelerators are available:

- [Wmi]: System.Management.ManagementObject
- [WmiClass]: System.Management.ManagementClass
- [WmiSearcher]: System.Management.ManagementObjectSearcher

Each of the WMI cmdlets uses the `ComputerName` parameter to aim the operation at another computer. The WMI cmdlets also support a credential parameter and other authentication options affecting the authentication method.

Both the `Wmi` and `WmiClass` type accelerator can be written to use a remote computer by including the computer name. For example:

```
[Wmi]"\\RemoteComputer\root\cimv2:Win32_Process.Handle=$PID"
[WmiClass]"\\RemoteComputer\root\cimv2:Win32_Process"
```

Getting instances

The `Get-WmiObject` command is used to execute queries for instances of WMI objects. For example:

```
Get-WmiObject -Class Win32_ComputerSystem
```

The type accelerator, `WmiSearcher`, may also be used to execute queries:

```
([WmiSearcher]"SELECT * FROM Win32_Process").Get()
```

Working with dates

The WMI cmdlets do not convert date-time properties found in WMI. Querying the `Win32_Process` class for the creation date of a process returns the date-time property as a long string:

```
PS> Get-WmiObject Win32_Process -Filter "ProcessId=$PID" | Select Name,
CreationDate
Name                CreationDate
----                ------------
powershell_ise.exe 20170209120229.941677+000
```

The .NET namespace used by the WMI cmdlet, `System.Management`, includes a class called `ManagementDateTimeConverter`, dedicated to converting date and time formats found in WMI.

The string in the preceding example may be converted as follows:

```
Get-WmiObject Win32_Process -Filter "ProcessId=$PID" |
    Select Name, @{Name='CreationDate'; Expression={
[System.Management.ManagementDateTimeConverter]::ToDateTime($_.CreationDate
) }}
```

Getting classes

The `Get-WmiObject` command is used to get classes:

```
Get-WmiObject Win32_Process -List
```

The WMI cmdlets are able to recursively list classes in namespaces. The following command lists classes in `root\cimv2` and any child namespaces:

```
Get-WmiObject -List -Recurse
```

In addition to the list parameter, the `WmiClass` type accelerator might be used:

```
[WmiClass]"Win32_Process"
```

Calling methods

Calling a method on an existing instance of an object found using `Get-WmiObject` is similar to any .NET method call.

The following example gets and restarts the `DNS Client` service. The following operation requires administrative access:

```
$service = Get-WmiObject Win32_Service -Filter "DisplayName='DNS Client'"
$service.StopService()    # Call the StopService method
$service.StartService()# Call the StartService method
```

The WMI class can be used to find details of a method, for example, the `Create` method of `Win32_Share`:

```
PS> (Get-WmiObject Win32_Share -List).Methods['Create']
Name          : Create
InParameters  : System.Management.ManagementBaseObject
OutParameters : System.Management.ManagementBaseObject
Origin        : Win32_Share
Qualifiers    : {Constructor, Implemented, MappingStrings, Static}
```

Where the `Invoke-CimMethod` command accepts a hashtable, the `Invoke-WmiMethod` command expects arguments to be passed as an array in a specific order. The order can be retrieved by using the `GetMethodParameters` method of the WMI class:

```
PS> (Get-WmiObject Win32_Share -List).GetMethodParameters('Create')


__GENUS          : 2
__CLASS          : __PARAMETERS
__SUPERCLASS     :
__DYNASTY        : __PARAMETERS
__RELPATH        :
__PROPERTY_COUNT : 7
__DERIVATION     : {}
__SERVER         :
__NAMESPACE      :
__PATH           :
Access           :
Description      :
MaximumAllowed   :
Name             :
Password         :
Path             :
Type             :
PSComputerName   :
```

To create a share, the argument list must therefore contain an argument for `Access`, then `Description`, then `MaximumAllowed`, and so on. If the argument is optional, it can be set to null; however, PowerShell is unable to say which are mandatory, so a trip to the MSDN is required:

`https://msdn.microsoft.com/en-us/library/aa389393(v=vs.85).aspx`

Having established that `Path`, `Name`, and `Type` are mandatory, an array of arguments can be created in the order described by `GetMethodParameters`:

```
$argumentList = $null,              # Access
                $null,              # Description
                $null,              # MaximumAllowed
                'Share1',           # Name
                $null,              # Password
                'C:\Temp\Share1',   # Path
                0                   # Type (Disk Drive)
Invoke-WmiMethod Win32_Share -Name Create -ArgumentList $argumentList
```

The `return` value describes the result of the operation; a `ReturnValue` of `0` indicates success. As this operation requires administrator privileges (run as administrator), a return value of `2` is used to indicate it was run without sufficient rights.

Adding the `ComputerName` parameter to `Invoke-WmiMethod` will create a share on a remote machine.

Arrays of null values are messy:
This method of supplying arguments to execute a method is difficult to work with for any but the simplest of methods. An alternative is to use the .NET method `InvokeMethod` on the `class` object:

```
$class = Get-WmiObject Win32_Share -List
$inParams = $class.GetMethodParameters('Create')
$inParams.Name = 'Share1'
$inParams.Path = 'C:\Temp\Share1'
$inParams.Type = 0
$return = $class.InvokeMethod('Create', $inParams, $null)
```

The last argument, set to null here, is `InvokeMethodOptions`, which is most often used to define a timeout for the operation. Doing so is beyond the scope of this chapter.
To create a share on a remote computer, use the `ComputerName` parameter with `Get-WmiObject`.

Creating instances

An instance of a WMI class can be created using the CreateInstance method of the class. The following example creates an instance of Win32_Trustee:

```
(Get-WmiObject Win32_Trustee -List).CreateInstance()
```

Associated classes

Objects returned by Get-WmiObject have a GetRelated method that can be used to find associated instances.

The GetRelated method accepts arguments that can be used to filter the results. The first argument, relatedClass, is used to limit the instances returned to specific classes, as shown here:

```
Get-WmiObject Win32_LogonSession | ForEach-Object {
    [PSCustomObject]@{
    LogonName = $_.GetRelated('Win32_Account').Caption
        SessionStarted =
[System.Management.ManagementDateTimeConverter]::ToDateTime($_.StartTime)
    }
}
```

Permissions

Working with permissions in WMI is more difficult than in .NET as the values in use are not given friendly names. However, the .NET classes can still be used, even if not quite as intended.

The following working examples demonstrate configuring the permissions.

Sharing permissions

Get-Acl and Set-Acl are fantastic tools for working with file system permissions, or permissions under other providers. However, these commands cannot be used to affect share permissions.

The SmbShare module:
The `SmbShare` module has commands that affect share permissions. This example uses the older WMI classes to modify permissions. It might be used if the `SmbShare` module cannot be.
The command `Get-SmbShareAccess` might be used to verify the outcome of this example.

The following operations require administrative privileges; run ISE or PowerShell as an administrator if attempting to use the examples.

Creating a shared directory

The following snippet creates a directory and shares that directory:

```
$path = 'C:\Temp\WmiPermissions'
New-Item $path -ItemType Directory
Invoke-CimMethod Win32_Share -MethodName Create -Arguments @{
    Name = 'WmiPerms'
    Path = $path
    Type = 0
}
```

Getting a security descriptor

When `Get-Acl` is used, the object it gets is a security descriptor. The security descriptor includes a set of control information (ownership, and so on), along with the discretionary and system access control lists.

The WMI class `Win32_LogicalShareSecuritySetting` is used to represent the security for each of the shares on a computer:

```
$security = Get-CimInstance Win32_LogicalShareSecuritySetting -Filter
"Name='WmiPerms'"
```

The security settings object can be used to retrieve a security descriptor by calling the `GetSecurityDescriptor` method:

```
$return = $security | Invoke-CimMethod -MethodName GetSecurityDescriptor
$aclObject = $return.Descriptor
```

The security descriptor held in the aclObject variable is very different from the result returned by Get-Acl:

```
PS> $aclObject

ControlFlags    : 32772
DACL            : {Win32_ACE}
Group           :
Owner           :
SACL            :
TIME_CREATED    :
PSComputerName  :
```

The DACL, or discretionary access control list, is used to describe the permission levels for each security principal (a user, group, or computer account). Each entry in this list is an instance of Win32_ACE:

```
PS> $aclObject.DACL

AccessMask                : 1179817
AceFlags                  : 0
AceType                   : 0
GuidInheritedObjectType   :
GuidObjectType            :
TIME_CREATED              :
Trustee                   : Win32_Trustee
PSComputerName            :
```

The Win32_ACE object has a Trustee property that holds the Name, Domain, and SID of the security principal--in this case, the Everyone principal:

```
PS> $aclObject.DACL.Trustee

Domain          :
Name            : Everyone
SID             : {1, 1, 0, 0...}
SidLength       : 12
SIDString       : S-1-1-0
TIME_CREATED    :
PSComputerName  :
```

AceFlags describes how an ACE is to be inherited. As this is a share, the AceFlags property will always be 0. Nothing can or will inherit this entry. .NET can be used to confirm this:

```
PS> [System.Security.AccessControl.AceFlags]0
None
```

`AceType` is either `AccessAllowed` (`0`) or `AccessDenied` (`1`). Again, .NET can be used to confirm this:

```
PS> [System.Security.AccessControl.AceType]0
AccessAllowed
```

Finally, the `AccessMask` property can be converted into a meaningful value with .NET as well. The access rights that can be granted on a share are a subset of those that might be assigned to a file or directory:

```
PS> [System.Security.AccessControl.FileSystemRights]1179817
ReadAndExecute, Synchronize
```

Putting this together, the entries in a shared `DACL` can be made much easier to understand:

```
using namespace System.Security.AccessControl

$aclObject.DACL | ForEach-Object {
    [PSCustomObject]@{
        Rights   = [FileSystemRights]$_.AccessMask
        Type     = [AceType]$_.AceType
        Flags    = [AceFlags]$_.AceFlags
        Identity = $_.Trustee.Name
    }
}
```

In the preceding example, the domain of the `trustee` is ignored. If this were something other than `Everyone`, it should be included.

Adding an access control entry

To add an **Access Control Entry** (**ACE**) to this existing list, an entry must be created. Creating an ACE requires a `Win32_Trustee`. The following `trustee` is created from the current user:

```
$trustee = New-CimInstance (Get-CimClass Win32_Trustee) -ClientOnly
$trustee.Domain = $env:USERDOMAIN
$trustee.Name = $env:USERNAME
```

The `SID` does not need to be set on the `trustee` object, but if the security principal is invalid, the attempt to apply the change to security will fail.

Then the Win32_ACE can be created. The following ACE grants full control of the share to the trustee:

```
$ace = New-CimInstance (Get-CimClass Win32_ACE) -ClientOnly
$ace.AccessMask = [UInt32][FileSystemRights]'FullControl'
$ace.AceType = [UInt32][AceType]'AccessAllowed'
$ace.AceFlags = [UInt32]0
$ace.Trustee = $trustee
```

The ACE is added to the DACL using the += operator:

```
$aclObject.DACL += $ace
```

Setting the security descriptor

Once the ACL has been changed, the modified security descriptor must be set. The instance returned by Win32_LogicalShareSecuritySetting contains a SetSecurityDescriptor method:

```
$security | Invoke-CimMethod -MethodName SetSecurityDescriptor -Arguments
@{
    Descriptor = $aclObject
}
```

WMI permissions

Getting and setting WMI security in PowerShell uses the same approach as share security. WMI permissions might be set using wmimgmt.msc if the GUI is used. The content of the DACL differs slightly.

The class __SystemSecurity is used to access the security descriptor. Each WMI namespace has its own instance of the __SystemSecurity class. For example:

```
Get-CimClass __SystemSecurity -Namespace root
Get-CimClass __SystemSecurity -Namespace root\cimv2
```

Getting a security descriptor

The security descriptor for a given namespace can be retrieved from the `__SystemSecurity` class. By default, administrator privileges are required to get the security descriptor:

```
$security = Get-CimInstance __SystemSecurity -Namespace root\cimv2
$return = $security | Invoke-CimMethod -MethodName GetSecurityDescriptor
$aclObject = $return.Descriptor
```

The access mask

The values of the access mask in the `DACL` are documented on MSDN:

`https://msdn.microsoft.com/en-us/library/aa392710(v=vs.85).aspx`

The standard access rights `ReadSecurity` and `WriteSecurity` are also relevant.

The access mask is a composite of the values listed here:

- `EnableAccount`: 1
- `ExecuteMethods`: 2
- `FullWrite`: 4
- `PartialWrite`: 8
- `WriteProvider`: 16
- `RemoteEnable`: 32
- `ReadSecurity`: 131072
- `WriteSecurity`: 262144

WMI and SDDL

Security Descriptor Definition Language (**SDDL**), is used to describe the content of a security descriptor as a string.

A security descriptor returned by `Get-Acl` has a method that can convert the entire security descriptor to a string:

```
PS> (Get-Acl C:\).GetSecurityDescriptorSddlForm('All')
O:S-1-5-80-956008885-3418522649-1831038044-1853292631-2271478464G:S-1-5-80-
956008885-3418522649-1831038044-1853292631-2271478464D:PAI(A;;LC;;;AU)(A;OI
CIIO;SDGXGWGR;;;AU)(A;;FA;
;;SY)(A;OICIIO;GA;;;SY)(A;OICIIO;GA;;;BA)(A;;FA;;;BA)(A;OICI;0x1200a9;;;BU)
```

A security descriptor defined using `SDDL` can also be imported. If the `sddlString` variable is assumed to hold a valid security descriptor, the following command might be used:

```
$acl = Get-Acl C:\
$acl.SetSecurityDescriptorSddlForm($sddlString)
```

The imported security descriptor will not apply to the directory until `Set-Acl` is used.

WMI security descriptors can be converted to and from different formats, including `SDDL`. WMI has a specialized class for this: `Win32_SecurityDescriptorHelper`. The methods for the class are as shown following:

```
PS> (Get-CimClass Win32_SecurityDescriptorHelper).CimClassMethods
Name                 ReturnType Parameters              Qualifiers
----                 ---------- ----------              ----------
Win32SDToSDDL            UInt32 {Descriptor, SDDL}      {implemented, static}
Win32SDToBinarySD        UInt32 {Descriptor, BinarySD} {implemented, static}
SDDLToWin32SD            UInt32 {SDDL, Descriptor}      {implemented, static}
SDDLToBinarySD           UInt32 {SDDL, BinarySD}        {implemented, static}
BinarySDToWin32SD        UInt32 {BinarySD, Descriptor} {implemented, static}
BinarySDToSDDL           UInt32 {BinarySD, SDDL}        {implemented, static}
```

A WMI security descriptor might be converted to `SDDL` to create a backup before making a change:

```
$security = Get-CimInstance __SystemSecurity -Namespace root\cimv2
$return = $security | Invoke-CimMethod -MethodName GetSecurityDescriptor
$aclObject = $return.Descriptor

$return = Invoke-CimMethod Win32_SecurityDescriptorHelper -MethodName
Win32SDToSDDL -Arguments @{
    Descriptor = $aclObject
}
```

If the operation succeeds (that is, if the ReturnValue is 0), the security descriptor in SDDL form will be available:

```
PS> $return.SDDL
O:BAG:BAD:AR(A;CI;CCDCWP;;;S-1-5-21-2114566378-1333126016-908539190-1001)(A
;CI;CCDCLCSWRPWPRCWD;;;BA)(A;CI;CCDCRP;;;NS)(A;CI;CCDCRP;;;LS)(A;CI;CCDCRP;
;;AU)
```

A security descriptor expressed as an SDDL string can be imported:

```
$sddl =
'O:BAG:BAD:AR(A;CI;CCDCWP;;;S-1-5-21-2114566378-1333126016-908539190-1001)(
A;CI;CCDCLCSWRPWPRCWD;;;BA)(A;CI;CCDCRP;;;NS)(A;CI;CCDCRP;;;LS)(A;CI;CCDCRP
;;;AU)'
$return = Invoke-CimMethod Win32_SecurityDescriptorHelper -MethodName
SDDLToWin32SD -Arguments @{
    SDDL = $sddl
}
$aclObject = $return.Descriptor
```

If the ReturnValue is 0, the aclObject variable will contain the imported security descriptor:

```
PS> $aclObject

ControlFlags   : 33028
DACL           : {Win32_ACE, Win32_ACE, Win32_ACE, Win32_ACE...}
Group          : Win32_Trustee
Owner          : Win32_Trustee
SACL           :
TIME_CREATED   :
PSComputerName :
```

Summary

In this chapter, we have explored working with WMI classes, the different commands available, and the WMI query language. Both the CIM and WMI cmdlets were explored as a means of working with WMI. We explored getting and setting permissions using WMI, using shared security and WMI security as examples.

The Chapter 13, *HTML, XML, and JSON*, explores working with the **Component Object Model (COM)**.

13
HTML, XML, and JSON

PowerShell has a number of commands for working with HTML, XML, and JSON. These commands, combined with some of the available .NET classes, provide a rich set of tools for creating or modifying these formats.

In this chapter, the following topics are covered:

- HTML
- XML
- `System.Xml`
- `System.Xml.Linq`
- JSON

HTML

HTML is frequently used in PowerShell as a means of generating reports by email. PowerShell includes `ConvertTo-Html`, which may be used to generate HTML content.

ConvertTo-Html

`ConvertTo-Html` generates an HTML document with a table based on an input object. The following example generates a table based on the output from `Get-Process`:

```
Get-Process |
ConvertTo-Html -Property Name, Id, WorkingSet
```

Multiple tables

`ConvertTo-Html` may be used to build more complex documents by using the `Fragment` parameter. The `Fragment` parameter generates an HTML table only (instead of a full document). Tables may be combined to create a larger document:

```
# Create the body
$body = '<h1>Services</h1>'
$body += Get-Service |
    Where-Object Status -eq 'Running' |
ConvertTo-Html -Property Name, DisplayName -Fragment
$body += '<h1>Processes</h1>'
$body +=  Get-Process |
    Where-Object WorkingSet -gt 50MB |
ConvertTo-Html -Property Name, Id, WorkingSet-Fragment
# Create a document with the merged body
ConvertTo-Html -Body $body -Title Report |
    Out-File report.html
```

Adding style

HTML content can be enhanced by adding a **Cascading Style Sheet** (**CSS**) fragment. When CSS is embedded in an HTML document, it is added between style tags in the head element.

The following style uses CSS to change the font, color the table headers, define the table borders, and justify the table content:

```
$css = @'
<style>
body { font-family: Arial; }
table {
width: 100%;
border-collapse: collapse;
    }
table, th, td {
border: 1px solid Black;
padding: 5px;
    }
th {
text-align: left;
background-color: LightBlue;
    }
tr:nth-child(even) {
background-color: GainsBoro;
```

```
    }
</style>
'@
```

The Head parameter of ConvertTo-Html is used to add the element to the document:

```
Get-Process |
ConvertTo-Html -Property Name, Id, WorkingSet -Head $css|
    Out-File report.html
```

The CSS language is complex, and very capable. The elements used in the preceding code, and many more, are documented with examples on the w3schools website:

https://www.w3schools.com/css/

Different browsers support different parts of the CSS language, and email clients tend to support a smaller set still. Testing in the expected client is an important part of developing content.

ConvertTo-Html and Send-MailMessage:
ConvertTo-Html outputs an array of strings, while Send-MailMessage will only accept a body as a string. Attempting to use the output from ConvertTo-Html with Send-MailMessage directly will raise an error. The Out-String command may be added to ensure the output from ConvertTo-Html is a string:

```
$messageBody = Get-Process |
ConvertTo-Html Name, Id, WorkingSet -Head $css |
Out-String
```

HTML and special characters

HTML defines a number of special characters; for example, a literal ampersand (&) in HTML must be written as &.

ConvertTo-Html will handle the conversion of special characters in input objects, but it will not work with special characters in raw HTML that are added using the Body, Head, PreContent, or PostContent parameters.

The Sytem.Web.HttpUtility class includes methods that are able to convert strings containing such characters.

Before `System.Web.HttpUtility` can be used, the assembly must be added:

```
Add-Type -AssemblyName System.Web
```

The static method `HtmlEncode` will take a string and replace any reserved characters with an HTML code. For example, the following snippet will replace > with `>`:

```
PS>'<h1>{0}</h1>' -f [System.Web.HttpUtility]::HtmlEncode('Files > 100MB')

<h1>Files &gt; 100MB</h1>
```

The static method `HtmlDecode` can be used to reverse the process:

```
PS> [System.Web.HttpUtility]::HtmlDecode("<h1>Files &gt; 100MB</h1>")
<h1>Files > 100MB</h1>
```

XML

eXtensible Markup Language (**XML**), is a plain text format used to store structured data. XML is written to be both human and machine readable.

XML documents often begin with a declaration, as shown here:

```
<?xml version="1.0"?>
```

The declaration has three possible attributes. The version attribute is mandatory when a declaration is included:

- `version`: The XML version, 1.0 or 1.1
- `encoding`: The file encoding, most frequently `utf-8` or `utf-16`
- `standalone`: Whether or not the XML file uses an internal or external **Document Type Definition** (**DTD**), permissible values are yes or no

Elements and attributes

XML is similar in appearance to HTML. Elements begin and end with a tag name. The tag name describes the name of an element. For example:

```
<?xml version="1.0"?>
<rootElement>value</rootElement>
```

An XML document can only have one `root` element, but an element may have many descendants:

```
<?xml version="1.0"?>
<rootElement>
<firstChild>1</firstChild>
<secondChild>2</secondChild>
</rootElement>
```

An element may also have attributes. The element `rootElement` in the following example has an attribute named `attr`:

```
<?xml version="1.0"?>
<rootElementattr="value">
   <child>1</child>
</rootElement>
```

Namespaces

XML documents can use one or more namespaces that can be used to provide uniquely named elements within a document.

XML namespaces are declared in an attribute with a name prefixed by `xmlns:`. For example:

```
<?xml version="1.0"?>
<rootElementxmlns:item="http://namespaces/item">
<item:child>1</item:child>
</rootElement>
```

The XML namespace uses a URL as a unique identifier. The identifier is often used to describe an element as belonging to a schema.

Schemas

An XML schema can be used to describe and constrain the elements, attributes, and values within an XML document.

About DTD:
A document type definition, or DTD, may be used to constrain the content of an XML file. As DTD has little bearing on the use of XML in PowerShell, it is considered beyond the scope of this book.

XML schema definitions are saved with an XSD extension. Schema files can be used to validate the content of an XML file.

The following is a simple schema that validates the item namespace:

```
<?xml version="1.0"?>
<xs:schemaxmlns:xs="http://www.w3.org/2001/XMLSchema"
targetNamespace="http://namespaces/item"
xmlns="https://www.w3schools.com"
elementFormDefault="qualified">
<xs:element name="rootElement">
<xs:element name="child" type="xs:string" />
</xs:element>
</xs:schema>
```

System.Xml

PowerShell primarily uses the `System.Xml.XmlDocument` object to work with XML content.

ConvertTo-Xml

The `ConvertTo-XML` command creates an XML representation of an object as an `XmlDocument`. For example, the current PowerShell process object might be converted to XML:

```
Get-Process -Id $pid | ConvertTo-Xml
```

XML is text:
The command used in the previous code creates an XML representation of the object. All numeric values are stored as strings. The following example shows that the `WorkingSet` property, normally an integer, is held as a string:

```
$xml = Get-Process -Id $pid | ConvertTo-Xml
$property = $xml.Objects.Object.Property |
Where-Object Name -eq WorkingSet
$property.'#text'.GetType()
```

XML type accelerator

The XML type accelerator (`[Xml]`) can be used to create instances of `XmlDocument`, as shown in the following code:

```
[Xml]$xml = @"
<?xml version="1.0"?>
<cars>
<car type="Saloon">
<colour>Green</colour>
<doors>4</doors>
<transmission>Automatic</transmission>
<engine>
<size>2.0</size>
<cylinders>4</cylinders>
</engine>
</car>
</cars>
"@
```

Elements and attributes of an `XmlDocument` object may be accessed as if they were properties. This is a feature of the PowerShell language rather than the .NET object:

```
PS> $xml.cars.car

type         : Saloon
colour       : Green
doors        : 4
transmission : Automatic
engine       : engine
```

If the document contained more than one `car` element, each of the instances will be returned.

XPath and Select-Xml

XPath can be used to navigate or search an XML document. PowerShell (and .NET) uses XPath 1.0.

The structure and format of XPath queries are beyond the scope of this chapter. However, a number of web resources are available, including: `https://msdn.microsoft.com/en-us/library/ms256115(v=vs.110).aspx`

Terms and values used in `XPath` queries, and XML in general, are casesensitive.

Given the following XML snippet, `Select-Xml` might use an `XPath` expression to select the engines of green cars:

```
$string = @"
<?xml version="1.0"?>
<cars>
<car type="Saloon">
<colour>Green</colour>
<doors>4</doors>
<transmission>Automatic</transmission>
<engine>
<size>2.0</size>
<cylinders>4</cylinders>
</engine>
</car>
</cars>
"@
```

The `XPath` expression and the result are shown here:

```
PS>Select-Xml -XPath '//car[colour="Green"]/engine' -Content $string |
    Select-Object -ExpandProperty Node

size cylinders
---- ---------
2.0  4
```

A similar result can be achieved using the `SelectNodes` method of an XML document:

```
([Xml]$string).SelectNodes('//car[colour="Green"]/engine')
```

`Select-Xml` has an advantage in that it can be used to work against files directly using the `Path` parameter:

SelectNodes and XPathNodeList:
If the `SelectNodes` method is called, and there are no results, an empty `XPathNodeList` object is returned. The following condition is flawed:

```
$nodes = $xml.SelectNodes('//car[colour="Blue"]')
if ($nodes) {
Write-Host "A blue car record exists"
}
```

In this case, using the Count property is a better approach:

```
if ($nodes.Count -gt 1) {
Write-Host "A blue car record exists"
}
```

If the search is only concerned with the first matching entry, or the search always returns a unique result, the `SelectSingleNode` method can be used instead.

Working with namespaces

If an XML document includes a namespace, then queries for elements within the document are more difficult. Not only must the namespace tag be included, but an `XmlNamespaceManager` must be defined.

`Select-Xml` builds a namespace manager based on the content of a hashtable when the `Namespace` parameter is used:

```
$xml = @"
<?xml version="1.0"?>
<cars xmlns:c="http://example/cars">
<car type="Saloon">
<c:colour>Green</c:colour>
<c:doors>4</c:doors>
<c:transmission>Automatic</c:transmission>
<c:engine>
<size>2.0</size>
<cylinders>4</cylinders>
</c:engine>
</car>
</cars>
"@
Select-Xml '//car/c:engine' -Namespace @{c='http://example/cars'} -Xml $xml
```

If the `SelectNodes` method is being used, the `XmlNamespaceManager` must be built and then passed as an argument:

```
$namespaceManager = New-Object
System.Xml.XmlNamespaceManager($xml.NameTable)
$namespaceManager.AddNamespace('c', 'http://example/cars')
$xml.SelectNodes(
    '//car[c:colour="Green"]/c:engine',
    $namespaceManager
)
```

XML documents, such as group policy reports, are difficult to work with as they often contain many different namespaces. Each of the possible namespaces must be added to a namespace manager.

Creating documents

PowerShell can be used to create XML documents from scratch. One possible way to do this is by using the `XmlWriter` class:

```
$writer = [System.Xml.XmlWriter]::Create("$pwd\newfile.xml")
$writer.WriteStartDocument()
$writer.WriteStartElement('cars')
$writer.WriteStartElement('car')
$writer.WriteAttributeString('type', 'Saloon')
$writer.WriteElementString('colour', 'Green')
$writer.WriteEndElement()
$writer.WriteEndElement()
$writer.Flush()
$writer.Close()
```

Elements opened by `WriteStartElement` must be closed to maintain a consistent document.

The `XmlWriter` class is a buffered writer. The `Flush` method is called at the end to push the content of the buffer back to the file.

The format of generated XML can be changed by supplying an `XmlWriterSettings` object when calling the `Create` method. For example, it might be desirable to write line breaks and indent elements as shown in the following example:

```
$writerSettings = New-Object System.Xml.XmlWriterSettings
$writerSettings.Indent = $true
$writer = [System.Xml.XmlWriter]::Create(
    "$pwd\newfile.xml",
    $writerSettings
)
$writer.WriteStartDocument()
$writer.WriteStartElement('cars')
$writer.WriteStartElement('car')
$writer.WriteAttributeString('type', 'Saloon')
$writer.WriteElementString('colour', 'Green')
$writer.WriteEndElement()
$writer.WriteEndElement()
$writer.Flush()
$writer.Close()
```

Modifying element and attribute values

Existing elements within an XML document can be modified by assigning a new value. For example, the misspelling of `Appliances` could be corrected:

```
[Xml]$xml = @"
<?xml version="1.0"?>
<items>
<item name='Fridge'>
<category>Appliancse</category>
</item>
<item name='Cooker'>
<category>Appliances</category>
</item>
</items>
"@
($xml.items.item | Where-Object name -eq 'Fridge').category = 'Appliances'
```

Attributes may be changed in the same way; the interface does not distinguish between the two value types.

A direct assignment of a new value cannot be used if the XML document contains more than one element or attribute with the same name (at the same level). For example, the following XML snippet has two values with the same name:

```
[Xml]$xml = @"
<?xml version="1.0"?>
<list>
<name>one</name>
<name>two</name>
</list>
"@
```

The first value may be changed if it is uniquely identified and selected:

```
$xml.list.SelectSingleNode('./name[.="one"]').'#text' = 'three'
```

The following example shows a similar change made to the value of an attribute:

```
[Xml]$xml = @"
<?xml version="1.0"?>
<list name='letters'>
<name>1</name>
</list>
"@
$xml.SelectSingleNode('/list[@name="letters"]').SetAttribute('name',
'numbers')
```

The `@` symbol preceding `name` in the `XPath` expression denotes that the value type is an attribute. If the attribute referred to by the `SetAttribute` method does not exist, it will be created.

Adding elements

Elements must be created before they can be added to an existing document. Elements are created in the context of a document:

```
[Xml]$xml = @"
<?xml version="1.0"?>
<list type='numbers'>
<name>1</name>
</list>
"@
$newElement = $xml.CreateElement('name')
$newElement.InnerText = 2
$xml.list.AppendChild($newElement)
```

Complex elements may be built up by repeatedly using the `Create` methods of the `XmlDocument` (held in the variable, `$xml`).

If the new node is substantial, it may be easier to treat the new node set as a separate document and merge one into the other.

Copying nodes between documents

Nodes (elements, attributes, and so on) may be copied and moved between different XML documents. To bring a node from an external document into another, it must first be imported.

The following example creates two simple XML documents. The first (the variable `xml`) is the intended destination. The `newNodes` variable contains a set of elements that should be copied:

```
[Xml]$xml = @"
<?xml version="1.0"?>
<list type='numbers'>
<name>1</name>
</list>
"@
[Xml]$newNodes = @"
<root>
<name>2</name>
<name>3</name>
<name>4</name>
</root>
"@
```

To copy the name nodes requires each node to be selected (in turn), imported into the original document, and added to the desired node:

```
foreach ($node in $newNodes.SelectNodes('/root/name')) {
    $newNode = $xml.ImportNode($node, $true)
$null = $xml.list.AppendChild($newNode)
}
```

The `ImportNode` method requires two parameters: the node from the foreign document (`newNodes`) and whether or not the import is deep (one level or fully recursive).

The resulting XML can be viewed by inspecting the `OuterXml` property of the `xml` variable:

```
PS> $xml.OuterXml
<?xml version="1.0"?><list
type="numbers"><name>1</name><name>2</name><name>3</name><name>4</name></li
st>
```

Removing elements and attributes

Elements may be removed from a document by selecting the node, then calling the `RemoveChild` method on the parent:

```
[Xml]$xml = @"
<?xml version="1.0"?>
<list type='numbers'>
<name>1</name>
<name>2</name>
<name>3</name>
</list>
"@
$node = $xml.SelectSingleNode('/list/*[.="3"]')
$null = $node.ParentNode.RemoveChild($node)
```

The `RemoveAll` method is also available; however, this removes all children (and attributes) of the selected node.

Attributes are similarly easy to remove from a document:

```
$xml.list.RemoveAttribute('type')
```

Schema validation

XML documents that reference a schema can be validated.

PowerShell itself comes with a number of XML files with associated schemas in the help files. For example, the help file for `ISE` is available:

```
PS>Get-Item $pshome\modules\ISE\en-US\ISE-help.xml

    Directory: C:\Windows\System32\WindowsPowerShell\v1.0\modules\ISE\en-US

Mode                LastWriteTime         Length Name
----                -------------         ------ ----
-a----         29/11/16     07:57          33969 ISE-help.xml
```

The schema documents used by the help content are saved in `$pshome\Schemas\PSMaml`.

The following snippet may be used to load the schema files and then test the content of the document:

```
$path = Resolve-Path "$pshome\modules\ISE\en-US\*-help.xml"
[Xml]$document = Get-Content $path -Raw
$document.Schemas.Add(
    'http://schemas.microsoft.com/maml/2004/10',
    "$pshome\Schemas\PSMaml\maml.xsd"
)
$document.Validate( {
param($sender, $eventArgs)

if ($eventArgs.Severity -in 'Error', 'Warning') {
        Write-Host $eventArgs.Message
    }
} )
```

The argument for `Validate` is a script block that is executed each time an error is encountered. `Write-Host` is used to print a message to the console. A value cannot be directly returned as the script block is executed in the background.

Line number and line position information is not available using this technique for a number of reasons. The first is that the `XmlDocument` object is built from a string (returned by `Get-Content`) and not attached to the file.

System.Xml.Linq

The `System.Xml.Linq` namespace was added with .NET 3.5. This is known as LINQ to XML. **Language Integrated Query** (**LINQ**) is used to describe a query in the same language as the rest of a program. Therefore, interacting with a complex XML document does not require the use of `XPath` queries.

PowerShell can make use of `System.Xml.Linq` once the required assembly has been added:

```
Add-Type -AssemblyName System.Xml.Linq
```

This can also be phrased as:

```
using assembly System.Xml.Linq
```

As a newer interface, `System.Xml.Linq` tends to be more consistent. The same syntax is used to create a document from scratch that is used to add elements and so on.

Opening documents

The `XDocument` class is used to load or parse a document. XML content may be cast to an `XDocument` in the same way that content is cast using the `[Xml]` type accelerator:

```
using assembly System.Xml.Linq
[System.Xml.Linq.XDocument]$xDocument = @"
<?xml version="1.0"?>
<cars>
<car type="Saloon">
<colour>Green</colour>
<doors>4</doors>
<transmission>Automatic</transmission>
<engine>
<size>2.0</size>
<cylinders>4</cylinders>
</engine>
</car>
</cars>
"@
$xDocument.Save("$pwd\cars.xml")
```

If the content has been saved to a file, the `Load` method may be used with a file name:

```
$xDocument = [System.Xml.Linq.XDocument]::Load("$pwd\cars.xml")
```

Selecting nodes

LINQ to XML uses PowerShell to query the content of XML files. This is achieved by combining the methods made available through an `XDocument` (or `XContainer`, or `XElement`). Methods are available to find attributes and elements, either as immediate children, or deeper within a document:

```
$xDocument = [System.Xml.Linq.XDocument]::Load("$pwd        2;cars.xml")
$xDocument.Descendants('car').
Where( { $_.Element('colour').Value -eq 'Green' } ).
Element('engine')
```

The XML-specific methods are supplemented by `.Linq` extension methods, such as the `Where` method, to filter content.

As the query, a script block encapsulated by the `Where` method, is native PowerShell, the comparison operation (`-eq`) is caseinsensitive. The selection of the element by name is casesensitive.

Although it is not the preferred approach, `XPath` can still be used by calling the static method `XPathSelectElements`, as shown here:

```
[System.Xml.XPath.Extensions]::XPathSelectElements(
    $xDocument,
    '//car[colour="Green"]/engine'
)
```

Creating documents

`System.Xml.Linq` can be used to create a document from scratch. For example:

```
using assembly System.Xml.Linq
using namespace System.Xml.Linq

$xDocument = [XDocument]::new(
    [XDeclaration]::new('1.0', 'utf-8', 'yes'),
    [XElement]::new('list', @(
        [XAttribute]::new('type', 'numbers'),
        [XElement]::new('name', 1),
        [XElement]::new('name', 2),
        [XElement]::new('name', 3)
    ))
)
```

Converting the `xDocument` object to a string shows the document without the declaration:

```
PS> $xDocument.ToString()

<list type="numbers">
<name>1</name>
<name>2</name>
<name>3</name>
</list>
```

The `Save` method may be used to write the document to a file:

```
$xDocument.Save("$pwd\test.xml")
```

Reviewing the document shows the declaration:

```
PS> Get-Content test.xml
```

```
<?xml version="1.0" encoding="utf-8" standalone="yes"?>
<list type="numbers">
<name>1</name>
<name>2</name>
<name>3</name>
</list>
```

Working with namespaces

LINQ to XML handles the specification of namespaces by adding an `XNamespace` object to an `XName` object. For example:

```
PS> [XNameSpace]'http://example/cars' + [XName]'engine'

LocalName Namespace           NamespaceName
--------- ---------           -------------
engine    http://example/cars http://example/cars
```

As `XNamespace` expects to have an `XName` added to it, casting to that type can be skipped, simplifying the expression:

```
[XNamespace]'http://example/cars' + 'engine'
```

A query for an element in a specific namespace will use the following format:

```
using namespace System.Xml.Linq

[XDocument]$xDocument = @"
<?xml version="1.0"?>
<cars xmlns:c="http://example/cars">
<car type="Saloon">
<c:colour>Green</c:colour>
<c:doors>4</c:doors>
<c:transmission>Automatic</c:transmission>
<c:engine>
<size>2.0</size>
<cylinders>4</cylinders>
</c:engine>
</car>
</cars>
"@

$xNScars = [XNameSpace]'http://example/cars'
$xDocument.Descendants('car').ForEach( {
    $_.Element($xNScars+ 'engine')
} )
```

Modifying element and attribute values

Modifying an existing node, whether it is an attribute or an element value, can be done by assigning a new value:

```
[XDocument]$xDocument = @"
<?xml version="1.0"?>
<items>
<item name='Fridge'>
<category>Appliancse</category>
</item>
<item name='Cooker'>
<category>Appliances</category>
</item>
</items>
"@
$xDocument.Element('items').
Elements('item').
Where( { $_.Attribute('name').Value -eq 'Fridge' } ).
ForEach( { $_.Element('category').Value = 'Appliances' } )
```

Modifying the value of an attribute uses the same syntax:

```
[XDocument]$xDocument = @"
<?xml version="1.0"?>
<list name='letters'>
<name>1</name>
</list>
"@
$xDocument.Element('list').Attribute('name').Value = 'numbers'
```

If the attribute does not exist, an error will be thrown:

```
PS> $xDocument.Element('list').Attribute('other').Value = 'numbers'

The property 'Value' cannot be found on this object. Verify that the
property exists and can be set.
At line:1 char:1
+ $xDocument.Element('list').Attribute('other').Value = 'numbers'
+ ~~~~~~~~~~~~~~~~~~~~~~~~~~~~~~~~~~~~~~~~~~~~~~~~~~~~~~~~~~~~~~~
    + CategoryInfo          : InvalidOperation: (:) [], RuntimeException
    + FullyQualifiedErrorId :PropertyNotFound
```

Adding nodes

Nodes can be added by using the Add methods, which include Add, AddAfterSelf, AddBeforeSelf, and AddFirst. For example:

```
[XDocument]$xDocument = @"
<?xml version="1.0"?>
<list type='numbers'>
<name>1</name>
</list>
"@
$xDocument.Element('list').
Element('name').
AddAfterSelf(@(
                    [XElement]::new('name', 2),
                    [XElement]::new('name', 3),
                    [XElement]::new('name', 4)
               ))
```

The different Add methods afford a great deal of flexibility over the content of a document; in this case, the new elements appear after the <name>1</name> element.

Removing nodes

The Remove method of an XElement or XAttribute is used to remove the current node.

In the following example, the first name element is removed from the document:

```
[XDocument]$xDocument = @"
<?xml version="1.0"?>
<list type='numbers'>
<name>1</name>
<name>2</name>
<name>3</name>
</list>
"@
$xDocument.Element('list').FirstNode.Remove()
```

Schema validation

LINQ to XML can be used to validate an XML document against a schema file.

The XML document `ISE-help.xml` is validated against its schema in the following example:

```
using namespace System.Xml.Linq

$path = Resolve-Path "$pshome\modules\ISE\en-US\*-help.xml"
$xDocument = [XDocument]::Load($path, [LoadOptions]::SetLineInfo)

$xmlSchemaSet = [System.Xml.Schema.XmlSchemaSet]::new()
$null = $xmlSchemaSet.Add(
    'http://schemas.microsoft.com/maml/2004/10',
    "$pshome\Schemas\PSMaml\maml.xsd"
)
[System.Xml.Schema.Extensions]::Validate(
    $xDocument,
    $xmlSchemaSet,
    {
param($sender, $eventArgs)

if ($eventArgs.Severity -in 'Error', 'Warning') {
            Write-Host $eventArgs.Message
            Write-Host ('  At {0} column {1}' -f
                $sender.LineNumber,
                $sender.LinePosition
            )
        }
    }
)
```

Positional information is made available by loading the `XDocument` with the `SetLineInfo` option.

JSON

JavaScript Object Notation (**JSON**), is similar to XML in some respects. It is intended to be both human and machine readable, and is written in plain text.

Much similar as a hashtable, JSON-formatted objects are made up of key and value pairs. For example:

```
{
    "key1":  "value1",
    "key2": "value2"
}
```

ConvertTo-Json

The `ConvertTo-Json` command can be used to convert a PowerShell object (or hashtable) to JSON:

```
PS> Get-Process -Id $PID |
    Select-Object Name, Id, Path |
ConvertTo-Json

{
    "Name":  "powershell_ise",
    "Id":  3944,
    "Path":
"C:\\Windows\\System32\\WindowsPowerShell\\v1.0\\powershell_ise.exe"
}
```

By default, `ConvertTo-Json` will convert objects to a depth of two. Running the following code will show how the value for three is simplified as a string:

```
@{
one = @{     # 1st iteration
two = @{     # 2nd iteration
three = @{
four = 'value'
            }
        }
    }
} | ConvertTo-Json
```

The property three is present, but the value is listed as `System.Collections.Hashtable` as acquiring the value would need a third iteration. Setting the value of the `Depth` parameter to `three` allows `ConvertTo-Json` to fully inspect the properties of three.

Going too deep:
JSON serialization is a recursive operation. The depth may be increased, which is useful when converting a complex object.
Some value types may cause `ConvertTo-Json` to apparently hang. This is caused by the complexity of those value types. Such value types may include circular references.
A `ScriptBlock` object, for example, cannot be effectively serialized as JSON. The following command takes over 15 seconds to complete and results in a string over 50 million characters long:
`Measure-Command { { 'ScriptBlock' } | ConvertTo-Json -Depth 6 -Compress }`
Increasing the recursion depth to 7 results in an error as keys (property names) begin to duplicate.

ConvertFrom-Json

The `ConvertFrom-Json` command is used to turn a JSON document into an object. For example:

```
'{ "Property": "Value" }' | ConvertFrom-Json
```

`ConvertFrom-Json` creates a `PSCustomObject`.

JSON understands a number of different data types, and each of these types is converted to an equivalent .NET type. The following example shows how each different type might be represented:

```
$object = @"
{
    "Decimal": 1.23,
    "String": "string",
    "Int32": 1,
    "Int64": 2147483648,
    "Boolean": true
}
"@ | ConvertFrom-Json
```

Inspecting individual elements after conversion reflects the type, as demonstrated in the following example:

```
PS> $object.Int64.GetType()
$object.Boolean.GetType()

IsPublic IsSerial Name                                     BaseType
-------- -------- ----                                     --------
True     True     Int64                                    System.ValueType
True     True     Boolean                                  System.ValueType
```

JSON serialization within PowerShell is useful, but it is not perfect. For example, consider the result of converting `Get-Date`:

```
PS> Get-Date | ConvertTo-Json
{
    "value":  "\/Date(1489321529249)\/",
    "DisplayHint":  2,
    "DateTime":  "12 March 2017 12:25:29"
}
```

The value includes a `DisplayHintNoteProperty` and a `DateTimeScriptProperty`, added to the `DateTime` object. These add an extra layer of properties when converting back from JSON:

```
PS> Get-Date | ConvertTo-Json | ConvertFrom-Json

valueDisplayHintDateTime
-----                  ----------- --------
12/03/2017 12:27:25              2 12 March 2017 12:27:25
```

The `DateTime` property can be removed using the following:

```
Get-TypeData System.DateTime | Remove-TypeData
```

`DisplayHint` is added by `Get-Date`, and therefore the command cannot be used in this context.

Any extraneous members such as this would have to be tested for invalid members prior to conversion, which makes the solution more of a problem:

```
PS> Get-TypeData System.DateTime | Remove-TypeData
[DateTime]::Now | ConvertTo-Json | ConvertFrom-Json | Select-Object *


Date        : 12/03/2017 00:00:00
Day         : 12
```

```
DayOfWeek   : Sunday
DayOfYear   : 71
Hour        : 12
Kind        : Utc
Millisecond : 58
Minute      : 32
Month       : 3
Second      : 41
Ticks       : 636249187610580000
TimeOfDay   : 12:32:41.0580000
Year        : 2017
```

Summary

This chapter took a brief look at working with HTML content, and how HTML content is formatted.

Working with XML content is a common requirement. This chapter introduced the structure of XML, along with two different approaches to working with XML.

Finally, JSON serialization was introduced, along with the `ConvertTo-Json` and `ConvertFrom-Json` commands.

The `Chapter 14`, *Working with REST and SOAP*, explores working with REST and SOAP.

14
Working with REST and SOAP

REST and SOAP are often used as labels to refer to two different approaches to implementing a web-based **Application Programming Interface** (**API**).

The growth of cloud-based services in recent years has pushed the chances of working with such interfaces from rare to almost certain.

In this chapter, we are going to cover the following topics:

- Web requests
- Working with REST
- Working with SOAP

Web requests

A background in web requests is valuable before delving into interfaces that run over the top of **Hyper-Text Transfer Protocol** (**HTTP**).

PowerShell can use `Invoke-WebRequest` to send HTTP requests. For example, the following command will return the response to a `GET` request for the Hey, Scripting Guy blog:

```
Invoke-WebRequest -UseBasicParsing
https://blogs.technet.microsoft.com/heyscriptingguy/
```

HTTP methods

HTTP supports a number of different methods, including:

- `GET`
- `HEAD`
- `POST`
- `PUT`
- `DELETE`
- `CONNECT`
- `OPTIONS`
- `TRACE`
- `PATCH`

These methods are defined in the HTTP 1.1 specification:

`https://www.w3.org/Protocols/rfc2616/rfc2616-sec9.html`

It is common to find that a web server only supports a subset of these. In many cases, supporting too many methods is deemed to be a security risk. The `Invoke-WebRequest` command can be used to verify the list of HTTP methods supported by a site, for example:

```
PS> Invoke-WebRequest www.indented.co.uk -Method OPTIONS |
    Select-Object -ExpandProperty Headers

Key            Value
---            -----
Allow          OPTIONS, TRACE, GET, HEAD, POST
Public         OPTIONS, TRACE, GET, HEAD, POST
Content-Length 0
```

HTTPS

If a connection to a web service uses HTTPS (HTTP over **Secure Sockets Layer** (**SSL**)) the certificate must be validated before a connection can complete and a request can be completed. If a web service has an invalid certificate an error will be returned.

How PowerShell reacts to different scenarios can be tested. The `badssl` site can be used to test how PowerShell might react to different SSL scenarios:

```
https://badssl.com/
```

For example, when attempting to connect to a site with an expired certificate (using `Invoke-WebRequest`) the following message will be displayed:

```
PS> Invoke-WebRequest https://expired.badssl.com/
Invoke-WebRequest : The underlying connection was closed: Could not
establish trust relationship for the SSL/TLS secure channel.
At line:1 char:1
+ Invoke-WebRequest https://expired.badssl.com/
+ ~~~~~~~~~~~~~~~~~~~~~~~~~~~~~~~~~~~~~~~~~~~~~~
    + CategoryInfo          : InvalidOperation:
(System.Net.HttpWebRequest:HttpWebRequest) [Invoke-WebRequest],
WebException
    + FullyQualifiedErrorId :
WebCmdletWebResponseException,Microsoft.PowerShell.Commands.InvokeWebReques
tCommand
```

`Invoke-WebRequest` cannot bypass or ignore an invalid certificate on its own (using a parameter). Certificate validation behavior may be changed by adjusting the `CertificatePolicy` on the `ServicePointManager`:

```
https://msdn.microsoft.com/en-us/library/system.net.servicepointmanager(v=vs.11
0).aspx
```

Bypassing SSL errors

If a service has an invalid certificate, the best response is to fix the problem. When it is not possible or practical to address the real problem, a workaround can be created.

This modification applies to the current PowerShell session and will reset to default behavior every time a new PowerShell session is opened.

The certificate policy used by the `ServicePointManager` may be replaced with a customized handler by writing a class (PowerShell, version 5) that replaces the `CheckValidationResult` method:

```
Class AcceptAllPolicy: System.Net.ICertificatePolicy {
    [Boolean] CheckValidationResult(
        [Net.ServicePoint] $servicePoint,
        [Security.Cryptography.X509Certificates.X509Certificate]
$certificate,
```

```
            [Net.WebRequest] $webRequest,
            [Int32] $problem)
        {
    return $true
        }
}
[System.Net.ServicePointManager]::CertificatePolicy =
[AcceptAllPolicy]::new()
```

Once the policy is in place, certificate errors will be ignored as the previous method returns `true` no matter its state:

```
Invoke-WebRequest "https://expired.badssl.com/"

StatusCode        : 200
StatusDescription : OK
...
```

CertificatePolicy is marked as obsolete:
The `CertificatePolicy` property is marked as obsolete in the documentation on MSDN.
Until recently, adjusting the `ServerCertificateValidationCallback` was sufficient. However, with PowerShell 5 this appears to only fix part of the problem for `Invoke-WebRequest`.
Requests made by `System.Net.WebClient` are satisfied by this simpler approach which trusts all certificates:
`[System.Net.ServicePointManager]::ServerCertificateValidationCallback = { $true }`

Capturing SSL errors

The `ServerCertificateValidationCallback` process provides the opportunity to analyze errors during certificate validation.

The method is called asynchronously (in response to an event), therefore the variables created within either the class or script block are not available to PowerShell itself. Information may be exported to a file using a command such as `Export-Clixml`.

`Invoke-WebRequest` might throw an error if the validation callback is used. However, if the goal to validate the certificate and response to the web request is less important, `System.Net.WebClient` might be used.

A number of arguments are passed to the `ServerCertificateValidationCallback`. The following example provides parameters for each of the arguments:

```
using namespace System.Security.Cryptography.X509Certificates

[System.Net.ServicePointManager]::ServerCertificateValidationCallback = {
param(
        [Object]$sender,
        [X509Certificate2]$certificate,
        [X509Chain]$chain,
        [System.Net.Security.SslPolicyErrors]$sslPolicyErrors
    )

    [PSCustomObject]@{
        Sender          = $sender
        Certificate     = $certificate
        Chain           = $chain
SslPolicyErrors = $sslPolicyErrors
    } | Export-Clixml $env:TEMP\CertValidation.xml

return $true
}

$webClient = New-Object System.Net.WebClient
$webClient.DownloadString('https://expired.badssl.com/') | Out-Null

$certValidation = Import-Clixml $env:TEMP\CertValidation.xml
```

Once the content of the XML file has been loaded, the content may be investigated. For example, the certificate that was exchanged can be viewed:

```
$certValidation.Certificate
```

Or the response can be used to inspect all of the certificates in the key `Chain`:

```
$certValidation.Chain.ChainElements | Select-Object -ExpandProperty
Certificate
```

The `ChainStatus` property exposes details of any errors during chain validation:

```
$certValidation.Chain.ChainStatus
```

The `ChainStatus` is summarized by the `SslPolicyErrors` property.

PowerShell should be restarted to reset the certificate policies to system defaults.

Working with REST

A **REpresentational State Transfer** (**REST**), it compliant web service allows a client to interact with the service using a set of predefined stateless operations. REST is not a protocol, it is an architectural style.

Whether or not an interface is truly REST-compliant is not particularly relevant when the goal is to use one in PowerShell. Interfaces must be used according to any documentation that has been published.

Invoke-RestMethod

The `Invoke-RestMethod` command is able to execute methods exposed by web services. The name of a method is part of the **Uniform Resource Identifier** (**URI**), it is important not to confuse this with the `Method` parameter. The `Method` parameter is used to describe the HTTP method. By default, `Invoke-RestMethod` uses the `HTTP GET`.

Simple requests

The REST API provided by GitHub may be used to list the repositories made available by the PowerShell team.

The API entry point is `https://api.github.com` as documented in the reference:

`https://developer.github.com/v3/`

The specific method being called is documented on a different page of the reference:

`https://developer.github.com/v3/repos/#list-user-repositories`

The name of the user forms part of the URI; there are no arguments for this method. Therefore, the following command will execute the method and return a list of repositories:

```
Invoke-RestMethod -Uri https://api.github.com/users/powershell/repos
```

Requests with arguments

Arguments are passed to REST methods in one of two possible ways: in a query string or using the Body parameter.

The Google geocoding API expects address as an argument:

https://developers.google.com/maps/documentation/geocoding/start

When using a query string any reserved characters must be replaced. For example, spaces in a query string must be replaced with %20 or +. The .NET framework provides a means of changing reserved characters using the HttpUtility class:

```
# HttpUtility is not available without loading System.Web
Add-Type -AssemblyName System.Web
$address = '221b Baker St, Marylebone, London NW1 6XE'
$address = [System.Web.HttpUtility]::UrlEncode($address)
Invoke-RestMethod -Uri
"https://maps.googleapis.com/maps/api/geocode/json?address=$address"
```

These additional steps may be avoided by using the Body parameter of the Invoke-RestMethod. Any encoding changes that may be required will be handled automatically:

```
$body = @{
address = '221b Baker St, Marylebone, London NW1 6XE'
}
Invoke-RestMethod -Uri "https://maps.googleapis.com/maps/api/geocode/json"
-Body $body
```

In this case, the arguments are described by a hashtable.

The previous syntax is much easier to work with than a long query string, but it is not necessarily clear this is possible from the developer guides for REST interfaces.

It is critical to note that REST interfaces are case sensitive; using a parameter named Address would result in an error message as shown following:

```
PS> $body = @{
    Address = '221b Baker St, Marylebone, London NW1 6XE'
}
Invoke-RestMethod -Uri "https://maps.googleapis.com/maps/api/geocode/json"
-Body $body
Invoke-RestMethod : The remote server returned an error: (400) Bad Request.
At line:4 char:1
+ Invoke-RestMethod -Uri "https://maps.googleapis.com/maps/api/geocode/ ...
+ ~~~~~~~~~~~~~~~~~~~~~~~~~~~~~~~~~~~~~~~~~~~~~~~~~~~~~~~~~~~~~~~~~~~~~~~~~~~
    + CategoryInfo          : InvalidOperation:
```

```
(System.Net.HttpWebRequest:HttpWebRequest) [Invoke-RestMethod],
WebException
    + FullyQualifiedErrorId :
WebCmdletWebResponseException,Microsoft.PowerShell.Commands.InvokeRestMetho
dCommand
```

Working with authentication

There are a large number of authentication systems that might be used when working with web services.

For services which expect to use the current user account to authenticate, the `UseDefaultCredential` parameter may be used to pass authentication tokens without explicitly passing a username and password. A service that is integrated into an Active Directory domain, expecting to use Kerberos authentication, might be an example of such a service.

Implementation of authentication in REST-based web services varies enormously.

REST interfaces written to provide automation access tend to offer reasonably simple approaches to automation, often including basic authentication.

Interfaces written as an endpoint for other clients, for example the REST interface provided by `Spotify`, require complex client-implementation specific authentication and authorization exchanges. One of the most popular of these processes is OAuth.

Walking through OAuth

The following example is based on the REST API provided by `Spotify` (using a free account). The goal of this process is to get the content of a private playlist named `Classical` that exists in my account, and to do that the application must be authorized.

The details of this process will vary slightly between APIs; the lessons learnt here can be translated to many different web APIs. For example, GitHub implements a very similar process to support OAuth:

`https://developer.github.com/v3/oauth/#web-application-flow`

Creating an application

Before starting with the code, to use OAuth an application has to be registered with `Spotify`. This is done using the developer portal:

```
https://developer.spotify.com/my-applications/#!/applications
```

An application must be created to acquire a **Client ID** and **Client Secret**. The following screenshot is of a temporary application created for this process:

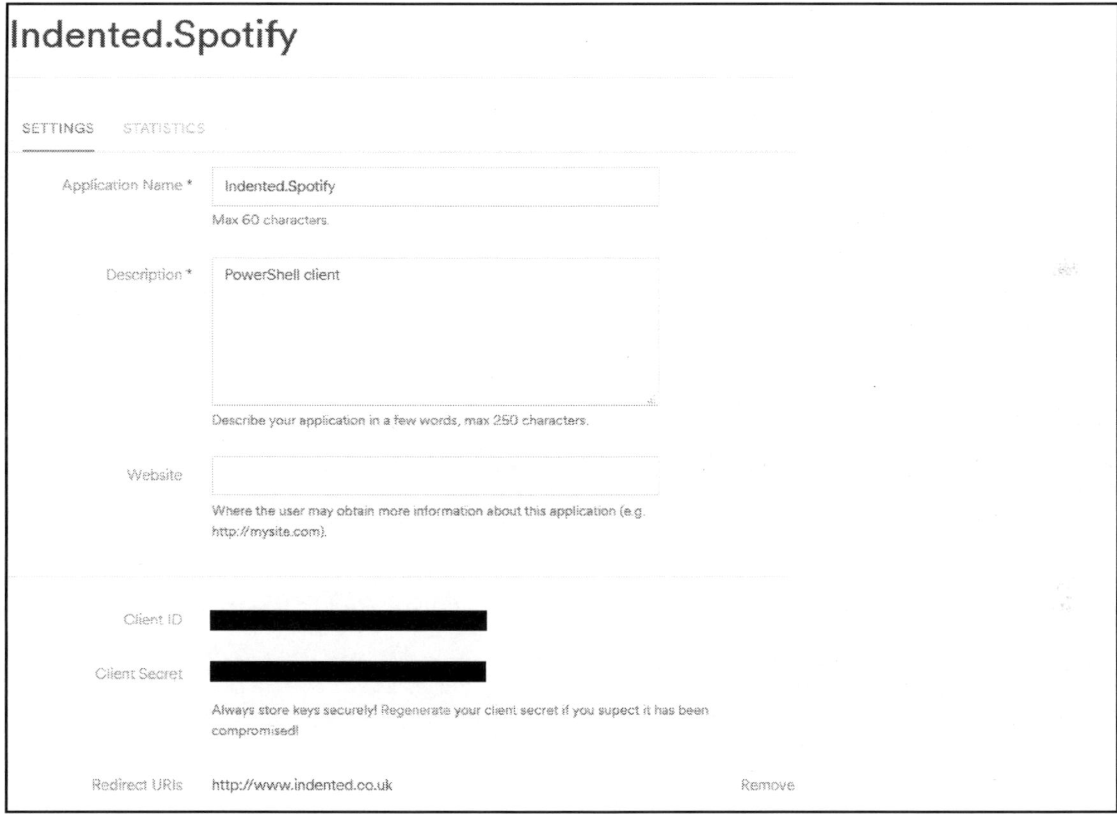

The values from the web page will fill three variables:

```
$clientId = 'FromSpotify'
$clientSecret = 'FromSpotify'
$redirectUrl = 'AnyURL'
```

Getting an authorization code

Once an application is registered an authorization code is required. Obtaining the authorization code gives the end-user the opportunity to grant the application access to a `Spotify` account. The process is described in the web API guide:

https://developer.spotify.com/web-api/authorization-guide/#authorization-code-flow

Before starting, two assemblies must be imported:

```
using assembly PresentationFramework
using assembly System.Web
```

The **Windows Presentation Framework** is used to create a very small interface to load the authorization request page.

A URL must be created that will prompt for authorization:

```
$authorize =
'https://accounts.spotify.com/authorize?client_id={0}&response_type=code&redirect_uri={1}&scope={2}' -f
    $clientId,
    $redirectUrl,
    'playlist-read-private'
```

Scope describes the rights the application would like to have; the user request page will include details of the requested rights. The web API guide contains a list of possible scopes:

https://developer.spotify.com/web-api/using-scopes/

The URL will be added to a `WebBrowser` control that is displayed to the user:

```
$window = New-Object System.Windows.Window
$window.Height = 650
$window.Width = 450
$browser = New-Object System.Windows.Controls.WebBrowser
# Add an event handler to close the window when
# interaction with Spotify is complete.
$browser.add_Navigated( {
if ($args[0].Source -notlike '*spotify*') {
        $args[0].Parent.Close()
    }
} )
$browser.Navigate($authorize)
$window.Content = $browser
$null = $window.ShowDialog()
```

The window will close as soon as it leaves the `Spotify` pages. That should be when it hits the redirect URL.

If the application has already been authorized the window will close without prompting for user interaction.

The URL it navigates to contains the authorization code in a query string. `HttpUtility` is used to extract the code from the query string:

```
$authorizationCode =
[System.Web.HttpUtility]::ParseQueryString($window.Content.Source.Query)['c
ode']
```

Requesting an access token

The next step is to create an access token. The access token is valid for a limited time. The `clientSecret` is sent with this request; if this were an application that was given to others, keeping the secret would be a challenge to overcome:

```
$accessToken = Invoke-RestMethod -Uri
https://accounts.spotify.com/api/token -Method POST -Body @{
grant_type    = 'authorization_code'
code          = $authorizationCode
redirect_uri  = $redirectUrl
client_id     = $clientId
client_secret = $clientSecret
}
```

The previous request used the HTTP method `POST`. The HTTP method, which should be used with a REST method, is documented in the developer guides for an interface.

Each of the requests that follow will use the access token from the previous request. The access token is placed in an HTTP header field named `Authorization`. The `Authorization` field is created using a hashtable:

```
$headers = @{
    Authorization = 'Bearer {0}' -f $accessToken.access_token
}
```

Getting a list of playlists

The next step is to retrieve all of the playlists belonging to the current user. The method is described in the web API guide:

`https://developer.spotify.com/web-api/get-list-users-playlists/`

The user reference (`/user/id`) can be replaced with me (`/me`) for this request. Getting the list of tracks needs the user ID. The user ID can be taken from the playlist owner, avoiding a need to increase the number of rights requested (by scope).

The list of playlists is filtered to one named `Classical`:

```
$playlists = Invoke-RestMethod -Uri https://api.spotify.com/v1/me/playlists
-Headers $headers
$playlist = $playlists.items | Where-Object Name -eq 'Classical'
$user = $playlist.owner.id
$id = $playlist.id
```

The previous steps identify the ID of the playlist, the name of the user account is required as well for the next step, which lists the tracks in the playlist.

Getting a list of tracks

Finally, with the ID strings, the list of tracks can be retrieved. Again, the method is described in the web API guide:

`https://developer.spotify.com/web-api/get-playlists-tracks/`

The method call requires the authorization header:

```
$tracks = Invoke-RestMethod -Uri
https://api.spotify.com/v1/users/$user/playlists/$id/tracks -Headers
$headers
```

The tracks in this particular playlist are shown following:

```
PS> $tracks.items.track.name

The Planets, Op. 32: I. Mars, the Bringer of War
The Planets, Op. 32: II. Venus, the Bringer of Peace
The Planets, Op. 32: III. Mercury, the Winged Messenger
The Planets, Op. 32: IV. Jupiter, the Bringer of Jollity
The Planets, Op. 32: V. Saturn, the Bringer of Old Age
The Planets, Op. 32: VI. Uranus, the Magician
The Planets, Op. 32: VII. Neptune, the Mystic
```

The web API guide shows other methods that might be used when working with playlists. The application is authorized to use anything that reads information about playlists:

`https://developer.spotify.com/web-api/playlist-endpoints/`

Working with SOAP

Unlike REST, which is an architectural style, SOAP is a protocol. It is perhaps reasonable to compare working with SOAP to importing a .NET assembly (DLL) to work with the types inside. As a result, a SOAP client is much more strongly tied to a server than is the case with a REST interface.

SOAP uses XML to exchange information between client and server.

SOAP-based web APIs are, these days, quite rare.

New-WebServiceProxy

The `New-WebServiceProxy` command is used to connect a **Web Services Description Language** (**WSDL**) document. The document is written in XML and can be viewed in a browser.

The command accesses a service anonymously by default. If the current user should be passed on, the `UseDefaultCredential` parameter should be used. If explicit credentials are required, the `Credential` parameter can be used.

The following example creates a proxy, which is used to access a web service that exposes information about Mendeleev's periodic table of the elements:

```
$periodicTable= New-WebServiceProxy
http://www.webservicex.net/periodictable.asmx?WSDL -Namespace Mendeleev
```

The object returned by the command holds information about the connection:

```
PS>$periodicTable

SoapVersion                          : Default
AllowAutoRedirect                    : False
CookieContainer                      :
ClientCertificates                   : {}
EnableDecompression                  : False
UserAgent                            : Mozilla/4.0 (compatible; MSIE 6.0;
MS Web Services Client Protocol 4.0.30319.42000)
```

```
Proxy                                 :
UnsafeAuthenticatedConnectionSharing : False
Credentials                           :
UseDefaultCredentials                 : False
ConnectionGroupName                   :
PreAuthenticate                       : False
Url                                   :
http://www.webservicex.net/periodictable.asmx
RequestEncoding                       :
Timeout                               : 100000
Site                                  :
Container                             :
```

Methods

As well as describing the connection, the web service proxy object exposes methods used to interact with the web service.

`Get-Member` can be used to view the methods. The methods beginning with `Get` are shown following:

```
PS> $periodicTable | Get-Member Get* -MemberType Method | Select-Object
Name, Definition

Name                      Definition
----                      ----------
GetAtomicNumber           string GetAtomicNumber(string ElementName)
GetAtomicNumberAsync      voidGetAtomicNumberAsync(string ElementName), ...
GetAtomicWeight           string GetAtomicWeight(string ElementName)
GetAtomicWeightAsync      voidGetAtomicWeightAsync(string ElementName), ...
GetAtoms                  string GetAtoms()
GetAtomsAsync             void GetAtomsAsync(), ...
GetElementSymbol          string GetElementSymbol(string ElementName)
GetElementSymbolAsync void GetElementSymbolAsync(string ElementName), ...
GetHashCodeintGetHashCode()
GetLifetimeServiceSystem.ObjectGetLifetimeService()
GetType                   type GetType()
```

The `GetAtoms` method will list the names of each of the elements in the periodic table. The name of an element can be used to retrieve simple information using the other methods, for example:

```
PS> $periodicTable.GetAtomicNumber('Zirconium')
<NewDataSet>
<Table>
<AtomicNumber>40</AtomicNumber>
```

```
<ElementName>Zirconium</ElementName>
<Symbol>Zr</Symbol>
<AtomicWeight>91.22</AtomicWeight>
<BoilingPoint>3851</BoilingPoint>
<IonisationPotential>6.8500000000000005</IonisationPotential>
<EletroNegativity>1.22</EletroNegativity>
<AtomicRadius>1.45</AtomicRadius>
<MeltingPoint>2125</MeltingPoint>
<Density>6511</Density>
</Table>
</NewDataSet>
```

As this interface does not define structured types, the value returned is an XML string. PowerShell can use the XML type accelerator to turn this into an object:

```
PS> ([Xml]$periodicTable.GetAtomicNumber('Einsteinium')).NewDataSet.Table

AtomicNumber      : 99
ElementName       : Einsteinium
Symbol            : Es
AtomicWeight      : 255
BoilingPoint      : 1500
EletroNegativity : 1.2
MeltingPoint      : 860
```

The property values, such as the `MeltingPoint`, are strings and would need to be converted to numeric values if there was a need to compare values:

```
PS> $hydrogen =
([Xml]$periodicTable.GetAtomicNumber('Hydrogen')).NewDataSet.Table
$hydrogen.MeltingPoint.GetType()

IsPublic IsSerial Name                                     BaseType
-------- -------- ----                                     --------
True     True     String                                   System.Object
```

Types

A SOAP-based web service might encapsulate a response in a type. This allows the service to define value types for properties. In the case of the periodic table, this might have been used to convert values intended to be numeric into `Int32` (or another appropriate type).

The `sunsetrises` service is an example of a SOAP interface that uses a defined type. A proxy for this service is created as follows:

```
New-WebServiceProxy http://www.webservicex.net/sunsetriseservice.asmx?WSDL
```

The `GetSunSetRiseTime` method expects an object of type `LatLonDate` as an argument. The method returns an object of the same type. The assumption is that supplying latitude and longitude on this object will let the method fill in the rest of the details.

The Google geocoding service demonstrated when looking at REST was able to return latitude and longitude for an `address`:

```
# Use Google's service to find a latitude and longitude
$body = @{
address = '221b Baker St, Marylebone, London NW1 6XE'
}
$response = Invoke-RestMethod -Uri
"https://maps.googleapis.com/maps/api/geocode/json" -Body $body

# Connect to the SOAP service
$sun = New-WebServiceProxy
http://www.webservicex.net/sunsetriseservice.asmx?WSDL -Namespace Sun

# Create an instance of LatLonDate
$latLonDate = New-Object Sun.LatLonDate
# Populate the Latitude and Longitude
$latLonDate.Latitude = $response.results.geometry.location.lat
$latLonDate.Longitude = $response.results.geometry.location.ln
```

Once the properties have been filled in, the method can be called:

```
PS> $sun.GetSunSetRiseTime($latLonDate)

Latitude    : 51.52377
Longitude   : -0.1585369
SunSetTime  : 17.65245
SunRiseTime : 5.9284
TimeZone    : 0
Day         : 0
Month       : 0
Year        : 0
```

The `SunSetTime` and `SunRiseTime` might be considered to be hours expressed as a decimal. These can be speculatively converted to hours and minutes as follows:

```
$sunSetRiseTime = $sun.GetSunSetRiseTime($latLonDate)
$hour = [Math]::Floor($sunSetRiseTime.SunRiseTime)
$minute = [Math]::Round(60 * ($sunSetRiseTime.SunRiseTime % 1))
```

Using `Get-Date` turns that into a `DateTime` object:

```
PS> Write-Host "Sun rise:" (Get-Date -Hour $hour -Minute $minute)

Sun rise: 12/03/2017 05:56:50
```

This demonstrates that it is possible to work with SOAP methods that expect objects of a specific type.

Namespaces

The previous example uses `Sun` as a namespace. All types derived from the web service will appear beneath that namespace. The namespace, and types beneath, exist for the duration of the PowerShell session.

If an attempt is made to create the web service proxy a second time using the same namespace, PowerShell can become confused.

The following example creates the web service proxy twice:

```
# Create once
$sun = New-WebServiceProxy
http://www.webservicex.net/sunsetriseservice.asmx?WSDL -Namespace Sun
# Create again with the same namespace
$sun = New-WebServiceProxy
http://www.webservicex.net/sunsetriseservice.asmx?WSDL -Namespace Sun
$latLonDate = New-Object Sun.LatLonDate

$latLonDate.Latitude = 51.52377
$latLonDate.Longitude = -0.1585369
```

When the `GetSunSetRiseTime` method is called an error is thrown:

```
$sunSetRiseTime = $sun.GetSunSetRiseTime($latLonDate)
Cannot convert argument "L", with value: "Sun.LatLonDate", for
"GetSunSetRiseTime" to type "Sun.LatLonDate": "Cannot convert the
"Sun.LatLonDate" value of type
"Sun.LatLonDate" to type "Sun.LatLonDate"."
At line:10 char:1
+ $sunSetRiseTime = $sun.GetSunSetRiseTime($latLonDate)
+ ~~~~~~~~~~~~~~~~~~~~~~~~~~~~~~~~~~~~~~~~~~~~~~~~~~~~~
    + CategoryInfo          : NotSpecified: (:) [], MethodException
    + FullyQualifiedErrorId :MethodArgumentConversionInvalidCastArgument
```

At this point, PowerShell has two different versions of `Sun.LatLonDate`. The version that is created by `New-Object` cannot be made suitable for the second version of the web service proxy.

There are a number of possible solutions to this problem:

1. Restart the PowerShell session.
2. Create a unique namespace for each web service proxy.
3. Allow PowerShell to use a dynamic namespace.

The third option allows PowerShell to manage namespaces, it will not overlap these. Creating instances of objects will need the name of the dynamically generated namespace.

The following example retrieves the name of the namespace from the object returned by `New-WebServiceProxy`:

```
$sun = New-WebServiceProxy
http://www.webservicex.net/sunsetriseservice.asmx?WSDL
$namespace = $sun.GetType().Namespace
$latLonDate = New-Object "$namespace.LatLonDate"
$latLonDate.Latitude = 51.52377
$latLonDate.Longitude = -0.1585369
$sun.GetSunSetRiseTime($latLonDate)
```

The value held in the namespace variable may never change. Assigning the value as shown previously, is sufficient to correctly create the `LatLonDateobject`, even if the `New-WebServiceProxy` command has been run more than once.

Summary

This chapter has explored working with web requests before taking a look at REST and SOAP web interfaces.

`Chapter 15`, *Remoting and Remote Management*, explores remoting and remote management.

15
Remoting and Remote Management

Windows remoting came to PowerShell with the release of version 2.0. Windows remoting is a powerful feature that allows administrators to move away from RPC-based remote access.

PowerShell 6 includes plans to allow the use of SSH as a transport for remoting. A demonstration of this is available on GitHub:

```
https://github.com/PowerShell/PowerShell/tree/master/demos/SSHRemoting
```

In this chapter, the following topics are covered:

- WS-Management
- CIM sessions
- PS sessions
- The double-hop problem

WS-Management

Windows remoting uses WS-Management as its communication protocol. Support for WS-Management and remoting were introduced with PowerShell 2.0. WS-Management uses **Simple Object Access Protocol** (**SOAP**) to pass information between the client and the server.

Enabling remoting

Before remoting can be used, it must be enabled. In a domain environment, remoting can be enabled using a group policy:

- **Policy name:** `Allow remote server management through WinRM`
- **Path:** `Computer configuration \ Administrative Templates \ Windows Components \ Windows Remote Management (WinRM) \ WinRM Service`

If remoting is enabled using a group policy, a firewall rule should be created to allow access to the service:

- **Policy name:** `Define inbound port exceptions`
- **Path:** `Computer Configuration \ Administrative Templates \ Network \ Network Connections \ Windows Firewall \ Domain Profile`
- **Port exception example:** `5985:TCP:*:enabled:WSMan`

Windows remoting can be enabled on a per-machine basis using the `Enable-PSRemoting` command.

Remoting may be disabled in PowerShell using `Disable-PSRemoting`. Disabling remoting will show the following warning:

```
PS> Disable-PSRemoting

WARNING: Disabling the session configurations does not undo all the changes
made by the Enable-PSRemoting or Enable-PSSessionConfiguration cmdlet. You
might have to manually undo the changes by following these steps:
1. Stop and disable the WinRM service.
2. Delete the listener that accepts requests on any IP address.
3. Disable the firewall exceptions for WS-Management communications.
4.Restore the value of the LocalAccountTokenFilterPolicy to 0, which
restricts remote access to members of the Administrators group on the
computer.
```

Get-WSManInstance

`Get-WSManInstance` provides access to instances of resources at a lower level than commands such as `Get-CimInstance`.

For example, `Get-WSManInstance` can be used to get the WMI class `Win32_OperatingSystem`:

```
Get-WSManInstance -ResourceUri wmicimv2/win32_operatingsystem
```

The response is an `XmlElement` that PowerShell presents as an object with properties for each child element.

`Get-WSManInstance` has been superseded by `Get-CimInstance`, which was introduced in PowerShell 3.0.

WSMan drive

The `WSMan` drive is accessible when PowerShell is running as administrator. The drive can be used to view and change the configuration of remoting.

For example, the provider can be used to update settings such as the `MaxEnvelopeSize`, which affects the maximum permissible size of SOAP messages sent and received by WSMan:

```
Set-Item WSMan:\localhost\MaxEnvelopeSizekb 1024
```

The WinRM service may need to be restarted after values are changed:

```
Restart-Service winrm
```

Remoting and SSL

By default, Windows remoting requests are unencrypted. An HTTPS listener can be created to support encryption. Before attempting to create an HTTPS listener, a certificate is required.

Using a self-signed certificate is often the first step when configuring SSL. Windows 10 comes with a PKI module that can be used to create a certificate. In the following example, a self-signed certificate is created in the computer's personal store:

```
PS> New-SelfSignedCertificate -DnsName $env:COMPUTERNAME
PSParentPath: Microsoft.PowerShell.Security\Certificate::LocalMachine\MY
Thumbprint                               Subject
----------                               -------
D8D2F174EE1C37F7C2021C9B7EB6FEE3CB1B9A41 CN=SSLTEST
```

Once the certificate has been created, an HTTPS listener may be created using the WSMan drive:

```
New-Item -Path WSMan:\localhost\Listener -Address * -Transport HTTPS -
CertificateThumbprint 'D8D2F174EE1C37F7C2021C9B7EB6FEE3CB1B9A41'  -Force
```

The `Force` parameter is used to suppress a confirmation prompt.

Set-WSManQuickConfig

Certificates used by remoting have the following requirements:

- The subject must contain the computer name (without a domain)
- The certificate must support the server authentication enhanced key usage
- The certificate must not be expired, revoked, or self-signed

If a certificate that meets these requirements is present, the `Set-WSManQuickConfig` command may be used:

```
Set-WSManQuickConfig -UseSSL
```

HTTPS listeners may be viewed as follows:

```
PS> Get-ChildItem WSMan:\localhost\Listener\* | Where-Object { (Get-Item
"$($_.PSPath)\Transport").Value -eq 'HTTPS' }
WSManConfig: Microsoft.WSMan.Management\WSMan::localhost\Listener
Type      Keys                            Name
----      ----                            ----
Container {Transport=HTTPS, Address=*} Listener_1305953032
```

The preceding example may be extended by exploring the properties for the listener:

```
Get-ChildItem WSMan:\localhost\Listener | ForEach-Object {
    $listener = $_ | Select-Object Name
    Get-ChildItem $_.PSPath | ForEach-Object {
        $listener | Add-Member $_.Name $_.Value
    }
    $listener
} | Where-Object Transport -eq 'HTTPS'
```

The self-signed certificate can be assigned in this manner, but for an SSL connection to succeed, the client must trust, the certificate. Without trust the following error is shown:

```
PS> Invoke-Command -ScriptBlock { Get-Process } -ComputerName
$env:COMPUTERNAME -UseSSL
[SSLTEST] Connecting to remote server SSLTEST failed with the following
```

```
error message : The server certificate on the destination computer
(SSLTEST:5986) has the following errors:
The SSL certificate is signed by an unknown certificate authority. For more
information, see the about_Remote_Troubleshooting Help topic.
+ CategoryInfo : OpenError: (SSLTEST:String) [],
PSRemotingTransportException
+ FullyQualifiedErrorId : 12175,PSSessionStateBroken
```

A number of options are available to bypass this option:

- Disable certificate verification
- Add the certificate from the remote server to the local root certificate store

Disabling certificate verification can be achieved by configuring the options of a PS session:

```
$options = New-PSSessionOption -SkipCACheck
$session = New-PSSession computerName -SessionOptions $options
```

Either of the preceding options will allow the connection to complete. This can be verified using `Test-WSMan`:

```
Test-WSMan -UseSSL
```

If a new certificate is obtained, the certificate for the listener may be replaced by using `Set-Item`:

```
Set-Item
WSMan:\localhost\Listener\Listener_1305953032\CertificateThumbprint
'D8D2F174EE1C37F7C2021C9B7EB6FEE3CB1B9A41'
```

Remoting and permissions

By default, Windows remoting requires administrative access. A summary of granted permissions may be viewed using `Get-PSSessionConfiguration`. The summary does not include the permission level:

```
Get-PSSessionConfiguration Microsoft.PowerShell
```

Remoting permissions GUI

Permissions can be changed using the graphical interface. The interface will be displayed when the following command is run:

```
Set-PSSessionConfiguration microsoft.powerShell -ShowSecurityDescriptorUI
```

This displays a standard GUI for assigning permissions.

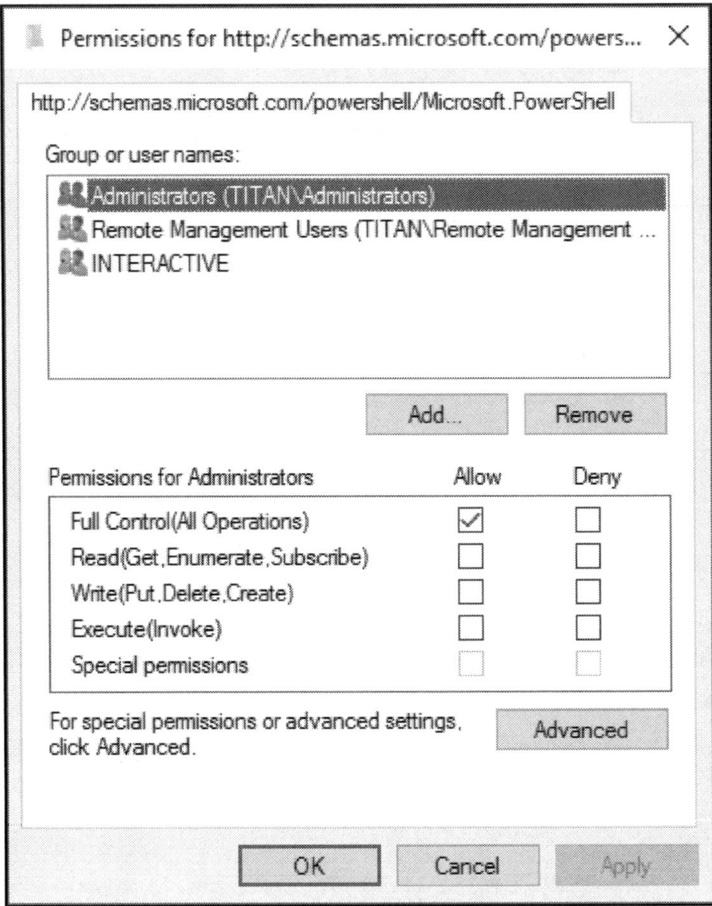

The session configuration defines four different permission levels:

- `Full`
- `Read`
- `Write`
- `Execute`

Remoting permissions by script

Permissions may also be changed using a script. The following commands retrieve the current security descriptor:

```
using namespace System.Security.AccessControl

$sddl = Get-PSSessionConfiguration microsoft.powerShell |
    Select-Object -ExpandProperty SecurityDescriptorSddl
$acl = New-Object CommonSecurityDescriptor(
    $false,
    $false,
$sddl
)
$acl.DiscretionaryAcl
```

The object created here does not translate access masks into meaningful names. There are a small number of possible values for the access mask (shown here as 32-bit integers):

- `Full` (`All` operations): `268435456`
- `Read` (`Get`, `Enumerate`, `Subscribe`): `-2147483648`
- `Write` (`Put`, `Delete`, `Create`): `1073741824`
- `Execute` (`Invoke`): `536870912`

Permissions may be combined by using the `-bor` operator. For example, read and write may be defined using:

```
$readAndWrite = -2147483648 -bor 1073741824
```

Granting `Read`, `Write`, and `Execute` individually should be equivalent to `Full Control`. However, the result of binary (or the composite of all values) is `-536870912`, not the expected value for Full.

Understanding these values allows the current settings to be displayed in more detail than `Get-PSSessionConfiguration` displays. The function adds two script properties to each of the access control entries in the discretionary ACL. The first translates the SID into an account name; the second translates the access mask into a name (or set of names).

The example uses an enumeration (`enum`) to describe the possible access rights:

```
using namespace System.Security.AccessControl; using namespace
System.Security.Principal
[Flags()]
enum SessionAccessRight {
    All      = -536870912
```

```
        Full    = 268435456
        Read    = -2147483648
        Write   = 1073741824
        Execute = 536870912
    }

    function Get-PSSessionAcl {
        param (
            [String[]]$Name
        )
    Get-PSSessionConfiguration -Name $Name |
            ForEach-Object {
        New-Object CommonSecurityDescriptor(
                    $false,
                    $false,
    $_.SecurityDescriptorSddl
    )
            }
    }

    function Get-PSSessionAccess {
        param (
            [String[]]$Name
        )

        (Get-PSSessionAcl -Name $Name).DiscretionaryAcl |
            Add-Member Identity -MemberType ScriptProperty -Value {
    $this.SecurityIdentifier.Translate([NTAccount])
            } -PassThru |
            Add-Member AccessRight -MemberType ScriptProperty -Value {
              [SessionAccessRight]$this.AccessMask
    } -PassThru
    }
```

Additional access may by granted by using the `AddAccess` method on the `DiscretionaryAcl`. Granting access requires the SID of an account. The SID can be retrieved using the same `Translate` method that was used to get an account name from a SID. For example, the security identifier of the local administrator account may be retrieved:

```
using namespace System.Security.Principal

([NTAccount]"Administrator").Translate([SecurityIdentifier])
```

Adding to the discretionary ACL may be achieved as shown in the following snippet. The example makes use of the `Get-PSSessionAcl` function and `SessionAccessRight` enumeration created previously to grant access to the current user. The current user is identified using environment variables:

```
using namespace System.Security.AccessControl
 using namespace System.Security.Principal
 $identity = "$env:USERDOMAIN\$env:USERNAME"
 $acl = Get-PSSessionAcl -Name "Microsoft.PowerShell"
 $acl.DiscretionaryAcl.AddAccess(
 'Allow',
   ([NTAccount]$identity).Translate([SecurityIdentifier]),
   [Int][SessionAccessRight]'Full',
   'None', # Inheritance flags
   'None' # Propagation flags
   )
```

The updated ACL must be converted back to an SDDL string to apply the change:

```
$sddl = $acl.GetSddlForm('All')
Set-PSSessionConfiguration microsoft.powershell -SecurityDescriptorSddl
$sddl
```

User Account Control

User Account Control (UAC) restricts local (not domain) user accounts logging on using a remote connection. The remote connection will be made as a standard user account by default, that is, a user without administrative privileges.

The `Enable-PSRemoting` command disables UAC remote restrictions. If another method has been used to enable remoting, and a local account is being used to connect, it is possible that remote restrictions are still in place.

The current value can be viewed using:

```
Get-ItemPropertyValue
HKLM:\SOFTWARE\Microsoft\Windows\CurrentVersion\Policies\System -Name
LocalAccountTokenFilterPolicy
```

If the key or value is missing, an error will be thrown.

UAC remote restrictions can be disabled as follows. Using the `Force` parameter will allow the creation of both the key and the value:

```
Set-ItemProperty
HKLM:\SOFTWARE\Microsoft\Windows\CurrentVersion\Policies\System -Name
LocalAccountTokenFilterPolicy -Value 1 -Force
```

The change used previously, and UAC remote restrictions, are described in Microsoft's Knowledge Base article 951016:

https://support.microsoft.com/en-us/help/951016/description-of-user-account-control-and-remote-restrictions-in-windows-vista

Trusted hosts

If a remote system is not part of a domain, or is part of an untrusted domain, an attempt to connect using remoting may fail. The remote system must either be listed in trusted hosts or must use SSL.

Use of trusted hosts also applies when connecting from a computer on a domain to another computer using a local user account.

Trusted hosts are set on the client, the system making the connection. The following command gets the current value:

```
Get-Item WSMan:\localhost\Client\TrustedHosts
```

The value is a comma-delimited list. Wildcards are supported in the list. The following function may be used to add a value to the list:

```
function Add-TrustedHost {
    param (
        [String]$Hostname
    )

    $item = Get-Item WSMan:\localhost\Client\TrustedHosts
    $trustedHosts = @($item.Value -split ',')
    $trustedHosts = $trustedHosts + $Hostname |
        Where-Object { $_ } |
Select-Object -Unique

$item | Set-Item -Value ($trustedHosts -join ',')
}
```

CIM sessions

CIM sessions are used to work with CIM services, predominantly WMI or commands that base their functionality on WMI. Such commands include those in the `NetAdapter` and `Storage` modules available on Windows 2012 and Windows 8. A list of commands that support CIM sessions may be viewed as follows:

```
Get-Command -ParameterName CimSession
```

The list will only include commands from modules that have been imported.

New-CimSession

CIM sessions are created using the `New-CimSession` command. The following example creates a CIM session using the current system as the computer name using WSMan as the protocol:

```
PS> New-CimSession -ComputerName $env:COMPUTERNAME
Id           : 1
Name         : CimSession1
InstanceId   : bc03b547-1051-4af1-a41d-4d16b0ec0402
ComputerName : CIMTEST
Protocol     : WSMAN
```

If the computer name parameter is omitted, the protocol will be set to `DCOM`:

```
PS> New-CimSession
Id           : 2
Name         : CimSession2
InstanceId   : 804595f4-0144-4590-990a-92b2f22f894f
ComputerName : localhost
Protocol     : DCOM
```

`New-CimSession` can be used to configure operation timeout settings and whether or not an initial network test should be performed.

The protocol used by `New-CimSession` can be changed using `New-CimSessionOption`. Changing the protocol can be useful if there is a need to interact with systems where WinRM is not running or configured:

```
PS> New-CimSession -ComputerName $env:COMPUTERNAME -SessionOption (New-
CimSessionOption -Protocol Dcom)
Id           : 3
Name         : CimSession3
InstanceId   : 29bba117-c899-4389-b874-5afe43962a1e
```

```
ComputerName : CIMTEST
Protocol     : DCOM
```

Get-CimSession

Sessions created using `New-CimSession` persist until the CIM session is removed (by `Remove-CimSession`) or the PowerShell session ends:

```
PS> Get-CimSession | Select-Object Id, ComputerName, Protocol
Id   ComputerName Protocol
--   ------------ --------
 1   CIMTEST      WSMAN
 2   localhost    DCOM
 3   CIMTEST      DCOM
```

Using CIM sessions

Once a CIM session has been created, it can be used for one or more requests. In the following example, a CIM session is created and then used to gather disk and partition information:

```
$ErrorActionPreference = 'Stop'
try {
    $session = New-CimSession -ComputerName $env:COMPUTERNAME
    Get-Disk -CimSession $session
    Get-Partition -CimSession $session
} catch {
    throw
}
```

In the preceding script, if the attempt to create the session succeeds, the session will be used to get disk and partition information.

Error handling with `try` and `catch` is discussed in `Chapter 17`, *Error Handling*. The block is treated as a transaction; if a single command fails, the block will stop running. If the attempt to create a new session fails, `Get-Disk` and `Get-Partition` will not run.

PS sessions

PS sessions use Windows remoting to communicate between servers. PS sessions can be used for anything from remote command and script execution to providing a remote shell.

New-PSSession

Sessions are created using the `New-PSSession` command. In the following example, a session is created on a computer named `PSTEST`:

```
PS> New-PSSession -ComputerName PSTEST
Id Name ComputerName State ConfigurationName Availability
-- ---- ------------ ----- ----------------- ------------
1  Session1 PSTEST  Opened Microsoft.PowerShell Available
```

Get-PSSession

Sessions created using `New-PSSession` persist until the PS session is removed (by `Remove-PSSession`) or the PowerShell session ends. The following example returns sessions created in the current PowerShell session:

```
PS> Get-PSSession | Select-Object Id, ComputerName, State
Id ComputerName State
-- ------------ -----
 1 PSTEST       Opened
```

If the `ComputerName` parameter is supplied, `Get-PSSession` will show sessions created on that computer. For example, if a session is created in one PowerShell console as follows:

```
$session = New-PSSession -ComputerName PSTest -Name Example
```

A second administrator console session will be able to view details of that session:

```
PS> Get-PSSession -ComputerName PSTest| Select-Object Name, ComputerName,
State
Name      ComputerName  State
----      ------------  -----
Example   PSTest        Disconnected
```

Invoke-Command

`Invoke-Command` may be used with a PS session to execute a command or script on a remote system:

```
$session = New-PSSession -ComputerName $env:COMPUTERNAME
Invoke-Command { Get-Process -Id $PID } -Session $session
```

$env:COMPUTERNAME is localhost:
Connecting to a session requires administrative access by default. The preceding command will fail if PowerShell is not running with an administrative token (run as administrator).
A PowerShell session with the administrator token can be started using the following command:
`Start-Process powershell -Verb RunAs`

`Invoke-Command` has a wide variety of different uses, as shown in the command help. For example, a single command can be executed against a list of computers:

```
Invoke-Command { Get-Process -Id $PID } -ComputerName 'first', 'second',
'third'
```

This technique can be useful when combined with `AsJob`. Pushing the requests into the background allows each server to get on with its work, pushing it back when the work is complete.

Once the job created by the previous command has completed, any data may be retrieved using the `Receive-Job` command.

A number of advanced techniques may be used with `Invoke-Command`.

Local functions and remote sessions

The following example executes a function created on the local machine in a remote system using positional arguments:

```
function Get-FreeSpace {
    param (
        [Parameter(Mandatory = $true)]
        [String]$Name
    )

    [Math]::Round((Get-PSDrive $Name).Free / 1GB, 2)
}
Invoke-Command ${function:Get-FreeSpace} -Session $session -ArgumentList c
```

This technique succeeds because the body of the function is declared as a script block. `ArgumentList` is used to pass a positional argument into the `DriveLetter` parameter.

If the function depends on other locally defined functions, the attempt will fail.

Using splatting with ArgumentList

The `ArgumentList` parameter of `Invoke-Command` does not offer a means of passing named arguments to a command.

Splatting allows parameters to be defined using a hashtable. Splatting uses the following format:

```
$params = @{
    ID = $PID
}
Get-Process @params
```

The at symbol (`@`) is used to instruct PowerShell that the hashtable contains a set of parameters to a command.

The following example uses splatting to pass parameters. The function is defined on the local system, and the definition of the function is passed to the remote system:

```
# A function which exists on the current system
function Get-FreeSpace {
    param (
        [Parameter(Mandatory = $true)]
        [String]$Name
    )

    [Math]::Round((Get-PSDrive $Name).Free / 1GB, 2)
}

# Define parameters to pass to the function
$params = @{
    Name = 'c'
}

# Execute the function with a named set of parameters
Invoke-Command -ScriptBlock {
param ( $definition, $params )

&amp; ([ScriptBlock]::Create($definition)) @params
} -ArgumentList ${function:Get-FreeSpace}, $params -ComputerName
$computerName
```

In the preceding example, the definition of the `Get-FreeSpace` function is passed as an argument along with the requested parameters. The script block used with `Invoke-Command` converts the definition into a `ScriptBlock` and executes it.

The AsJob parameter

The AsJob command can be used with Invoke-Command. For example:

```
$session = New-PSSession PSTest
Invoke-Command {
    Start-Sleep -Seconds 120
    'Done sleeping'
} -Session $session -AsJob
```

The command finishes immediately, returning the job that has been created.

While the job is running, the session availability is set to Busy as follows:

```
PS> $session | Select-Object Name, ComputerName, Availability
Name      ComputerName  Availability
----      ------------  ------------
Session1  PSTest        Busy
```

Attempts to run another command against the same session will result in an error message.

Once the job has completed, the Receive-Job command may be used.

Disconnected sessions

The InDisconnectedSession of Invoke-Command starts the requested script and immediately disconnects the session. This allows a script to be started and collected from a different console session or a different computer.

The session parameter cannot be used with InDisconnectedSession; Invoke-Command creates a new session for a specified computer name. The session is returned by the following command:

```
Invoke-Command{ Start-Sleep -Seconds 120; 'Done' } -ComputerName PSTest -
InDisconnectedSession
```

A second PowerShell session or computer is able to connect to the disconnected session to retrieve the results. The following command assumes that only one session exists with the computer PSTest:

```
Get-PSSession -ComputerName PSTest |
    Connect-PSSession |
    Receive-PSSession
```

Tasks started with `AsJob` will also continue to run if a session is disconnected. The following example creates a session, starts a long-running process, and disconnects the session:

```
$session = New-PSSession PSTest -Name 'Example'
Invoke-Command { Start-Sleep -Seconds (60 * 60) } -Session $session -AsJob
Disconnect-PSSession $session
```

Once the session has been created and disconnected, the PowerShell console can be closed. A second PowerShell console can find and connect to the existing session:

```
$session = Get-PSSession -ComputerName PSTest -Name 'Example'
Connect-PSSession $session
```

Reviewing the details of the session will show that it is busy running `Start-Sleep`:

```
PS> Get-PSSession | Select-Object Name, ComputerName, State, Availability
Name    ComputerName State  Availability
----    ------------ -----  ------------
Example PSTest       Opened Busy
```

The using variable scope

When working with `Invoke-Command`, PowerShell makes the `using` variable scope available.

The `using` variable scope allows access to variables created on a local machine within a script block used with `Invoke-Command`.

The following example shows the use of a variable containing parameters for `Get-Process`. The local variable may contain any reasonable value:

```
$params = @{
    Name            = 'powershell'
    IncludeUserName = $true
}
Invoke-Command {
    $params = $using:params
    Get-Process @params
} -ComputerName PSTest
```

The `using` scope is a handy alternative to the `ArgumentList` parameter.

Enter-PSSession

The `Enter-PSSession` command may be used to use a session as a remote console. By default, `Enter-PSSession` accepts a computer name as the first argument:

```
Enter-PSSession $env:COMPUTERNAME
```

In a similar way, an existing session might be used:

```
$session = New-PSSession -ComputerName $env:COMPUTERNAME
Enter-PSSession -Session $session
```

`Enter-PSSession` uses WS-Management as a means of exchanging information between the client and the server. Once a command is typed and the return key is pressed, the entire command is sent to the remote host. The result of the command is sent back using the same mechanism. This exchange can inject a small amount of latency into the shell.

Import-PSSession

`Import-PSSession` brings commands from a remote computer into the current session. Microsoft Exchange uses this technique to provide remote access to the Exchange Management Shell.

The following example imports the `NetAdapter` module from a remote server into the current session:

```
$computerName = 'PSTest'
$session = New-PSSession -ComputerName $computerName
Import-PSSession -Session $session -Module NetAdapter
```

Any commands used within this module are executed against the session target, not against the local computer.

If the session is removed, the imported module and its commands will be removed from the local session.

Export-PSSession

In the preceding example, `Import-PSSession` is used to immediately import commands from a remote system into a local session. `Export-PSSession` writes a persistent module that can be used to achieve the same goal.

The following example creates a module in the current user's module path:

```
$computerName = 'PSTest'
$session = New-PSSession -ComputerName $computerName
Export-PSSession -Session $session -Module NetAdapter -OutputModule
"NetAdapter-$computerName"
```

Once the module has been created, it can be imported by name:

```
Import-Module "NetAdapter-$computerName"
```

This process replaces the need to define and import a session, and is useful for remote commands that are used on a regular basis.

Copying items between sessions

PowerShell 5 introduced the ability to copy between sessions using the `Copy-Item` command.

The `FromSession` parameter is used to copy a file to the local system:

```
$session1 = New-PSSession PSTest1
Copy-Item -Path C:\temp\doc.txt -Destination C:\Temp -FromSession $session1
```

In the preceding example, `Path` is on `PSTest1`.

The `ToSession` parameter is used to copy a file to a remote system:

```
$session2 = New-PSSession PSTest2
Copy-Item -Path C:\temp\doc.txt -Destination C:\Temp -ToSession $session2
```

In the previous example, the path used for the destination parameter is on `PSTest2`.

The `FromSession` and `ToSession` parameters cannot be specified together; two separate commands are required to copy a file between two remote sessions.

The double-hop problem

The double-hop problem describes a scenario in PowerShell where remoting is used to connect to a host and the remote host tries to connect to another resource. In this scenario, the second connection, the second hop, fails because authentication cannot be implicitly passed.

There have been numerous articles discussing this problem over the years. Ashley McGlone published a blog post in 2016 that describes the problem and each of the possible solutions:

`https://blogs.technet.microsoft.com/ashleymcglone/2016/08/30/powershell-remoting-kerberos-double-hop-solved-securely/`

This section briefly explores using `CredSSP`, as well as how to pass explicit credentials to a remote system. Neither of these options is considered secure, but they require the least amount of work to implement.

The two options discussed as follows are therefore useful when:

- The remote endpoint is trusted and has not been compromised.
- Critical authentication tokens can be extracted by any administrator on the remote system
- They are not used for wide-scale regular or scheduled automation, as the methods significantly increase exposure

CredSSP

A session can be created using `CredSSP` as the authentication provider:

```
New-PSSession -ComputerName PSTest -Credential (Get-Credential) -
Authentication CredSSP
```

`CredSSP` must be enabled on the client to support passing credentials to a remote system. The `DelegateComputer` parameter can be used with either a specific name, or with a wildcard (`*`):

```
Enable-WSManCredSSP -Role Client -DelegateComputer PSTest
```

`CredSSP` must also be enabled on the server to receive credentials:

```
Enable-WSManCredSSP -Role Server
```

If this approach is used as a temporary measure, the `CredSSP` roles might be removed afterward.

On the server making the connection, the `Client` role can be disabled:

```
Disable-WSManCredSSP -Role Client
```

On the remote system, the `Server` role can be disabled:

```
Disable-WSManCredSSP -Role Server
```

Passing credentials

Passing credentials into a remote session means the second hop can authenticate without being dependent on authentication tokens from the original system.

In this example, the `using` variable scope is used to access a credential variable. The credential is used to run a query against Active Directory from a remote system:

```
$Credential = Get-Credential
Invoke-Command -ComputerName PSTest -ScriptBlock {
    Get-ADUser -Filter * -Credential $using:Credential
}
```

Summary

This chapter explored remoting in PowerShell, starting with WS-Management and then moving onto CIM sessions and PS sessions.

Finally, the double-hop problem was introduced, along with a number of possible ways to work around the issue.

16
Testing

The goal of testing in PowerShell is to ensure that code works as it has been designed. Automatic testing ensures that this continues to be the case as code is changed over time.

Testing often begins before code is ready to execute. `PSScriptAnalyzer` can look at code and provide advice on best practices. This technique is known as static analysis.

Unit tests pick up when code is ready to execute. Tests may exist before the code when following practices such as **Test-Driven Development** (**TDD**). A unit test focuses on the smallest parts of a script, function, module, or class. A unit test strives to validate the inner workings of a unit of code, ensuring that conditions evaluate correctly, that it terminates or returns where it should, and so on.

Testing might extend into systems and acceptance testing, although this often requires a test environment to act against. Acceptance testing may include black-box testing, used to verify that a command accepts known parameters and generates an expected set of results. Black-box testing, as the name suggests, does not concern itself with understanding how a block of code arrives at a result.

The following topics are covered in this chapter:

- Static analysis
- Testing with Pester

Static analysis

Static analysis is the process of evaluating code without executing it. Static analysis in PowerShell makes use of an **Abstract Syntax Tree** (**AST**): a tree-like representation of a block of code.

Abstract syntax tree

The AST in PowerShell is available for any script block, for example:

```
{ Write-Host 'content' }.Ast
```

The script block that defines a function can be retrieved via `Get-Command`:

```
function Write-Content { Write-Host 'content' }
(Get-Command Write-Content).ScriptBlock
```

Or the script block defining a function can be retrieved using `Get-Item`:

```
function Write-Content { Write-Host 'content' }
(Get-Item function:\Write-Content).ScriptBlock
```

It is possible to work down through the content of the script block using AST. For example, the first argument for the command `Write-Host` might be accessed:

```
{ Write-Host 'content' }.Ast.
                         Endblock.
                         Statements.
                         PipelineElements.
                         CommandElements[1]
```

The approach used previously is rough and simply extracts the second command element from the first statement in the end block.

Rather than following the tree so literally, it is possible to execute searches against the tree. For example, the `Write-Host` command is not necessarily a sensible inclusion; a search for occurrences of the command can be constructed:

```
{ Write-Host 'content' }.Ast.FindAll( {
        param ( $ast )

        $ast -is [Management.Automation.Language.CommandAst] -and
$ast.GetCommandName() -eq 'Write-Host'
    },
    $true
)
```

In the preceding command, the `FindAll` method expects two arguments:

- The first argument is a script block predicate. The predicate is a script block that accepts a single argument, an element from the tree. In the preceding example, a parameter is declared to give the argument a name. The argument is tested by a comparison that will return `true` or `false`
- The second argument is used to decide whether the search should extend to include nested script blocks

PSScriptAnalyzer

The evaluation of elements in the abstract syntax tree is the method used by the `PSScriptAnalyzer` tool. The tool can be installed using:

```
Install-Module PSScriptAnalyzer
```

`PSScriptAnalyzer` can be used to inspect a script with the command `Invoke-ScriptAnalzyer`. For example, the tool will flag warnings and errors about use of the `Password` parameter and variable, as it is not considered to be a good practice:

```
[CmdletBinding()]
param (
    [Parameter(Mandatory = $true)]
    [String]$Password
)

$Credential = New-Object PSCredential(
    '.\user',
    $Password | ConvertTo-SecureString -AsPlainText -Force
)
$Credential.GetNetworkCredential().Password
```

The results of running `PSScriptAnalyzer` are shown as follows:

```
PS> Invoke-ScriptAnalyzer $psISE.CurrentFile.FullPath | Format-List
RuleName : PSAvoidUsingConvertToSecureStringWithPlainText
Severity : Error
Line     : 8
Column   : 17
Message  : File 'password.ps1' uses ConvertTo-SecureString with plaintext.
This will expose secure information. Encrypted standard strings should be
used instead.
RuleName : PSAvoidUsingPlainTextForPassword
Severity : Warning
```

```
Line     : 3
Column   : 5
Message  : Parameter '$Password' should use SecureString, otherwise this
will expose sensitive information.
See ConvertTo-SecureString for more information.
```

Suppressing rules

It is rarely realistic to expect any significant piece of code to pass all of the tests `PSScriptAnalyzer` will throw at it.

Individual tests can be suppressed at function, script, or class level. The following demonstrative function creates a `PSCustomObject`:

```
function New-Message {
    [CmdletBinding()]
    param (
        $Message
    )

    [PSCustomObject]@{
        Name  = 1
        Value = $Message
    }
}
```

Running `PSScriptAnalyzer` against a file containing the function will show the following warning:

```
PS> Invoke-ScriptAnalyzer $psISE.CurrentFile.FullPath | Format-List
RuleName : PSUseShouldProcessForStateChangingFunctions
Severity : Warning
Line     : 1
Column   : 10
Message  : Function 'New-Message' has verb that could change system state.
Therefore, the function has to support 'ShouldProcess'.
```

Given that this function creates a new object in memory, and does not change the system state, the message might be suppressed. This is achieved by adding a `SuppressMessage` attribute before a `param` block:

```
function New-Message {
[Diagnostics.CodeAnalysis.SuppressMessage('PSUseShouldProcessForStateChangi
ngFunctions', '')]
    [CmdletBinding()]
    param (
```

```
        $Message
    )

    [PSCustomObject]@{
        Name  = 1
        Value = $Message
    }
}
```

Rules are typically suppressed as it becomes evident one will be triggered. The list of rules may be viewed using the `Get-ScriptAnalyzerRule` command.

Testing with Pester

The PowerShell module Pester can be used to build unit tests for scripts and functions. Unit tests target the smallest possible unit of code, which, in PowerShell, is likely to be a function or a method in a PowerShell class.

Pester tests are saved in a file named ending with `.tests.ps1` and executed using the command `Invoke-Pester`. `Invoke-Pester` finds files named `*.tests.ps1` under a given path and executes all tests in each.

`Describe` and `Should` statements may also be entered in the console when exploring syntax, but this is not the normal method of defining and running tests.

While `Pester` is included with Windows 10, it is not the latest version. The latest version may be installed from the `PSGallery`:

```
Install-Module Pester -Force
```

Why write tests?

A set of tests can help when:

- Debugging
- Refactoring

A set of tests can prevent a bug making it out of a development environment, whether as the result of a change, or because the feature is new.

Refactoring, or restructuring, existing code has a high chance of introducing bugs. If a script or function already has tests, the risk is reduced. Tests that verify overall functionality (not necessarily unit tests) should continue to pass after refactoring.

What to test

How extensive tests should be is debatable. Striving for 100% code coverage does not necessarily mean a block of code has been effectively tested.

Consider testing:

- Any complex conditions
- Acceptance of different input or expected values; including complex parameter validation
- Exit conditions (especially raised errors or exceptions)
- When writing a unit test, resist the temptation to test other functions or commands. A unit test is not responsible for making sure every command it calls works. That comes later

Describe and It

Groups of tests are written within a `describe` block. The `describe` block must be given a name. A `describe` block is often named after the subject of the tests.

Tests are declared using `It` followed by a description. The `It` statement contains assertions that are declared using `Should`.

Pester 4:
Pester 3 expected assertion keywords (`Be`, `BeLike`, and so on) to be written as a bare word. For example:

```
$value | Should Be 0
```

Pester 4 supports the syntax used by 3 as legacy syntax. The assertion names are now also presented as dynamic parameters. For example:

```
$value | Should -Be 0
```

This allows tools such as ISE and Visual Studio Code to provide auto-completion when `Should -` is typed.
The tests used as examples in this section use the syntax native to Pester 4.

The following function calculates the square root of a value. This particular function does not draw in information, except from the single parameter; testing is limited to validating output:

```
function Get-SquareRoot {
    param (
        [Decimal]$Value
    )

    if ($Value -lt 0) { throw 'Invalid value' }

    $result = $Value
    $previous = 0
    while ([Math]::Abs($result - $previous) -gt 1e-300) {
        $previous = $result
        $result = ($result + $Value / $previous) / 2
    }
    return $result
}
```

Tests may be written to verify that the function does what it is expected to do:

```
Describe Get-SquareRoot {
    It 'Returns a square root of 0 for a value of 0' {
        Get-SquareRoot 0 | Should -Be 0
    }

    It 'Returns simple square root values' {
        Get-Squareroot 1 | Should -Be 1
        Get-SquareRoot 4 | Should -Be 2
        Get-SquareRoot 9 | Should -Be 3
        Get-SquareRoot 16 | Should -Be 4
    }
}
```

Pester displays output showing the state of each of the tests:

```
Describing Get-SquareRoot
[+] Returns a square root of 0 for a value of 0 47ms
[+] Returns simple square root values 24ms
```

Each test, defined using `It`, returns a single line expressing the result of the test. A test may fail for two reasons:

- The subject of the test has an error
- The test has an error

For example, if an error is injected into the first test, the result will change, showing what about the test failed:

```
Describing Get-SquareRoot
[-] Returns a square root of 0 for a value of 0 42ms
Expected: {9}
But was: {0}
at <ScriptBlock>, : line 19
19: Get-SquareRoot 0 | Should Be 9
[+] Returns simple square root values 21ms
```

If a single test contains multiple `Should` assertions, conditions are evaluated in order until the first fails, or all pass.

For example, if two errors are injected into the last test, Pester is expected to indicate the test fails when it reaches the assertion that the square root of `9` is `33`:

```
It 'Returns simple square root values' {
    Get-Squareroot 1 | Should -Be 1
    Get-SquareRoot 4 | Should -Be 2
    Get-SquareRoot 9 | Should -Be 33
    Get-SquareRoot 16 | Should -Be 44
}
```

Executing the tests shows an error once Pester reaches the third assertion, that the square root of `9` should be `33`:

```
Describing Get-SquareRoot
[+] Returns a square root of 0 for a value of 0 32ms
[-] Returns simple square root values 30ms
Expected: {33}
But was: {3}
at <ScriptBlock>, : line 31
31: Get-SquareRoot 9 | Should Be 33
```

In this context, Pester will never execute the last assertion; the test has already failed.

Test cases

When the inputs and outputs of a function are being repetitively tested, the `TestCases` parameter of `It` can be used. Test cases are defined in a hashtable, which is splatted into `It` as a set of parameters.

The four test cases used in the preceding example might be rewritten as follows:

```
$testCases = @(
    @{ Value = 1;  ExpectedResult = 1 }
    @{ Value = 4;  ExpectedResult = 2 }
    @{ Value = 9;  ExpectedResult = 33 }
    @{ Value = 16; ExpectedResult = 44 }
)

It 'Calculates the square root of <Value>to be<ExpectedResult>' -TestCases
$testCases {
    param (
        $Value,
        $ExpectedResult
    )

    Get-SquareRoot $Value | Should -Be $ExpectedResult
}
```

The preceding tests still contain errors; the advantage of this approach is that Pester will report success or failure for each of the test cases individually:

```
Describing Get-SquareRoot
[+] Returns a square root of 0 for a value of 0 37ms
[+] Calculates the square root of 1 to be 1 20ms
[+] Calculates the square root of 4 to be 2 11ms
[-] Calculates the square root of 9 to be 33 16ms
Expected: {33}
But was: {3}
at <ScriptBlock>, : line 41
41: Get-SquareRoot $Value | Should Be $ExpectedResult
[-] Calculates the square root of 16 to be 44 35ms
Expected: {44}
But was: {4}
at <ScriptBlock>, : line 41
41: Get-SquareRoot $Value | Should Be $ExpectedResult
```

Pester automatically replaces values enclosed in angular braces (< and `>`) with names from the hashtable describing each test case.

Using test cases can save time spent debugging code and tests, as fewer runs are needed to highlight problems.

Independent verification

It is common to find that there is more than one way to achieve a result in PowerShell. In the case of the `Get-SquareRoot` function, .NET has a `Math.Sqrt` static method that can be used to produce a similar result.

The availability of an alternative approach (which is known to work) allows a result to be dynamically validated, either in place of or in addition to statically defined values.

The set of test cases might be adjusted to use `Math.Sqrt` to verify that the function is working as intended:

```
$values = 81, 9801, 60025, 3686400, 212255761, 475316482624
$testCases = foreach ($value in $values) {
    @{ Value = $value; ExpectedResult = [Math]::Sqrt($value) }
}
It 'Calculates the square root of <Value> to be <ExpectedResult>' -
TestCases $testCases {
    param (
        $Value,
        $ExpectedResult
    )
    Get-SquareRoot $Value | Should -Be $ExpectedResult
}
```

Independent verification has limitations if two approaches return different data types. For example, the following assertion will fail, despite using the same input values:

```
PS> (Get-SquareRoot 200) | Should -Be ([Math]::Sqrt(200))
Expected: {14.142135623731}
But was: {14.1421356237309504880168872421}
At ...
```

It may be possible to overcome the limitation of the verification by converting both to the same data type. Whether or not this action is appropriate depends on the nature of, and reason for, the test.

Assertions

Pester comes with support for a variety of assertion types. These assertion types are exposed as parameters for `Should`. Several of these assertion types grant access to additional parameters.

Be

`Be` performs a direct comparison, somewhat equivalent to `-eq`. `Be` can also be used to test equality between arrays:

```
0 | Should -Be 0
$true | Should -Be $true
@(1, 2, 3) | Should -Be @(1, 2, 3)
```

BeIn

`BeIn` tests for the presence of a value within an array:

```
'Harry' | Should -BeIn 'Tom', 'Richard', 'Harry'
```

BeLessThan

`BeLessThan` uses the `-lt` operator to perform a comparison:

```
1 | Should -BeLessThan 20
```

BeLike

`BeLike` performs a case-insensitive comparison using the `-like` operator:

```
'Value' | Should -BeLike 'v*'
```

BeLikeExactly

`BeLikeExactly` performs a case-sensitive comparison using the `-clike` operator:

```
'Value' | Should -BeLikeExactly 'V*'
```

BeNullOrEmpty

`BeNullOrEmpty` compares `null` to the value. Array values are tested using the `Count` property; arrays with zero elements will satisfy the assertion:

```
@() | Should -BeNullOrEmpty
'' | Should -BeNullOrEmpty
```

BeOfType

`BeOfType` can be used to ensure a value is of a specific .NET type. It is equivalent to the `-is` `operator`:

```
[IPAddress]"1.2.3.4" | Should -BeOfType [IPAddress]
```

FileContentMatch

`Contain` is used to perform a case-insensitive comparison against the content of a text file. `Contain` is not used to test the content of an array:

```
'hello world' | Out-File 'file.txt'
'file.txt' | Should -Contain 'World'
```

FileContentMatchExactly

Contain exactly performs a case-sensitive comparison against the content of a text file:

```
'hello world' | Out-File 'file.txt'
'file.txt' | Should -FileContentMatchExactly 'world'
```

FileContentMatchMultiline

`ContainMultiline` is used to perform a case-insensitive comparison against the content of a text file. `ContainsMultiline` does not strip end-of-line characters; to pass the test, the assertion must include correct end of line character sequences:

```
Set-Content file.txt -Value "1`n2`n3`n4"
'file.txt' | Should -FileContentMatchMultiline "2`n3"
```

Exist

`Exist` is used to test for the existence of a path using `Test-Path`. `Exist` does not differentiate between different object types:

```
'c:\Windows' | Should -Exist
```

Match

`Match` tests a value against a case-insensitive regular expression:

```
'value' | Should Match '^V.+e$'
```

MatchExactly

`MatchExactly` tests a value against a case-sensitive regular expression:

```
'value' | Should Match '^v.+e$'
```

Throw

`Throw` is used to test whether or not a block of code throws a terminating error. `Throw` has a number of different usage scenarios. The simplest is detecting whether a terminating error (of any kind) is thrown:

```
function Invoke-Something { throw }
Describe Invoke-Something {
    It 'Throws a terminating error' {
{ Invoke-Something } | Should Throw
    }
}
```

When testing for terminating errors, the subject of the test is placed in a script block (curly braces).

Pester allows testing of the error message:

```
function Invoke-Something { throw 'an error' }
Describe Invoke-Something {
    It 'Throws a terminating error' {
{ Invoke-Something } | Should Throw 'an error'
    }
}
```

Pester also allows testing of the fully qualified error ID:

```
function Invoke-Something {
    $errorRecord = New-Object System.Management.Automation.ErrorRecord(
        (New-Object Exception('an error')),
        'AnErrorID',
        'OperationStopped',
        $null
```

```
    )
    throw $errorRecord
}
Describe Invoke-Something {
    It 'Throws a terminating error' {
{ Invoke-Something } | Should -Throw -ErrorId 'AnErrorId'
    }
}
```

If a function is written such that it writes a non-terminating error (using `Write-Error`), and generation of that error must be tested, the following pattern might be used:

```
function Invoke-Something {
    [CmdletBinding()]
    param ( )

    Write-Error 'Error'
}
Describe Invoke-Something {
    It 'Throws a non-terminating error' {
{ Invoke-Something -ErrorAction SilentlyContinue }| Should -Not -Throw
{ Invoke-Something -ErrorAction Stop } | Should -Throw
    }
}
```

Not

`Not` is used to negate any of the previous terms, for example:

```
function Invoke-Something { return 1}
Invoke-Something | Should -Not -Be 0
Invoke-Something | Should -Not -BeNullOrEmpty
```

Context

`Context` blocks are nested under `describe`. `Context` blocks allow tests to be grouped together.

`Context` blocks are useful when there is a fundamental difference in how groups of tests should be handled, for example, where the setup method for each test is more extensive.

Before and After

Pester includes keywords that hold code that will execute before or after either each test or all tests. The following keywords are available:

- `BeforeAll`: Executed once, before all other content
- `AfterAll`: Executed once, after all other content
- `BeforeEach`: Executed immediately before each individual test
- `AfterEach`: Executed immediately after each individual test

Each of the keywords should be followed by a script block.

When using `Before` or `After` it is important to be aware of the order in which a section is executed. In the following list, `Loose code` refers to anything that is not part of a `Before`, `After`, or `It`:

- `Describe\BeforeAll`
- `Describe\Loose code`
- `Context\BeforeAll`
- `Context\Loose code`
- `Describe\BeforeEach`
- `Context\BeforeEach`
- `Context\Loose code`
- `It`
- `Context\AfterEach`
- `Describe\AfterEach`
- `Context\AfterAll`
- `Describe\AfterAll`

It is important to note that if `Mocks` are created under a `describe` block, they are categorized as `Loose code` in the context of this list. A command called in `Describe\BeforeAll` will not have access to mocks that are only created further down the list.

Loose code:
When using `Before` or `After`, consider enclosing `Mocks` in `BeforeAll` or `It` (if `Mocks` are specific to a single test) to ensure `Mocks` are always available where they might be used.

The following function is used to demonstrate how `Before` and `After` might be used. The function deletes files in a specified path where the last access time was defined at least a number of days ago:

```
function Remove-StaleFile {
    param (
        [Parameter(Mandatory = $true)]
        [String]$Path,
        [String]$Filter = '*.*',
        [Int32]$MaximumAge = 90
    )

    Get-ChildItem $Path -Filter $Filter |
        Where-Object LastWriteTime -lt (Get-Date).AddDays(-$MaximumAge) |
        Remove-Item
}
```

To test the function, a number of test cases might be constructed. `BeforeAll`, `BeforeEach`, and `AfterAll` might be used to ensure everything is ready for an individual test. Each of the following elements is contained within a single `Describe` block.

`BeforeAll` is used to create a temporary working path:

```
BeforeAll {
    $extensions = '.txt', '.log', '.doc'
    $Path = 'C:\Temp\StaleFiles'
    $null = New-Item $Path -ItemType Directory
    Push-Location $Path
}
```

`AfterAll` is used to clean up:

```
AfterAll {
    Pop-Location
    Remove-Item C:\Temp\StaleFiles -Recurse -Force
}
```

And `BeforeEach` is used to create a known set of files before each test executes:

```
    BeforeEach {
        foreach ($extension in $extensions) {
            $item = New-Item "stale$extension" -ItemType File -Force
            $item.LastWriteTime = (Get-Date).AddDays(-92)
}
foreach ($extension in $extensions) {
  $item = New-Item "new$extension" -ItemType File -Force
   $item.LastWriteTime = (Get-Date).AddDays(-88)
```

```
    }
        }
```

The tests themselves are simplified, needing only the code required to execute and test the impact of the function:

```
        It 'Removes all files older than 90 days' {
            Remove-StaleFile $Path
            Test-Path "stale.*" | Should -Be $false
            Get-ChildItem "new.*" | Should -Not -BeNullOrEmpty
        }

        $testCases = $extensions | ForEach-Object { @{ Extension = $_ } }
        It 'Removes all <Extension> files older than 90 days' -TestCases
    $testCases {
            param ( $Extension )

            Remove-StaleFile $Path -Filter "*$Extension"
            Test-Path "stale$Extension" | Should -Be $false
            Get-ChildItem "stale.*" | Should -Not -BeNullOrEmpty
            Get-ChildItem "new.*" | Should -Not -BeNullOrEmpty
        }
```

TestDrive

When testing commands that work with the filesystem, Pester provides a `TestDrive`. The `TestDrive` is a temporary folder created in the current user's temporary directory.

The folder is created when `describe` runs and is destroyed afterwards.

Using the `TestDrive` would simplify the setup process for the `Remove-StaleFile` function, for example, `BeforeAll` might become:

```
        BeforeAll {
            $extensions = '.txt', '.log', '.doc'
            Push-Location 'TestDrive:\'
        }
```

And `AfterAll` becomes:

```
        AfterAll {
            Pop-Location
        }
```

In the event that a command cannot work with the `TestDrive` label, as is the case with .NET types and methods, as well as native executables, the full path can be resolved using `Get-Item`:

```
(Get-Item 'TestDrive:\').FullName
```

Mock

The ability to mock commands is a prominent feature of Pester. Mocking is used to reduce the scope of a set of tests.

Creating a `Mock` overrides a command by taking a partial copy. The copy includes the `param` and `dynamic param` blocks, but excludes the any command implementation.

Mocks can be created under `Describe` or `Context` keywords.

Commands are mocked using the `Mock` keyword:

```
Mock Get-Date
```

If a command returns a value, a body can be defined for the `Mock` to simulate the normal operation of the command. In the following example, the string `01/01/2017` is returned in place of any normal response from `Get-Date`:

```
Mock Get-Date {
'01/01/2017'
}
```

Assert-MockCalled

Pester tracks calls made to mocked commands. The number of times a `Mock` has been called by a `command` can be tested using the `Assert-MockCalled` command. The following function makes a single call to `Get-CimInstance`:

```
function Get-OperatingSystemName{
    (Get-CimInstance Win32_OperatingSystem).Caption
}
```

If a `Mock` of `Get-CimInstance` is created, the number of times the command is called can be `tested`. In this example, the test asserts that `Get-CimInstance` is called at least once.

```
Describe Get-OperatingSystemName {
    Mock Get-CimInstance {
        [PSCustomObject]@{
            Caption = 'OSName'
        }
    }
    It 'Gets the name of the operating system' {
        Get-OperatingSystemName | Should -Be 'OSName'
        Assert-MockCalled Get-CimInstance
    }
}
```

If a test is to verify that a mocked command is never called, the `Times` parameter of `Assert-MockCalled` can be set to `0`:

```
Assert-MockCalled Get-CimInstance -Times 0
```

If a command is used in several different ways, it might be important to ensure that the command is called a specific number of times. In this instance, the `Exactly` parameter can be added to ensure the `Mock` is called that number of times only:

```
Assert-MockCalled Get-CimInstance -Times 1 -Exactly
```

Parameter filtering

Parameter filters can be applied to mocks to limit the scope of the `Mock`.

A parameter filter is a script block that tests the parameters passed when the `Mock` is called. For example, a mock for `Test-Path` might only apply to a specific path:

```
Mock Test-Path { $true } -ParameterFilter { $Path -eq 'C:\Somewhere' }
```

If Pester cannot find a `Mock` with a matching parameter filter, it will default to a mock without a parameter filter.

If there are no mocks available, the real command will be called. In the following example when the value of the `Path` parameter is `C:\`, the value will be returned from the `Mock`. Otherwise, the value returned by the `real` command will be used:

```
Describe TestPathMocking {
    Mock Test-Path { $false } -ParameterFilter { $Path -eq 'C:\' }
```

```
        It 'Uses the mock' {
            Test-Path 'C:\' | Should -Be $false
        }

        It 'Uses the real command' {
            Test-Path 'C:\Windows' | Should -Be $true
        }
    }
```

Mocking objects

It is not uncommon for a function to expect to work with the properties and methods of an object returned by a command.

Fabricating objects

Objects with specific properties can be simulated by creating a PS custom object (or `PSObject`):

```
[PSCustomObject]@{
    Property = "Value"
}
```

New methods can be added to an object using `Add-Member`:

```
[PSCustomObject]@{} | Add-Member MethodName -MemberType ScriptMethod -Value
{ }
```

This approach can be extended to include objects instantiated by `New-Object`. The following function creates and uses instances of two different .NET types:

```
function Write-File {
    $fileStream = New-Object System.IO.FileStream("C:\Temp\test.txt",
'OpenOrCreate')
    $streamWriter = New-Object System.IO.StreamWriter($fileStream)
    $streamWriter.WriteLine("Hello world")
    $streamWriter.Close()
}
```

The following mocks replace the first with `null`, and the second with an object that supports the methods used by the script:

```
Mock New-Object { } -ParameterFilter { $TypeName -eq 'System.IO.FileStream'
}
Mock New-Object {
```

```
    [PSCustomObject]@{} |
        Add-Member WriteLine -MemberType ScriptMethod -Value { } -PassThru
|
        Add-Member Close -MemberType ScriptMethod -Value { } -PassThru
} -ParameterFilter { $TypeName -eq 'System.IO.StreamWriter' }
```

Mocking methods

If an object is completely replaced with a fabrication, the constraints associated with the creation of that object are ignored. Perhaps more importantly, the object type is lost; this is important where another command expects an object of a specific type.

In cases where a specific object type is required, it is worth considering attempting to override properties and methods on a real instance of the object.

The following snippet instantiates an instance of an SQL connection, then overrides the `Open` method and `State` properties:

```
$sqlConnection = New-Object System.Data.SqlClient.SqlConnection
$sqlConnection | Add-Member State -MemberType NoteProperty -Force -Value
'Closed'
$sqlConnection | Add-Member Open -MemberType ScriptMethod -Force -Value {
    $this.State = 'Open'
}
```

This technique may be used to return a disarmed object of the correct type.

CIM objects

Commands that require instances of CIM objects can be provided with empty instances:

```
$cimInstance = New-Object
Microsoft.Management.Infrastructure.CimInstance('Null')
```

The string value used by the constructor is not validated against existing WMI classes. Commands that accept CIM instances as parameters typically validate using the `PSTypeNames` attribute. Additional type names can be added to the list for any object as follows:

```
$cimInstance = New-Object
Microsoft.Management.Infrastructure.CimInstance('Null')
$cimInstance | Add-Member -TypeName
'Microsoft.Management.Infrastructure.CimInstance#MSFT_Something'
```

`TypeNames` are held as an array in a hidden property of the object instance:

```
PS> $cimInstance.PSObject.TypeNames
Microsoft.Management.Infrastructure.CimInstance#MSFT_Something
Microsoft.Management.Infrastructure.CimInstance#Null
Microsoft.Management.Infrastructure.CimInstance
System.Object
```

Pester in practice

The following function sets a computer description by modifying values in the registry:

```
function Set-ComputerDescription {
    [CmdletBinding()]
    param (
        [Parameter(Mandatory = $true)]
        [AllowEmptyString()]
        [String]$Description
    )

    $erroractionpreference = 'Stop'

    try {
        $path =
'HKLM:\System\CurrentControlSet\Services\LanmanServer\Parameters'

        if ((Get-Item $path).GetValue('srvcomment') -ne $Description) {
            if ($Description) {
                Set-ItemProperty $path -Name 'srvcomment' -Value
$Description
            } else {
                Clear-ItemProperty $path -Name 'srvcomment'
                Remove-ItemProperty $path -Name 'srvcomment'
            }
        }
    } catch {
        throw
    }
}
```

When the function interacts with the registry, it does so using the following commands:

- `Get-Item`
- `Set-ItemProperty`
- `Clear-ItemProperty`
- `Remove-ItemProperty`

Testing the actions undertaken by each of the previous commands is not the responsibility of a unit test for `Set-ComputerDescription`. The unit tests are limited to ensuring that each of the commands is with the right parameters and at the right time. Each of the previous commands will be mocked.

The function reacts to a combination of the value of the `Description` parameter and the current state of the value.

A set of context blocks is appropriate for this division of the test. The difference between the blocks is the response from `Get-Item` and is therefore the implementation of the `Mock`:

```
Describe Set-ComputerDescription {
    Mock Set-ItemProperty
    Mock Clear-ItemProperty
    Mock Remove-ItemProperty
```

The first context is used to describe what happens when the current description is blank. A `Mock` for `Get-Item` is created, which returns a blank result:

```
    Context 'Description is blank' {
        Mock Get-Item {
            [PSCustomObject]@{} | Add-Member GetValue -MemberType
ScriptMethod -
Value {
                return ''
            }
        }
```

Each of the subsequent tests will use the `Get-Item` mock. These tests do not explicitly verify that `Get-Item` was called; it is perhaps unnecessary, as it sits in all possible code paths (except an error prior to it being called):

```
        It 'Updates the description with a new value' {
            Set-ComputerDescription -Description 'New description'
            Assert-MockCalled Set-ItemProperty -Scope It
        }

        It 'Does nothing if the description has not changed' {
```

```
            Set-ComputerDescription -Description ''
            Assert-MockCalled Set-ItemProperty -Times 0 -Scope It
            Assert-MockCalled Clear-ItemProperty -Times 0 -Scope It
            Assert-MockCalled Remove-ItemProperty -Times 0 -Scope It
        }
    }
```

The previous tests may be enhanced to ensure that `Clear` and `Remove-ItemProperty` are not called when updating with a new value. Given that the code paths are mutually exclusive, this is unlikely to be necessary.

The next context tests the actions that should be taken if a description is set. The `Mock` for `Get-Item` is replaced with one which returns a value:

```
    Context 'Description is set' {
        Mock Get-Item {
            [PSCustomObject]@{} | Add-Member GetValue -MemberType
ScriptMethod -Value {
                return 'Current description'
            }
        }
```

The next set of tests explores the possible actions, which may result in changing the description in this state:

```
        It 'Updates the description with a new value' {
            Set-ComputerDescription -Description 'New description'
            Assert-MockCalled Set-ItemProperty -Scope It
        }

        It 'Does nothing if the description has not changed' {
            Set-ComputerDescription -Description 'Current description'
            Assert-MockCalled Set-ItemProperty -Times 0 -Scope It
            Assert-MockCalled Clear-ItemProperty -Times 0 -Scope It
            Assert-MockCalled Remove-ItemProperty -Times 0 -Scope It
        }

        It 'Clears a description' {
            Set-ComputerDescription -Description ''
            Assert-MockCalled Clear-ItemProperty -Times 1 -Scope It
            Assert-MockCalled Remove-ItemProperty -Times 1 -Scope It
        }
    }
```

The preceding tests might be enhanced to verify that an error will trigger the `catch` statement. For example, if `Set-ItemProperty` were to throw a non-terminating error with `ErrorActionPreference` set to `Stop`, a non-terminating error would be raised as a terminating error. The terminating error can be tested:

```
Mock Set-ItemProperty { Write-Error -Message 'Non-terminating error' }

It 'Throws a terminating error if a terminating or non-terminating error is
raised' {
    { Set-ComputerDescription -Description 'New description' } | Should
Throw
}
```

The previous test will need to be placed in such a context that `Set-ItemProperty` is called. For example, this test might appear at the end of the first `context` block.

Summary

This chapter has explored static analysis with `PSScriptAnalyzer`. Testing with Pester was explored in detail, with a focus on using Pester for unit testing.

17
Error Handling

Errors are used to communicate unexpected conditions, an exceptional circumstance. Errors often contain useful information that can be used to diagnose a condition.

Handling errors is a critical part of working with the language, not least because PowerShell defines two different types of errors and several different ways to raise them.

As well as presenting different types of error, PowerShell has a number of different ways to handle errors, from ignoring errors to graceful handling.

During the course of this chapter, self-contained blocks of code are described as scripts. The terms function, script block, and script can be considered interchangeable in the context of error handling.

The following topics are covered in this chapter:

- Error types
- Error actions
- Raising errors
- Catching errors

Error types

PowerShell defines two different types of errors: terminating and non-terminating errors.

Terminating errors

A terminating error stops a pipeline processing; once an error is thrown, everything stops. A terminating error might appear as the result of using `throw`. In the following function, the second `Write-Host` statement will never execute:

```
PS> function ThrowError {
Write-Host 'First'
throw 'Error'
Write-Host 'Second'
}
PS>ThrowError
First
Error
At line:3 char:5
+ throw 'Error'
+ ~~~~~~~~~~~~~
+ CategoryInfo : OperationStopped: (Error:String) [], RuntimeException
+ FullyQualifiedErrorId : Error
```

Terminating errors are typically used to convey that something unexpected and terminal has occurred, a catastrophic failure that prevents a script continuing.

Non-terminating errors

A non-terminating error is written, a type of informational output, without stopping a script. Non-terminating errors are often the result of using `Write-Error`. The following function shows that processing continues after the error:

```
PS> function WriteError {
Write-Host 'First'
Write-Error 'Error'
Write-Host 'Second'
}
PS>WriteError
First
WriteError : Error
At line:1 char:1
+ WriteError
+ ~~~~~~~~~~
+ CategoryInfo : NotSpecified: (:) [Write-Error], WriteErrorException
+ FullyQualifiedErrorId :
Microsoft.PowerShell.Commands.WriteErrorException,WriteError
```

Non-terminating errors are used to notify the user that something went wrong, but that it was not necessarily sufficient to warrant shutting down a script.

Error action

The `ErrorAction` parameter and the `ErrorActionPreference` variable are used to control what happens when a non-terminating error is written.

CmdletBinding:
The `ErrorAction` parameter is only available if a function declares the `CmdletBinding` attribute. `CmdletBinding` is automatically added is automatically added if the `Parameter` attribute is used.

By default, the `ErrorAction` is set to continue. Any non-terminating errors will be displayed, but a script or function will continue to run.

If the `ErrorAction` is set to `SilentlyContinue`, errors will be added to the automatic variable `$error`, but the error will not be displayed.

The following function writes a non-terminating error using `Write-Error`:

```
function Invoke-Something {
    [CmdletBinding()]
    param ( )

    Write-Error 'Something went wrong'
}
Invoke-Something-ErrorAction SilentlyContinue
```

The error is written, but hidden from view. The error may be viewed as the latest entry in the `$error` variable:

```
PS> $Error[0]
Invoke-Something : Something went wrong
At line:8 char:1
+ Invoke-Something -ErrorAction SilentlyContinue
+ ~~~~~~~~~~~~~~~~~~~~~~~~~~~~~~~~~~~~~~~~~~~~~~~
+ CategoryInfo : NotSpecified: (:) [Write-Error], WriteErrorException
+ FullyQualifiedErrorId :
Microsoft.PowerShell.Commands.WriteErrorException,SilentError
```

If the error action is set to Stop, a non-terminating error becomes a terminating error, for example:

```
PS> function StopError {
[CmdletBinding()]
param ( )
Write-Error 'Something went wrong'
}
StopError -ErrorAction Stop
StopError : Something went wrong
At line:1 char:1
+ StopError -ErrorAction Stop
+ ~~~~~~~~~~~~~~~~~~~~~~~~~~~
+ CategoryInfo : NotSpecified: (:) [Write-Error], WriteErrorException
+ FullyQualifiedErrorId :
Microsoft.PowerShell.Commands.WriteErrorException,StopError
```

Raising errors

When writing a script, it may be desirable to use errors to notify someone running the script of a problem. The severity of the problem might dictate whether an error is non-terminating or terminating.

If a script makes a single change to a large number of diverse, unrelated objects, a terminating error might be frustrating for anyone using the script.

On the other hand, if a script fails to read a critical configuration file, a terminating error is likely the right choice.

Error records

When an error is raised in PowerShell, an ErrorRecord object is created (explicitly or implicitly).

An ErrorRecord object contains a number of fields that are useful for diagnosing an error. An ErrorRecord can be explored using Get-Member. For example, an ErrorRecord will be generated when attempting to divide by 0:

```
100 / 0
$record = $Error[0]
```

The ErrorRecord that was generated includes a ScriptStackTrace:

```
PS> $record.ScriptStackTrace
at <ScriptBlock>, <No file>: line 1
As well as a .NET stack trace:
PS> $record.Exception.StackTrace
at System.Management.Automation.IntOps.Divide(Int32 lhs, Int32 rhs)
at System.Dynamic.UpdateDelegates.UpdateAndExecute2[T0,T1,TRet](CallSite
site, T0 arg0, T1 arg1)
at
System.Management.Automation.Interpreter.DynamicInstruction`3.Run(Interpret
edFrame frame)
at
System.Management.Automation.Interpreter.EnterTryCatchFinallyInstruction.Ru
n(InterpretedFrame frame)
```

In some cases, the TargetObject property of an ErrorRecord might contain the object being worked on.

For example, if the values for a division operation were dynamically set, an ErrorRecord might be created to return those values to assist with debugging:

```
$numerator = 10
$denominator = 0
try {
    $numerator / $denominator
} catch {
    $errorRecord = New-Object Management.Automation.ErrorRecord(
        (New-Object Exception($_.Exception.Message)),
        'InvalidDivision',    # ErrorId
'InvalidOperation',  # ErrorCategory
        ([PSCustomObject]@{   # TargetObject
            Numerator    = $numerator
            Denominator = $denominator
        })
    )
    Write-Error -ErrorRecord $errorRecord
}
```

The values pushed into the ErrorRecord may be viewed by exploring the TargetObject property:

```
PS> $Error[0].TargetObject
Numerator      Denominator
---------      -----------
       10                0
```

The try-catch statement used previously is covered in detail later in this chapter.

Write-Error

The `Write-Error` command can be used to write non-terminating error messages.

The `Write-Error` command can be used with nothing more than a message:

```
Write-Error 'Message'
```

Or it might include additional information, such as a category and error ID to aid diagnosis by someone using the script:

```
Write-Error -Message 'Message' -Category 'InvalidOperation' -ErrorId
'UniqueID'
```

The following example shows a non-terminating error raised while running a loop:

```
function Test-Error {
    for ($i = 0; $i -lt 5; $i++) {
        Write-Error -Message "Iteration: $i"
    }
 }
Test-Error
```

The error will be displayed five times without stopping execution.

The `CmdletBinding` attribute adds support for common parameters, including `ErrorAction`. `ErrorAction` can be used to change the response to the error message. For example, if setting the `ErrorAction` to `Stop` will end processing after the first iteration of the loop:

```
PS> function Test-Error {
[CmdletBinding()]
param( )
for ($i = 0; $i -lt 5; $i++) {
Write-Error -Message "Iteration: $i"
}
}
Test-Error -ErrorAction Stop
Test-Error : Iteration: 0
At line:1 char:1
+ Test-Error -ErrorAction Stop
+ ~~~~~~~~~~~~~~~~~~~~~~~~~~~~
+ CategoryInfo : NotSpecified: (:) [Write-Error], WriteErrorException
+ FullyQualifiedErrorId :
Microsoft.PowerShell.Commands.WriteErrorException,Test-Error
```

Alternatively, the error might be silent (`SilentlyContinue`) or ignored (`Ignore`) depending on the context in which the error appears.

Setting the `ErrorActionPreference` variable (either globally, or within the function) will have the same effect on the handling of the error.

Throw and ThrowTerminatingError

The keyword `throw` raises a terminating error, for example:

```
throw 'Error message'
```

`throw` may be used with a string, a message, as shown previously. `throw` may also be used with an exception object:

```
throw New-Object ArgumentException('Unsupported value')
```

Or it may be used with an `ErrorRecord`:

```
throw New-Object Management.Automation.ErrorRecord(
    (New-Object InvalidOperationException('Invalid operation')),
    'AnErrorID',
    [Management.Automation.ErrorCategory]::InvalidOperation,
    $null
)
```

Commands in binary modules (Cmdlets) cannot use `throw`, it has a different meaning in the languages that might be used to author a `Cmdlet`. Cmdlets use the .NET method `PSCmdlet.ThrowTerminatingError`.

The `ThrowTerminatingError` method can be used in PowerShell in conjunction with an `ErrorRecord` object provided the `CmdletBinding` attribute is declared, for example:

```
function Invoke-Something {
    [CmdletBinding()]
    param ( )

    $errorRecord = New-Object Management.Automation.ErrorRecord(
        (New-Object Exception('Failed')),
        'AnErrorID',
        [Management.Automation.ErrorCategory]::OperationStopped,
        $null
    )
    $pscmdlet.ThrowTerminatingError($errorRecord)
}
```

Error and ErrorVariable

The `Error` variable is a collection (`ArrayList`) of handled and unhandled errors raised in the PowerShell session.

> **Testing the content of error variables:**
> Testing the content of an error variable is not a robust way to test for error conditions.
> As the variable fills with both handled and unhandled errors, it is indeterminate at best. `Error` variables continue to have value when debugging less obvious problems with code.

The collection can be cleared using:

```
$Error.Clear()
```

The most recent error is first in the list:

```
$Error[0]
```

Errors will be added to the collection except when the `ErrorAction` is set to `Ignore`.

The `ErrorVariable` parameter can be used to name a variable that should be used as well as `Error` for a specific command. The `Error` variable, the value in the variable name is an `ArrayList`.

The following function writes an `Error`. If `ErrorVariable` is used, the errors are added to the variable name:

```
function Invoke-Something {
    [CmdletBinding()]
    param ( )

    Write-Error 'Failed'
}
```

Executing the function with a named variable will make the errors available:

```
Invoke-Something -ErrorVariable InvokeError -ErrorAction SilentlyContinue
```

The errors stored in the variable can be inspected:

```
PS> $InvokeError
Invoke-Something : Failed
At line:1 char:1
+ Invoke-Something -ErrorVariable InvokeError -ErrorAction SilentlyCont ...
+ ~~~~~~~~~~~~~~~~~~~~~~~~~~~~~~~~~~~~~~~~~~~~~~~~~~~~~~~~~~~~~~~~~~~~~~~~
+ CategoryInfo : NotSpecified: (:) [Write-Error], WriteErrorException
+ FullyQualifiedErrorId :
Microsoft.PowerShell.Commands.WriteErrorException,Invoke-Something
```

ErrorVariable is never null:
If no errors occur, the variable will still be created as an `ArrayList`, but the list will contain no elements. That the list exists means using the variable as an implicit Boolean is flawed.
That is, the following statement will return `false`:
`$null -eq $InvokeError`
The `Count` property might be inspected instead:
`$InvokeError.Count -eq 0`

Error messages written to an `ErrorVariable` are duplicated in `Error`:

```
PS> $error[0]
Invoke-Something : Failed
At line:1 char:1
+ Invoke-Something -ErrorVariable InvokeError -ErrorAction SilentlyCont ...
+ ~~~~~~~~~~~~~~~~~~~~~~~~~~~~~~~~~~~~~~~~~~~~~~~~~~~~~~~~~~~~~~~~~~~~~~~~
+ CategoryInfo : NotSpecified: (:) [Write-Error], WriteErrorException
+ FullyQualifiedErrorId :
Microsoft.PowerShell.Commands.WriteErrorException,Invoke-Something
```

Catching errors

PowerShell provides two different ways to handle terminating errors: using `try-catch-finally`, or using `trap`.

Try, catch, and finally

PowerShell 2.0 introduced `try-catch-finally` as a means of handling terminating errors.

Try

A `try` block must be followed by either one or more `catch` blocks, or a `finally` block, or both. Each of the following patterns is valid:

```
try { <script> } catch { <script> }
try { <script> } finally { <script> }
try { <script> } catch { <script> } finally { <script }
```

An error occurring within `try` will trigger the execution of `catch`.

Catch

`Catch` is used to respond to terminating errors raised within `try`. `catch` can be used to respond to any exception, or a specific set of exception types. Each of the following is valid:

```
try { } catch { 'Catches any exception' }
try { } catch [ExceptionType] { 'Catch an exception type' }
try { } catch [ExceptionType1], [ExceptionType2] {
    'Catch exception type 1 and 2'
}
```

In the following example, calling the `ToString` method on the `null` variable will throw an exception that triggers `catch`:

```
try {
    $null.ToString()
} catch {
    Write-Host 'This exception has been handled'
}
```

When working with `catch`, the error record that was thrown is made available by using either the variable `$_` or `$PSItem`:

```
try {
    $null.ToString()
} catch {
    Write-Host $_.Exception.Message      # This is the same as...
    Write-Host $PSItem.Exception.Message # ... this.
}
```

ForEach-Object and catch:
If `ForEach-Object` is used, the current object in the pipeline is stored in the variable `$_`. For the object from the input pipeline to be available inside `catch`, it must be assigned to another variable first.

`catch` statements can be limited to handle specific exception types:

```
$ErrorActionPreference = 'Stop'
try {
    # If the file does not exist, this will raise an exception of type
ItemNotFoundException
    $content = Get-Content C:\doesnotexist.txt
} catch [System.Management.Automation.ItemNotFoundException] {
    Write-Host 'The item was not found'
}
```

If more than one type of error might be thrown by a block of code, multiple `catch` statements are supported. In the following example, an unauthorized access exception is thrown in response to an attempt to read a directory like a file:

```
$ErrorActionPreference = 'Stop'
try {
    Get-ChildItem C:\Windows\System32\Configuration -Filter *.mof |
ForEach-Object {
        $content = $_ | Get-Content
    }
} catch [System.IO.FileNotFoundException] {
    Write-Host 'The item was not found'
} catch [System.Management.Automation.ItemNotFoundException] {
    Write-Host 'Access denied'
}
```

In a similar manner, `catch` statements can be layered, starting with the most specific error type, working down to a broader condition. The first matching `catch` block will be used:

```
using namespace System.Management.Automation

try {
    throw New-Object ItemNotFoundException ('Item not found')
} catch [ItemNotFoundException] {
    Write-Host 'Item not found exception thrown'
} catch {
    Write-Host 'Error thrown'
}
```

Finally

The `finally` block will invoke whether an error is thrown or not. This makes it ideal for handling situations where things must always be cleanly closed down.

The following function ignores errors, but will always close down an open SQL connection, whether the `ExecuteReader` method succeeds or not:

```
using namespace System.Data.SqlClient

$connectionString = 'Data Source=dbServer;Initial Catalog=dbName'
try {
    $sqlConnection = New-Object SqlConnection($connectionString)
    $sqlConnection.Open()
    $sqlCommand = $sqlConnection.CreateCommand()
    $sqlCommand.CommandText = 'SELECT * FROM Employee'
    $reader = $sqlCommand.ExecuteReader()
} finally {
    if ($sqlConnection.State -eq 'Open') {
        $sqlConnection.Close()
    }
}
```

When `catch` is used with `finally`, the content of `finally` is executed before errors are returned, but after the body of `catch` has executed. This is demonstrated by the following example:

```
try {
    Write-Host "Try"
    throw 'Error'
} catch {
    Write-Host "Catch, after Try"
    throw
} finally {
    Write-Host "Finally, after Catch, before the exception"
}
```

Rethrowing errors

An error might be rethrown within a `catch` block. This technique can be useful if a `try` block performs a number of dependent steps in a sequence where one or more might fail.

Rethrowing an error raised by a script can be as simple as using `throw` in a `catch` block:

```
try {
    'Statement1'
    throw 'Statement2'
    'Statement3'
} catch {
    throw
}
```

`ThrowTerminatingError` might be used instead, depending on the desired behavior:

```
Function Invoke-Something {
   [CmdletBinding()]
   Param ( )
try {
    'Statement1'
    throw 'Statement2'
    'Statement3'
} catch {
    $pscmdlet.ThrowTerminatingError($_)
}
}
```

When an error is rethrown in this manner, the second instance of the error (within the `catch` block) is not written to either `Error` or an error variable. In cases where the error is re-thrown without modification, this does not present a problem.

If the re-thrown error attempts to add information, such as an error ID, the modified error record will also not be available to the error variables. For example:

```
try {
    throw 'Error'
} catch {
    Write-Error -Exception $_.Exception -ErrorId 'GeneratedErrorId' -
Category 'InvalidOperation'
}
```

The error raised in the `try` block is added to the error variables, but not displayed in a console (as it is handled). The second error is displayed on the console, but not added to any error variables.

To resolve this problem, the new error record should return the original exception as an inner exception:

```
try {
    throw 'Error'
} catch {
    $exception = New-Object Exception(
        $_.Exception.Message,
        $_.Exception
    )
    Write-Error -Exception $exception -ErrorId 'GeneratedErrorId' -Category
'InvalidOperation'
}
```

In the case of `exception` and most, if not all, exception types, the first argument of the constructor is a message, and the second (optional) argument is an inner exception.

Using an inner exception has a number of advantages:

- `try-catch` statements testing the outcome of the preceding snippet will trigger based on either the exception type or inner exception type
- The other properties of the exception remain available (via the inner exception), such as the stack trace

Inconsistent error behavior

The different methods PowerShell exposes to terminate a script are not entirely consistent.

When `throw` is used to raise a terminating error, it will stop the current script and anything which called it. In the following example, `child2` will never execute:

```
$ErrorActionPreference = 'Continue'
function caller {
    child1
    child2
}
function child1 {
    throw 'Failed'
    'child1'
}
function child2 {
    'child2'
}
caller
```

When the `ThrowTerminatingError` method is used, processing within `child1` stops, but the function `caller` continues. This is demonstrated as follows:

```
function caller {
    child1
    child2
}
function child1 {
    [CmdletBinding()]
    param ( )

    $errorRecord = New-Object Management.Automation.ErrorRecord(
        (New-Object Exception('Failed')),
        'ID',
        'OperationStopped',
        $null
    )
    $pscmdlet.ThrowTerminatingError($errorRecord)
    'child1'
}
function child2 {
    'child2'
}
```

Executing the function `caller` shows that `child2` is executed:

```
child1 : Failed
At line:2 char:5
+ child1
+ ~~~~~~
+ CategoryInfo : OperationStopped: (:) [child1], Exception
+ FullyQualifiedErrorId : ID,child1
child2
```

The behavior of the preceding example is equivalent to the behavior seen when calling Cmdlets. For example, the command `ConvertFrom-Json` raises a terminating error when the content it is asked to convert is invalid.

When a `Cmdlet` throws a terminating error within another function, the caller script continues to execute unless `ErrorAction` is set to `Stop`:

```
function caller {
    ConvertFrom-Json -InputObject '{{'
    child1
}
function child1 {
    'Called'
```

```
}
caller
```

The same behavior is seen when calling .NET methods, shown as follows. The static method `IPAddress.Parse` will raise a terminating error because the use of the method is not valid:

```
function caller {
    [IPAddress]::Parse('this is not an IP')
    child1
}
function child1 {
    'Called'
}
caller
```

Throw and ErrorAction

The `throw` keyword raises a terminating error, terminating errors are not supposed to be affected by either `ErrorAction` or `ErrorActionPreference`.

Unfortunately, errors raised by `throw` are affected by `ErrorAction` when `ErrorAction` is set to `SilentlyContinue`. This behavior is an important consideration when designing scripts for others to use.

The following function throws an error first; the second command should never run:

```
function Invoke-Something {
    [CmdletBinding()]
    param ( )

    throw 'Error'
    Write-Host 'No error'
}
```

Running the function normally shows that the error is thrown, and the second command does not execute:

```
PS> Invoke-Something
Error
At line:5 char:5
+ throw 'Error'
+ ~~~~~~~~~~~~~
+ CategoryInfo : OperationStopped: (Error:String) [], RuntimeException
+ FullyQualifiedErrorId : Error
```

If `ErrorAction` is set to `SilentlyContinue`, `throw` will be ignored:

```
PS> Invoke-Something -ErrorAction SilentlyContinue
No error
```

Enclosing `throw` in a `try-catch` block will trigger `catch`:

```
PS> function Invoke-Something {
[CmdletBinding()]
param ( )
try {
throw 'Error'
Write-Host 'No error'
} catch {
Write-Host 'An error occurred'
}
}
Invoke-Something -ErrorAction SilentlyContinue
An error occurred
```

The problem described here also applies when `throw` is used within the `catch` block. The following example should result in an error being displayed, as the error is terminating:

```
PS> function Invoke-Something {
[CmdletBinding()]
param ( )
try {
throw 'Error'
Write-Host 'No error'
} catch {
throw 'An error occurred'
}
}
Invoke-Something -ErrorAction SilentlyContinue
```

For scripts that declare the `CmdletBinding` attribute, `ThrowTerminatingError` can be used. The `ThrowTerminatingError` method does not suffer from the same problem:

```
PS> function Invoke-Something {
[CmdletBinding()]
param ( )
try {
throw 'Error'
Write-Host 'No error'
} catch {
$pscmdlet.ThrowTerminatingError($_)
}
}
```

```
Invoke-Something -ErrorAction SilentlyContinue
Invoke-Something : Error
At line:12 char:1
+ Invoke-Something -ErrorAction SilentlyContinue
+ ~~~~~~~~~~~~~~~~~~~~~~~~~~~~~~~~~~~~~~~~~~~~~~
+ CategoryInfo : OperationStopped: (Error:String) [Invoke-Something],
RuntimeException
+ FullyQualifiedErrorId : Error,Invoke-Something
```

In the preceding example, `throw` is used to raise the original error condition (which will create an error record). `ThrowTerminatingError` is used to rethrow the terminating error correctly.

If a function does not use the `CmdletBinding` attribute, care should be taken when writing error handling. For example, the following function cannot use `ThrowTerminatingError` or the `ErrorAction` parameter, but it is still subject to `ErrorActionPreference`:

```
PS> function Invoke-Something {
throw 'Error'
Write-Host 'No error'
}
$ErrorActionPreference = 'SilentlyContinue'
Invoke-Something
No error
```

Workarounds for this problem include using `Write-Error` with `ErrorAction` set to `Stop`:

```
function Invoke-Something {
    try {
        throw 'Error'
    } catch {
        Write-Error -ErrorRecord $_ -ErrorAction Stop
        break
    }
}
```

`Break` or `return` might also be used to immediately end the function:

```
function Invoke-Something {
    try {
        throw 'Error'
    } catch {
        Write-Error -ErrorRecord $_ -ErrorAction Continue
        break
    }
```

```
    Write-Host "Function end"
}
```

The error raised by `Write-Error` is non-terminating unless the `ErrorAction` parameter for `Write-Error` is set to `Stop`.

Nesting try-catch-finally

A `try-catch-finally` statement can be nested beneath another. This is most appropriate when a different approach is required by a smaller section of code.

A script perform setup actions, then working on a number of objects in a loop is a good example of one that might require more than one `try-catch` statement. The script should terminate cleanly if something goes wrong during setup, but it might only notify if an error occurs within the loop.

The following functions can be used as a working example of such a script. The setup actions might include connecting to a management server of some kind:

```
function Connect-Server {}
```

Once the connection is established, a set of objects might be retrieved:

```
function Get-ManagementObject {
    1..10 | ForEach-Object {
[PSCustomObject]@{ Name = $_; Property = "Value$_" }
    }
}
```

The `Set` filter accepts an input pipeline and changes a value on the object:

```
filterSet-ManagementObject {
    [CmdletBinding()]
    param (
        [Parameter(Mandatory = $true, ValueFromPipeline = $true)]
        $InputObject,

$Property
    )
    $InputObject.Property = $Property
}
```

The following script uses the preceding functions. If a terminating error is raised during either the `Connect` or `Get` commands, the script will stop. If a terminating error is raised during `Set`, the script writes about the error and moves onto the next object:

```
try {
    Connect-Server
Get-ManagementObject | ForEach-Object {
        try {
            $_ | Set-ManagementObject -Property 'NewValue'
        } catch {
            Write-Error -ErrorRecord $_
        } finally {
            $_
        }
    }
} catch {
    throw
 }
```

Changing individual functions to throw errors will show how each block triggers.

Terminating or non-terminating

One of the challenges of writing error handling is determining whether the error is terminating or non-terminating.

A possible solution is to force all errors to be terminating by setting `ErrorActionPreference` to `Stop`.

Setting `ErrorActionPreference` to `Stop` is equivalent to adding `-ErrorAction Stop` to every command that supports it.

When exploring nesting `try-catch-finally`, the following snippet was used:

```
try {
    Connect-Server
    Get-ManagementObject | ForEach-Object {
        try {
            $_ | Set-ManagementObject -Property 'NewValue'
        } catch {
            Write-Error -ErrorRecord $_
        } finally {
            $_
        }
    }
```

```
} catch {
    throw
 }
```

Setting `ErrorActionPreference` to `Stop` would remove the need to set an `ErrorAction` parameter on each of the commands (if those commands wrote non-terminating errors). However, doing so would also cause any informational errors written by `Write-Error` to completely stop the script.

For a script that implements a process, where the error handling can be strictly defined, the following workaround might be used. The `ErrorAction` for `Write-Error` is forcefully set to `Continue`, overriding the value held in the `preference` variable:

```
$ErrorActionPreference = 'Stop'
try {
    Connect-Server
    Get-ManagementObject | ForEach-Object {
        try {
            $_ | Set-ManagementObject -Property 'NewValue'
        } catch {
            Write-Error -ErrorRecord $_ -ErrorAction Continue
        } finally {
            $_
        }
    }
} catch {
    throw
 }
```

Setting `ErrorActionPreference` to `Stop` is harder to apply when writing tools, for example, when writing the commands used by this script, doing so would remove the choice from the end user.

A need for complex error handling is often a sign that a script needs to be broken down into smaller units.

Trap

PowerShell 1.0 came with `trap`. `trap` is used to catch errors raised anywhere within the scope of the `trap` declaration. That is, the current scope, and any child scopes.

`trap` is a useful tool for capturing errors that are not accounted for by `try-catch` blocks. Much of its use has been superseeded by `try-catch-finally`.

Using trap

`trap` is declared in a similar manner to the `catch` block:

```
trap { <script> }
trap [ExceptionType] { <script> }
trap [ExceptionType1], [ExceptionType2] { <script> }
```

A script may contain more than one `trap` statement, for example:

```
trap [InvalidOperationException] {
    Write-Host 'An invalid operation'
}
trap {
    Write-Host 'Catch all other exceptions'
}
```

The ordering of the preceding `trap` statements does not matter; the most specific statement is used to handle a given error.

When using a script, function, or script block, the `trap` statement can appear anywhere. `trap` does not have to appear before the code it acts against. For example, `trap` is implemented in the script block that is called as follows:

```
& {
    Write-Host 'Statement1'
    throw 'Statement2'
    Write-Host 'Statement3'

    trap { Write-Host 'An error occurred' }
}
```

The error raised by `throw` causes the `trap` statement to execute and execution stops; `Statement3` is never written.

Trap, scope, and continue

By default, if an error is handled by `trap`, script execution stops. The `continue` keyword can be used to resume a script at the next statement.

The following example handles the error raised by `throw`, and continues onto the next statement:

```
& {
    Write-Host 'Statement1'
    throw 'Statement2'
```

```
        Write-Host 'Statement3'

        trap {
            Write-Host 'An error occurred'
            continue
        }
    }
```

The behavior of `continue` is dependent on the scope `trap` is used. In the preceding example, `continue` moves onto writing `Statement3` as the `trap` statement, and the statements being executed are in the same scope.

The following script declares a function that throws an error. `trap` is declared in the parent scope of the function:

```
    & {
        function Invoke-Something {
            Write-Host 'Statement1'
            throw 'Statement2'
            Write-Host 'Statement3'
        }

        Invoke-Something
        Write-Host 'Done'

        trap {
            Write-Host 'An error occurred'
            continue
        }
    }
```

The `Continue` keyword is used, but `Statement3` is not displayed. Execution can only continue in the same scope as the `trap` statement.

Summary

This chapter has explored the different ways of raising and handling errors in PowerShell.

The difference between terminating and non-terminating errors was explored.

Using `try-catch-finally`, introduced with PowerShell 2, was explored as the preferred means of handling terminating errors.

`trap`, the type of error handling available with PowerShell 1, was demonstrated to add to the error handling toolset.

Index

A

D

E

J

L

M

N

O

P

Q

R

S

T

X

Made in the USA
Lexington, KY
15 June 2018